BELIEVER, BEWARE

BELIEVER, BEWARE

First-Person Dispatches from the Margins of Faith

Selected by Jeff Sharlet, Peter Manseau,
and the editors of *Killing the Buddha*

Beacon Press
Boston

Beacon Press
25 Beacon Street
Boston, Massachusetts 02108-2892
www.beacon.org

Beacon Press books are published under the auspices of
the Unitarian Universalist Association of Congregations.

Library of Congress Cataloging-in-Publication Data

Believer, beware: first-person dispatches from the margins of faith /
Selected by Jeff Sharlet, Peter Manseau & the editors of Killing the Buddha.
    p. cm.
  Includes bibliographical references.
  ISBN-13: 978-0-8070-7739-9 (pbk. : alk. paper)
  ISBN-10: 0-8070-7739-9 (pbk. : alk. paper) 1. United States—Religion.
2. Faith. I. Sharlet, Jeff. II. Manseau, Peter.

  BL2525.B445 2009
  200.973--dc22   2008047403

Composition by Wilsted & Taylor Publishing Services

The editors of *Killing the Buddha* are:

Meera Subramanian, Laurel Snyder, Jeff Sharlet,
Paul W. Morris, Peter Manseau, Ashley Makar,
and Marissa Dennis

Contents

Introduction

The Apocalypse Is Always Now

Most books about religion aspire to revelation, divine or worldly. In other words, they're apocalyptic. For what does apocalypse mean—*apokálypsis,* in the pagan Greek from which the Bible borrowed the term—but "lifting of the veil"?

Think of it like this. It's your wedding day, and whether you are man or woman, straight, gay, lesbian, trans, or other, apocalypse promises you a bride. Not, however, of your choosing. It's an arranged marriage, a match made in heaven, as they say. You are filled with both anticipation and fear.

What will she look like? Will she be beautiful? Will her eyes be those of a dove, as Solomon sings in the Song of Songs, her hair like "a flock of goats, that appear from Mount Gilead" (goat hair being the gold standard of grooming in Solomon's time)? Or will she be terrifying—eyeballs growing on stalks from her tongue, fangs poking out all over her face, angry red eyes where breasts should be, and parched yellow skin as if made from the paper of an ancient scroll, like the Apocalypse Beast that the Fantastic Four defeated in "Fantastic Four/Iron Man: Big in Japan #3"? And while we're on the subject of the Fantastic Four, why is it that only our most earnest literature, scripture, and our campiest, comic books, really care about the end of the world?

By "comic books" I mean not just stories told through picture panels and onomatopoeia but also all the trash, pulp, and pixels expended on that which is fabulous or overblown, the absurd played not for laughs, or *just* for laughs, but for Art, for Truth, for—Revelation. In this category, we may safely include the Green

Lantern, Wonder Woman, and Dr. Strange, of course, and "science" fiction, *Lost,* and *24.* But also Pink Floyd, Deep Purple, and Black Sabbath, and Mahler, Wagner, and Aaron Copland; M.I.A., N.W.A., and the CIA as an actual institution; Thoreau's *The Maine Woods* (picture the prophet atop Mount Katahdin, too close to God, screaming "Contact! Contact!" like a nineteenth-century Carl Sagan) but not placid *Walden;* Augustine but not Aquinas; both liberation theology and *Left Behind;* the white whale, the Black Panthers, the pink triangle, and the yellow star—any symbol or label or term that marks its bearer for death or exile, especially those whose meanings have been inverted; the Golem, the Hulk, and John Henry; Jayne Mansfield, Marilyn, and, more important—most important, perhaps—*Buffy the Vampire Slayer,* who faced the end of the world every season only to start over the following autumn.

Caught between comics and scripture is the stuff of this collection, memoir. Memoir, after all, is a euphemistic label for testimony, a cleaned-up manifestation of the comic book sensibility. Testimony provides the bones and the flesh of scripture, of religion lived, embodied, inscribed, and scrawled; "I was lost, but now I'm found" is one of its most popular story lines. The testimonies gathered here give that formula a twist: "I was lost, then found, but now I'm lost again."

Which brings to mind, of course, the endlessly looping plots of comic books and scripture, heroes and villains rising and falling, sinners redeemed and backsliding, the Joker defeated by Batman once and for all only to return ten issues later, the Israelites delivered to the promised land only to be sent into exile. It's always back into the breach or back into the desert—until, that is, The End. The final battle, Armageddon, Apocalypse, *the Answer.* That's another necessary cliché of the memoir/testimony genre: "I was blind, but now I see." Now I get it. Whether the writer achieves this new vision through religion or reason, revelation—epiphany—is the climax of the tale.

It's not always a blessing, this sight. The Bible offers a sneak peek beneath the veil even more horrible than anything dreamed up by Stan Lee: "And I stood upon the sand of the sea," writes John the Revelator, "and saw a beast rise up out of the sea, having seven heads and ten horns, and upon his horns ten crowns, and upon his heads the name of blasphemy."

Cross your fingers. Hope for the best. Lift the veil.

The problem with revelation is that when brought down to earth, secularized, it loses all its grandeur and its absurdity—the inherent kitsch of a beast with ten heads, the melodrama of the end of the world, that campy veil. It is not humbled by secularization, it is hushed. This is nowhere more disconcerting than in stories about religion that assume, in our modern age, that belief is a quality or even a quantity, an option or maybe even a substance, *spirituality,* the sort of thing that one might buy in handsomely designed organic cardboard containers at Whole Foods. Back in 2000, when Peter Manseau, Jeremy Brothers, and I created *Killing the Buddha,* the online magazine from which the stories in this collection are gathered, we announced ourselves with a rejection of all that: "*Killing the Buddha,*" declared our "Manifesto," "is a religion magazine for people made anxious by churches, people embarrassed to be caught in the 'spirituality' section of a bookstore, people both hostile and drawn to talk of God." We might as well have spoken of the "deep sympathy modified by revulsion" with which Susan Sontag undertook her famous dissection of camp as a sensibility.

In 2000, we set out with the notion that our knowing attitudes would allow us to transcend the clichés of The Beginning and The End, the melodrama of religion as "merely" ritual, the tedium of belief as custom. But that belief itself, that Buddha, at least, we have killed; or perhaps that Buddha killed us.

When *Publishers Weekly,* reviewing the first book to grow out of

Killing the Buddha, called our *Heretic's Bible* "disjointed and freakish" (they meant it in a good way), Peter Manseau and I argued over which of us was which; the truth was we each wanted to be both. We created *Killing the Buddha* with the idea that writing about matters of "ultimate concern," as prim Paul Tillich labels all religion, in the image of his Protestant divine, should be not solemn but subversive. Subversive of what? The very endeavor we were engaging in. Hence the name of the magazine:

> After years on his cushion, a monk has what he believes is a breakthrough: a glimpse of nirvana, the Buddhamind, the big pay-off. Reporting the experience to his master, however, he is informed that what has happened is par for the course, nothing special, maybe even damaging to his pursuit. And then the master gives the student dismaying advice: If you meet the Buddha, he says, kill him.
>
> Why kill the Buddha? Because the Buddha you meet is not the true Buddha, but an expression of your longing. If this Buddha is not killed he will only stand in your way.

The Buddha you meet, of course, is the answer you come up with when faced with big questions about meaning. Ours are as ready for the ax as any others. Eight years on from our manifesto and, between the two of us, four books that are often shelved, sigh, in the spirituality section of the bookstore (as this one no doubt will be, too, unless we can persuade our publisher to label it "humor," perhaps, or maybe "automotive"), we've been forced to come to terms with our place on the same shelf as Deepak Chopra, Rick Warren, and *Chicken Soup for the Soul,* all of which sell more copies in a week than this book will between now and Armageddon. We should be so lucky as to be so banal; it is an art, a balancing act, which we have never achieved. But there is surely some wisdom in the awkwardness of the questions to which such books respond. "Avant-garde" writers, meanwhile, reproduce ad nauseam the secular and spiritual assumptions of the mildly liberal middle class; we thought we would trump them with dispatches from the margins. Instead, as the stories that follow reveal, we found ourselves wading through the muck of the ordinary, a mudslide of the mundane, an apocalyptic swamp of What Is—the Word made strange. Marginality, we learned, can't honestly be chosen—at best, it must simply be recognized as the only ground we have to stand on.

It's hardly stable turf. And yet, there's no steadiness to be found in the most common response to the problem of belief in a postmodern age: "Sheilaism," the personalized religion an informant named Sheila famously described to sociologist Robert Bellah. "Just my own little voice," she said, reducing her mental jambalaya of received wisdom from half a dozen traditions to a self-satisfied squeak. That's the "spirituality" that embarrassed us eight years ago when we created *Killing the Buddha*. We were ashamed of it because we knew it was a virus with which we ourselves were infected. It seemed impossible not to be. We are all Sheilas now.

There are, nonetheless, alternatives. First, there's tradition itself. When we started *Killing the Buddha,* we found ourselves fellow traveling with punk fundamentalists, true believers and new monastics, intellectual snobs with vulgar mouths and contempt for the milquetoastery of pluralism. I am thinking here of another online magazine, *The New Pantagruel,* and of the hipster Christians gathering their forces behind Sufjan Stevens's pretty warble on his Asthmatic Kitty label, and even, after a fashion, of the hedonistic asceticism of the antiglobalization movement that swirled around us at the beginning. "Environmental druids, anarchist ninjas, union organizers, policy grinders, pacifists, political prisoners, poor people, and squatters like Carlo Giuliani," we called them in *Killing the Buddha* after the 2001 murder of Giuliani by Italian police at a

Group of 8 Summit in Genoa. "A vast array opposed for various reasons to the neo-liberal attempt to enclose all that is alive and mysterious in a set of trade agreements and holding corporations."

But the anarchists and their allies, like the new traditionalists, were all too often utopian, drawn like the theologians of the Radical Orthodoxy movement—another inspiration for *Killing the Buddha*—toward a mythical past. For Radical Orthodoxy, the lure was a moment of pure mind, medieval scholasticism's anticipation of postmodern theology; for the anarchists at their most sentimental, it was a fantasy of pure flesh, wild men and women living like cavemen, abandoning the corruptions of the world. Even language would be jettisoned, according to the primitivists who swung through the trees around Eugene, Oregon. In the future, as in the past, they promised, we will communicate with clicks and grunts and humps and caresses.

It's silly enough—and sad enough—to drive you 180 degrees in the opposite direction. Counter to the new traditionalists, left and right, were the new atheists, the revitalized movement of angry rationalists that would bring screeds from Sam Harris, Christopher Hitchens, and Richard Dawkins. No Sheilas they! The new atheism is a movement built on rock-hard reason, throbbing with a weird mix of contempt for and attraction to soft superstition. It is not enough for the new atheists simply to not believe; what matters is making sure that you don't believe. They are evangelists, and like evangelicalism itself—a faith built around the Great Commission and a hope for the conversion of every man, woman, and child— their cause is hopeless. If evangelicalism is shaded by delusion, the new atheism is propped up by a false posture. As an alternative to Sheilaism, it ultimately offers more of the same, translated into macho: to "just my own little voice" it replies, "my own awesome— erm, *brain*."

Which brings me round to the third escape from Sheilaism, the third way. Third ways are a twentieth-century tradition themselves, one that's usually a cover for something cynical. The third way was the path of Pyle, the violently optimistic spook in Graham Greene's *The Quiet American,* and it was the hope of the real-world CIA when it financed a generation of the American avant-garde, hoping to out-art the Soviet Union, as documented in Frances Stonor Saunders's *The Cultural Cold War.* The third way, we could argue, was a rhetorical trick of that forty-years' war. Like the bomb, it lingers; like nuclear power, it still seduces. The third way in politics, we're told by Democrats who vote like Republicans, is an aggressive centrism; the third way in religion, we're told by evangelicals who vote like Democrats, is a mealy mush of faith and pluralism, neither right nor left nor, apparently, much of anything. It is a rejection of both certainty and secularism, an embrace of tradition without ideas, a commitment to continuity without history, a center without moorings.

Third ways, in other words, tend to be built on false promises, naive realpolitik, compromises that conceal their costs. And yet, too skeptical for new traditionalism, too bored by the new atheism, we had no other chance but to find a third way of our own. Fortunately, we knew what to do with it when we found it: kill it. Because the third way you meet is not the true path but merely an expression of your longing. Thus, *Killing the Buddha,* a magazine devoted to its own undoing, a disjointed and freakish revelation road that runs in a bumpy circle, all its epiphanies merely echoes of one another, each murmuring the same precious and useless knowledge: the apocalypse is *always* now. Which means, of course, that the ending of one story is simply the beginning of another. Believer, beware; our condition is incurable.

JEFF SHARLET
Honeoye Falls, New York
September 2008

Jew Like Me

Peter Manseau

For three years after college I worked with an organization that collected used Yiddish books. A few times a month we'd leave our warehouse in western Massachusetts and drive north, to Montreal, or south, often to New Jersey, mainly to New York: Brooklyn, Williamsburg, Co-op City. Wherever Jews grew old, they were afraid of leaving their books as orphans.

So they called us, and we came. Most of the books we collected were saved only to die among their own, destined not to be distributed to a university, but to crumble on our bookshelves.

But the books' owners always seemed gladdened by our efforts. At least once every trip I heard the same grateful sentiment: The very fact that we cared enough to come for the books proved that Hitler hadn't won; that young Jews came for the memories of the old and the lonely guaranteed the future of the Jewish people.

Trouble was, I'm not Jewish. I had studied religion as an undergrad, picked up some Hebrew, read Philip Roth and Bernard Malamud, and generally developed a Judaic literacy totally alien to my French-Irish-American upbringing. Without thinking too much about it, I ended up a Catholic moving through a Yiddish-speaking world.

Early on I made no effort to conceal myself. One old man laughed when I told him my name, saying "*S'iz a modne yidishe nomen*" (Peter is a strange name for a Jew)—to which I shrugged and answered, "*Ober bin ikh nisht keyn yid*" (Well, I'm not a Jew), which is so unlikely a sentence to hear in Yiddish that he stared at me, blinking for a full minute, before he switched to English and told me which books to take and which to leave behind.

At best I was seen as a curiosity. More often I was greeted with suspicion, sometimes hostility. Once, while picking up books in a Montreal elementary school, I was accused of being a missionary, sent to convert the children of Canada's hasidic community.

What to do in the face of such a bizarre, xenophobic accusation? What else could I do? Following the time-honored assimilationist tradition, I learned to pass.

Just as in my high school French class I was not Peter but Pierre, in the Yiddish class I was then taking I was known as Pesach. It didn't take much to begin using this name on all my book-collecting trips. "*Vi heystu?*" they'd ask. "*Ikh heys Pesach,*" I'd answer. Beyond that I said very little. It was assumed I was a Jew and so, in a way, I was.

During one collection trip to Crown Heights I happened to be invited to a Lubavitcher wedding on Eastern Parkway. Not a scene for Catholic eyes: concentric circles of black-clad hasidim, dancing madly, a mosh pit of piety. Each man's hands on another's shoulders. Even Pesach joined in, circling with the rest, drinking a *l'chaim* of schnapps when offered.

"Mazel tov! Mazel tov!" the hasidim shouted to no one in particular. They, we, were Jews at a Jewish wedding, another victory over death; everyone was to be congratulated.

As the dancing continued, its fervor increased—then exploded. Fists pumped in the air. Grown men locked arms, hands to wrists, and spun each other round and round the way girls did at junior high dances. The well-wishing shouts grew louder and louder until they seemed a collective battle cry.

"We want the Rebbe!" the hasidim shouted, "We want the Rebbe now! We want *moshiach*"—the messiah—"we want *moshiach* now!" Lubavitch hasidim believe that their late rebbe, or leader, Menachem Mendl Schneerson, was and is in fact the messiah, and they await his return.

Pesach collapsed onto a folding chair next to the dance floor. There is no belonging, Pesach thought, like the belonging of the spent.

From the crowd two hasidim the likes of which he could have never imagined approached the table. One was about four feet tall, dressed like all the rest but in miniature. The other, also dressed in full hasidic regalia, seemed to have Down syndrome. The midget hasid took off his fedora and swatted at a chair.

"Have a seat right there, Rabbi," he said, and the Down syndrome hasid sat down beside me.

Pesach knew to keep silent but Peter was baffled and had had a bit too much to drink.

"Excuse me," I said. "He's a rabbi?"

"Of course he's a rabbi," the midget hasid said. "Isn't that right?"

The Down syndrome hasid said nothing, staring still into the circling crowd, which danced closer and closer to the tables now, threatening to swallow us.

"And you know what else?" the midget hasid said. "I think he's more than a rabbi." His voice dropped to a drunken whisper. "I think he's the Rebbe. I think *moshiach* is chained up inside him and we've got to get him out." He stared at me hard, as if he could see just as clearly inside me. "Wouldn't that be just like *Hashem*?" he asked. "Hiding in silence, seeing what we'll do?"

Just then the hasidim engulfed us. Rather than ask us to move they simply surrounded us and lifted us into the dance. Chairs and all, the three of us floated over the sea of black, as if we all had been married that day.

The Temple Door

Danielle Trussoni

The French had come to Vietnam in search of a paradise of palm trees and sunshine. For centuries, foreigners have come. There were all of the usual guests—the Chinese, the Khmer, the French—as well as the more unusual ones, such as the Hindu Kingdom of Champa, who built Gaudi-esque temples in Central Vietnam. But the Vietnamese have never been polite hosts, receiving foreigners with steely suspicion. When the Chinese (who taught the proto-Vietnamese to grow rice) tried to reorganize Vietnamese society along Chinese lines, they resisted. Just as they resisted contact with the West in AD 166, when Marcus Aurelius's Romans arrived, and again in the sixteenth century when Portugal sent its missionaries. They resisted the British, who came and then left after an agent of the East India Company was murdered in Hanoi. The missionaries came; the natives killed them.

I walked through the afternoon heat, trying to stay in the shade of palm trees. At the end of the district, I found myself at the mouth of a dirt road. Following it through a grove of trees, I came to a bright yellow building, half hidden by bushes, a wooden fence surrounding it. A curved rooftop swooped above. Painted dragons arched below the eaves, peering down the slanted corners like watchdogs. Glass tiles formed pictures upon the dull yellow wall—a blue-and-white bird, a red dragon, a turtle—each one at a corner of the entrance. The bird's feathers spread geometrically, square by square, around the door frame.

I banged my hand upon a set of warm red-and-black lacquered doors. When there was no response, I pushed them open and walked into a large room with a peaked ceiling and cement floor. Huge wooden doors, big as barn doors, stood ajar at the opposite end of the room, letting in sunlight. Incense rose in ringlets, filling the air with layers of slim, evanescent smoke. A very old, bald man stood near the doorway. When the monk saw me, he motioned for me to come closer. He was wrapped in long drapes of maroon cloth that twisted from his bare feet to a knot at his collarbone. He offered me a cigarette. He was missing most of his teeth.

"*Asseyez-vous!*" he said, pushing a chair at me. The table was nothing more than a wooden wheel balanced on an oil barrel. Teacups and saucers sat around a china teapot.

"*Quel âge avez-vous?*" the monk said.

Although I had studied French in high school, I responded in English. "Twenty-four," I said.

The monk clucked his tongue. He did not approve of youth. "*Très jeune,*" he said. "*Trop jeune.*"

The monk did not seem to speak a word of English, and so when he told me (in French) that he had been at the monastery for sixty years, from the late thirties, I thought I must not have understood him correctly. But the monk drew a six and a zero on my palm, confirming that he had moved into the pagoda thirty-five years before I was born.

He poured me tea, and I looked around the temple: there were tiny shrines cut into the walls, each one painted gold and crimson. Hundreds of plaques (embossed with prayers) stood next to black-and-white photographs. Incense and butter lamps burned below them.

When the monk wanted to speak to me again, he waved over a group of younger monks, Vietnamese men who were my age or slightly older. The old monk opened my hand, pressed down my fingers, and stroked my palm, as if he might read my fortune. He said something in slow, ambling Vietnamese and one of the young monks translated it into perfect English. He said, "Our master welcomes you to our pagoda. He is sorry that he doesn't speak your language. He learned French very well, many years ago. But he never learned English."

The head monk waddled away, slow as a goose, and the younger monk led me by the arm. "He would like to show you our pagoda, yes?"

I had not been inside a church for over ten years, and I'd never seen a Buddhist temple before. The statues and funeral tablets were so strange that I wanted to take a picture. But, when I dug for my camera, the young monk said, "Please. It is not allowed to take photographs here. It is not good luck."

We followed the head monk through the cavernous temple. He took us to a row of Bodhisattvas, a group of semi-human figures lounging against a wall with demons and dragons and all sorts of strange animals twisting around them. He led me to the Quan The Am Bo Tat, the Goddess of Mercy, a white statue of a woman armed like an octopus. She had eyes where eyes shouldn't be—in her forehead and cheeks, each eye looking in a different direction. The monk showed me A Di Da, the Buddha of the Past, and Di Lac, Buddha of the Future, two fat golden statues high on a dais. A pyramid of smaller statues surrounded the Buddhas. Incense rose from clay pots below them, releasing whips of smoke through the room. An elderly woman prostrated on yellow satin cushions, her long thin arms stretched out before her.

The young monk asked me if I was Christian. I told him that I was raised Christian, but that I had no idea of what I believed any longer. He studied me, pity in his eyes, and said, "You must discover this. It is important to know who you are."

The praying woman began to chant. Her voice rose into a high-pitched moan.

"This is a very old pagoda," the young monk said. "I have been here since I was seven. It is a sanctuary for us."

The old woman's prayer—half song, half groan—made me nervous. I was just about to excuse myself and leave, when the old monk put three joss sticks of incense in my hand. He pointed to the Buddha statues and said something in French.

The young monk translated. "He says you must pray."

"Pray for what?" I asked, as he lit the incense with a plastic lighter.

"You will know," he said, guiding me to the altar, "when you begin."

I had not knelt in prayer in so long that my knees felt rigid as I bent next to the old woman. Up close, I could see that she had a weathered face, and that she was much older, and more battered, than I had originally thought. The sadness in her face made her voice less abrasive. I blew on the incense and the ends fired orange. The rich, sharp smoke blanketed the base of the altar. I felt clumsy as I leaned forward, over the wooden steps that led up to the Buddhas, and stuck the incense into the sand in a clay pot, all three at once. They stayed for a moment, wobbled, and then fell over. When I tried to extricate them from the mess of smoke—so many sticks of incense burning with prayers—I singed my knuckles. Trying again, I pushed in one stick in at a time. This time, they stayed.

Through the haze of the smoke and chanting, images of my childhood filled my mind. I remembered the reels of eight-millimeter film shot during the years I was growing up. When we lived on Trussoni Court, we used to watch them on the wall of the living room, all of us kids in our pajamas. We had forgotten these tapes after our parents' marriage broke up, but for some reason Dad had recently decided to transfer the film to video. My father always said that the best years of his life were those spent with my mother, raising us, and so it must have taken a lot of strength for him to sort through the hours and hours of this forever-lost past, watching each reel. But he went through them all, selecting the best scenes and preserving them.

Dad gave me the tape when I was in graduate school. I watched it one evening, the lights turned low, as I drank a glass of pinot noir. The video cut across ten years and presented me with a father that I had long forgotten. I saw my father at Matt's christening, holding my brother as if he were the thinnest, most delicate Christmas ornament. I saw him planting the trees in the front yard of the house, just after Matt was born. In another shot, I saw myself, at two years old, dressed in Oshkosh overalls, my hair drawn into pigtails. I was an apple-cheeked girl with big black eyes, gazing up at my father, adoring.

My favorite part of the tape was a clip of my father helping me learn to ride my bike. I didn't know it at the time, but my mother had stood in the lawn and taped the whole thing. Dad wore jeans and no shoes. A cigarette dangled from his lips as he walked alongside the banana-seat bicycle I used to share with my sister, holding it steady. The camera followed me down the driveway, as I looked over my shoulder, checking that my father was there, and began to pedal. Dad stayed alongside the bike, holding the bar of the seat so that I gained balance and momentum. With Dad next to me, I was confident. I pushed the pedals harder until I was riding down the driveway, and onto Trussoni Court. I remembered that when I looked back and saw Dad far behind, I wavered and lost my balance, sending the bicycle crashing, falling hard onto the blacktop, scraping a layer of skin on the stony pavement. But in the video, I never hit the pavement. I kept my feet stiff on the pedals. I gripped the plastic handlebars. I knew that Dad would save me if I tipped.

I was grateful that my father had made the videotape. It was a record of my childhood free of the distortions of memory. The tape helped me to see that many of my recollections had been colored by love and anger—that I had often made my father in the image of my emotions. I saw that my memory had wrapped itself through the battle scenes of my life, ignoring the moments of tranquility. There were many things about those years that I had forgotten—the tenderness that my father was capable of when he wasn't sad or drinking or lost in remembering. He had been pushed to the limit by the war—he looked defeated and worn out in every shot. The tape forced me to see that, more than anything, my father had been defeated by Vietnam. He had lost his war, his pride. Nothing would change that.

I folded my hands and asked for my father's illness to disappear. I prayed that all the terrible things that had happened in Vietnam—to Americans and Vietnamese alike—would never happen again. I prayed for the one thing my father and I had never shared—peace. Then, I stood and walked away from the altar.

On my way out of the temple, I dropped a bundle of dong notes into a box for donations. My eyes had filled with tears. I could hardly see by the time I pushed past the doors and left the temple. Outside, the afternoon had become hot and bright and overwhelming. I leaned my head against the sun-warmed door, letting the heat soothe me.

Zen Mind, Alkie Mind
Martha G.

I didn't go to Alcoholics Anonymous to find God. I didn't go to AA to get sober, even. In 1979, at the age of twenty-one, I went to my first AA meeting looking for bad boys in leather jackets, Lou Reed wannabes. My best friend, who I'd met in OA—Overeaters Anonymous—was the one who tipped me off. There was a meeting in one of the cooler neighborhoods in my dying steel town, a meeting where the air hung heavy with smoke and stories about Patti Smith waking people out of their junkie stupors. The people who attended even committed a big AA no-no—they mixed their talk of drinking with talk of drugs, just as they had when they were using.

Did I want to go?

Did I.

So I went to my first AA meeting the way most people I know did: for all the wrong reasons. Talk to most people who stick around AA for any length of time, and as the fumes clear from their brains, the story they tell of their early sobriety sounds less like an epiphany, and more like an earthquake they barely survived. No one marches proudly to a first meeting. There are courts and crawling and police and slithering involved.

I slunk to my first meeting. I didn't think I had a drinking problem. In my twenty-one years, I'd managed to eat my way up to 170 and starve myself down to 74 pounds (I'm five foot three), and when I entered Overeaters Anonymous, I was mildly overweight. You wouldn't have noticed me on the street, either for my heft or lack thereof. But I was plagued with rage flashbacks over my formerly anorexic state, and I couldn't control my eating. Overeaters Anonymous helped, though I wasn't sure why. I learned that the program itself was modeled after Alcoholics Anonymous, the granddaddy of recovery programs. This intrigued me.

OA was, at the time, overwhelmingly female. AA . . . well, it was started by a male stockbroker and a male doctor. If you pick up the book *Alcoholics Anonymous* (AA's famed "Big Book"), filled with AA stories, you'll notice that it's mostly about men and their drinking, circa the Depression. The text reeks of three-piece suits and hard liquor. There's even a charmingly antique chapter titled "To Wives." Decades after AA began, it still had a distinctly male cast to it. And for me, that was part of its appeal. I was horny and lonely and twenty-one, and my old drinking and eating buddies weren't cutting it anymore.

Also, AA stories are filled with dramatic brushes with death. In OA, you rarely heard much about that. (Now, with the uptick in anorexia and morbid obesity, I'm not so sure.) I'd never collapsed with a needle in my arm, but at my thinnest, I had passed out on a nurse taking blood—I hadn't eaten in two days. I'd starved myself so much I gave myself visual and auditory hallucinations. The nurse in my high school had warned me that if I got the flu once more, I'd be dead. During the worst parts of my anorexia, I had wished I was a heroin addict, so that I could be cool while I did my dying. I was a sick girl. I could, as they said in AA, identify.

But I wasn't crazy about the prayers that bookended any twelve-step meeting I attended—an Our Father at the beginning, the Serenity Prayer at the end—even if the invitation to pray the latter began with "Will all those who care to, please join me in the Serenity Prayer." But though it had been years since I'd attended Mass without duress, and though I felt that talking about God the Father just reinforced the patriarchy, I said all the prayers. Said them out loud. Held every hand that wanted to be held. Because in the end, I wanted to belong, I wanted to be part of the Lou Reed wannabe club.

Which didn't stop me from feeling like a big fake on two fronts. Drinking was number one: I didn't have the requisite big story. I'd broken up somebody's marriage when I was seventeen, but that was a mostly sober, if stupid, time. I'd slept with people I hadn't wanted to sleep with—but, with one flashy exception, I'd done that without boozing it up either. My drinking story was mostly about hanging around in gay bars with men who weren't going to sleep with me, and coming up with ideas for movies and novels I couldn't remember in the morning. My big failures were mostly about the incompletes I pulled in my English classes—which, thanks to the loosey-goosey liberal arts college I went to, just sat there, not even affecting my grades. I never ruined a business. I never threw a pet out a window. I never drove a car up the steps of a children's hospital. I never punched out a blind kid. In AA story terms, I felt like a piker.

Then there was the God thing. If you open the AA "Big Book," the cornerstone of AA philosophy, the language is both explicit and mysterious. Nobody gets better from alcoholism without a reliance on God—on something or someone bigger than your drunken, sorry self. AA is a spiritually spacious enough place to add the words "as you understand him" after the word "God." But in the meetings I went to, in my hometown, people were quite open about their faiths, and the meetings reflected that. Nobody questioned whether the prayers should be said, or that somebody upstairs was listening.

This was my dirty secret. I was a junkie for AA stories. When I thought about God, though, I thought about other people. The other people in the rooms. Their stories. How the stories all started the same way, and repeated, and repeated. That's what addiction is: the same old stupid story, told in body after body. Cars crashed, marriages wrecked, jobs ended. That was the way every AA story began. And then, there's the part that always woke me up: the day of stopping. That's the day when you stop thinking of your life in the passive voice, when things stop happening to you, and you realize that you did them. As a writer, this fascinated me. If you stayed sober, you got to tell new stories about your life; you got to move from object to subject, from secondary character to protagonist. Ongoing recovery is a cliffhanger: I kept coming back to see if people had really pulled it off another hour, another day, another week.

By Christmas, I had joined the club, calling myself an alcoholic, though I hadn't quite stopped drinking. In AA lingo, I was a "periodic," someone who could go long days, longer weeks, without drinking, and fool myself that I had no problem, though the bottle sat square in the middle of my mind.

Then I went to a Christmas party, a big shindig at a local hotel, with booze and food and booze and food. The party marked the end of a temp job I'd had—one of three I'd had since I graduated from college six months before. The only thing I had to look forward to was more unemployment, more strange days in my parents' big, sad house.

AA is a perverse little thing. One of the things they tell you in AA is that if you're not sure you're an alcoholic, go out and drink some more, try it on for size. In meetings, I'd hear people say piously, "AA ruined my drinking," and I'd think, "What bullshit." But as I ate and drank my way through the party, I kept waiting without results for the mixed drinks to give me that sweet, wild lift. I kept waiting for the chocolate to make me wired and smart. I waited for the gin to take me to the place I used to go.

Someone gave me a ride home. In the living room, my father slept, while on the stereo, Charlie Parker, Dad's favorite addict jazzman, played so loud that you could hear him four houses away.

I stumbled around the kitchen, looking for something to put in my mouth. I finished the dregs of one of my father's drinks, a martini with a lemon twist. All I could taste was metal.

"Oh, God," I said. And put it down for good.

That was it for my epiphany. That was the white light moment that people often talk about when they tell their AA stories in church basements and synagogue social halls. The taste of metal, and Charlie Parker wailing in the next room, and using the name of the deity as a curse word.

I stopped drinking and waited for God to show up again. Through the years I said the prayers. One of my twelve-step friends confessed that for her, God was a black woman with a big lap, the Aunt Jemima of Jesus figures. When I imagined God at all I saw a blur. I was too much a self-aware feminist to see God as Big Daddy, even if I did say the Our Father. And I was too skeptical of the goddess culture to see Her as the Venus of Willendorf.

But I did do the things that are supposed to get you "conscious contact" with a God "as you understand him." I did a "fearless and searching moral inventory" with a woman who looked like a cross between Joni Mitchell and Mimi Rogers. I made a list of my character defects, as AA suggests, and I burned it, as my AA sponsor, slightly Wiccan, recommended. Then I made amends—I sought out those who had been harmed by those character defects.

I was raised Roman Catholic in the middle of the 1960s, just old enough to memorize the Mass in Latin in first grade and then never use it again. I never liked confession—in fact, very early on, I began to make up my sins, just to see if the priest would catch me. He never did, which made me cynical and smug: I was a good storyteller.

When I made amends to people, it never quite worked out the way I planned it. I didn't get that neat and tidy resolution that being in the confessional used to give me. People spilled or sprawled or spit at me. And yet somehow, I felt better than I ever did exiting confession.

But God wasn't a piece of this, either. Making amends to people I had harmed, either on a periodic or a daily basis, didn't show me my Higher Power. It just made my story that much more interesting.

Perhaps the central miracle of my sober life isn't, in fact my own. It was—it is—my father's sobriety. Three months after I gave up the drinking ghost, my father checked himself into rehab. He had wandered away from an important business lunch, driven without a license, smashed up a car, and finally, while detoxing, slit an artery in his head as he convulsed, reaching for a Diet 7-Up in a refrigerator.

Dad and I rarely went to meetings together. But we often encountered each other, with surprise and pleasure, like old buddies bumping into each other at a bar. Dad fell in love with AA, so much so that some of his friends referred to him as "the Mayor." He dressed for meetings, with jaunty hat and an extra handkerchief, he said, to wipe off the lipstick of all the ladies who wanted to kiss him hello.

Then doctors found a lump of cancer in my father's brain. The size of a baseball, they said, the cliché especially infuriating because Dad loathed sports. But Dad got the picture. He threatened suicide. He urinated on a Barcalounger chair in his hospital room and didn't even notice. One of Dad's dearest AA pals was in the room when it happened. Dad's pal acted as if nothing was wrong. And indeed, nothing was. The air smelled of urine, and they went on talking. If they'd been drunk together, they wouldn't have mentioned the pee, either.

During that year, I staggered back to some kind of faith. It is either a good thing or a very bad thing that Dad got cancer just as new age medical folks were starting to make the mind–body connection. I bought it big-time. I wanted to believe that Dad's brain was strong enough to talk back to the cancer. After all, he'd rewired himself for sobriety, hadn't he?

Dad and I now visualized like bastards, imagining the cancer beaten back by a series of military metaphors. But that's when Dad's mostly dormant Catholic imagery came to the fore.

"I'm a piece of coal, and God's dropped me from his airplane, and I'm plunging through the earth," Dad said.

Meanwhile, AA folks attended my father in droves. It was not unusual to for a crew to show up at our house to literally lift Dad into a car to get him to a meeting. When Dad lost the ability to walk, Dad's sponsor created an ad hoc meeting at our house. When Dad fell into a coma, AA members read to him in the hospital room, as the smell of his bedsores filled the room.

When he died, we buried him with his hat.

Even during the year of my father's cancer, the idea of drinking didn't really occur to me. The idea of suicide did, though, especially after my live-in boyfriend had a drunken romp with a man with herpes, in the house of a mutual friend. It wasn't so much I wanted to die, as I just didn't want to be alive anymore. I went to meetings in a state of fury. I spoke in tongues. I could barely hear what people said, but I didn't drink.

I wasn't angry with God that year, only cancer. I didn't think God was all that interested in cancer. But every time I would admire His Handiwork, I would also spot some place where His Chaos was in full bloom. After my father's death, the idea of God stopped making any sense to me at all.

When people first come to AA, shaking and dry and wrecked, they are urged to "use the group," to "act as if," to "fake it until you make it." In the beginning, I found most of these slogans loathsomely saccharine. Now, I use them incessantly. I've gone from thinking that AA was mostly made of morons to becoming convinced that AA founders Dr. Bob and Bill W. managed to careen their way to a kind of elegant American Buddhism. Kind of Zen Mind, Alkie Mind.

Because when I go to meetings now, I feel more at home than ever. I live in a big city where it is possible to find all flavors of AA meetings, including those aimed at the agnostic. But that isn't why I feel at home. I don't believe in God, and I say so, and no one throws me out. Because ultimately, the only requirement for AA membership, as I hear in every meeting, is a desire to stop drinking. And I still want that.

Some people may thank me for my sharing. Still others, I am sure, think I will drink soon. It has been twenty-one years since I did, but they may be right. It matters less and less to me what I believe, and more and more to me that I show up, a day at a time, in my life, and listen to the stories of others doing the same thing. Occasionally, I offer advice, mostly in the form of—stories about my life. My most usual prayer is the AA short form of the Serenity Prayer, which is: "Fuck it." This feels like enough.

AA is short on absolutes, but there is a portion of the AA "Big Book" that suggests that if you stick around, your life will change, and get better. Mine certainly has. I'm married now, to a man I love, and I have a mother-in-law I adore.

More than fifty years ago, my Jewish mother-in-law survived her time in the concentration camps by pretending to be Christian. She memorized the "Hail Mary" in Polish, and she has never, to this day, forgotten it. She never believed in the prayer, but it still saved her life.

What's Past Jersey?

Seth Castleman

I have seen Jeffrey twice a week for the past three and a half months. He is one of sixteen young men who await their trials on D Hall at Horizon Juvenile Detention Facility in the South Bronx. I see the D Hall guys twice a week for ninety minutes. They live in a brand-new multimillion-dollar prison facility in Mott Haven, one of New York's poorest neighborhoods and one of the four 'hoods in the city that collectively account for almost all youth arrests. (If you are underage and live elsewhere in the city, you are fairly safe from arrest.)

Jeffrey is Dominican, sixteen, with big puppy-dog eyes. His main man inside is Chris, a Puerto Rican kid with enough dignity and sincerity to be sainted. The two slide around the unit like cats. They slide, they smile, and they don't say much. Today I slip into a chair next to Chris and Jeffrey. No class today, just some personal time with a couple young men.

"How many times we seen each other, man?" I ask Jeffrey. "How many classes you come to?"

"Your classes?" he counts by tapping his fingers on the armrest of the massive wooden and plastic chair. Called bricks inside juvie, these chairs weigh well over a hundred pounds, designed to make it impossible to pick one up and smash another kid over the head.

"I'd say twenty-four. Yeah, twenty-four classes."

I am surprised he knows with such accuracy. "What's it done?"

He pauses a long time, smirking. He taps his fingers on the armrest. "I guess, well . . ." He doesn't seem to have anything to say to this.

"You can say nothing if that's the truth," I tell him. "You won't hurt my feelings."

"No. . . . You know, it relaxes me. I'm more relaxed when I'm hype." He pauses a while and we stare at the TV. "I been doing it in my room often."

"What do you mean?"

"The breathing thing, I been doing it often. You know, rising and falling." He makes a motion in front of his belly as if he were breathing deeply.

"What, every once in a while, like once a week?"

"No, often."

"Often?"

"Yeah, like every day."

"Every day?! You're shitting me."

"Nah, every night I go into my room and I read for a while. Then I turn out the light and do the breathing stuff you taught us. In, out, in, out. Fifteen, twenty minutes. Then I do my prayers and I go to sleep." He nods his head, then looks back at the TV. "Every night."

I am astounded. Jeffrey would show up each Monday and Thursday afternoon. He would sit in the back and rarely would he say anything. Only in the session on anger did he have lots to say. I never was quite sure if he was even doing the meditation or not.

He continues, "There's this place I can get alone in my room. I get into the zone. He puts his hand up between his eyes like a knife and moves it forward, making a slight sound, like a ball hitting a wall. "It's like duuuunh." He gives me a glance. "You know what I mean?"

"I do."

"Yeah. I get there. It's real still. I can get there in my room and just hang out there for a while." He is smiling now. "However long I want. Well, sometimes I can, not always."

He is silent for a while. "Reading, doing my prayers, the meditation, or just hanging out, it's like I can have everything I want in there, total freedom. It is real strong like, like I was . . . well, you know, like at peace."

"That's great, man."

"Yeah, but they don't let me stay in there. The staff kicks us out, they say we shouldn't be all alone. All day we got to sit out here on the unit. It fucking sucks, you know. I can't be happy out here. All this noise. All these assholes. The TV is blaring all the time. I don't watch TV, I listen to the radio, but there ain't no radio here. And people always coming up and bothering you, saying hey, what this, what that. No peace, man. No way I can be in the zone out here."

"That's why it's called a practice."

"Huh?"

"Inside your room you got it, man. And that's great, keep it up. But that isn't the training. The training isn't about finding a quiet place and escaping, that's too easy. The real training is, can you do it anywhere, anytime? Now that you have found it, the real practice begins. You do it in your room to strengthen it, to develop it. You with me?"

"Yeah." He looks away at the ceiling in the corner of the room above the supply closet.

"But then you come out here to practice so that eventually you can do it anywhere. The peace is within you, Jeffrey, not within your room."

"Yeah," he says, shaking his head and looking down. "You don't understand."

"Oh really? Let me tell you, I know just what you mean. All the noise, all the assholes, all the distractions. You remember when I started coming here? Well, that was when I moved to New York City, just a few months ago. Before that I had never lived in a city before. In fact I lived out, really out, in the woods where it was totally peaceful and quiet and alone. I practiced out there and got real still, like you in your room. It was great. Then I came to New

York, and it's crowded and smelly and noisy, and there sure are a lot of assholes."

"Wow. You never lived in a city before?"

"Not really. I was living out in the woods where there are only trees and mountains, in a little hut doing my meditation practice."

"You mean like Jersey?"

I had to laugh. "No. I mean way past Jersey."

"Nah. What's past Jersey?"

It would have been funny, but he was serious. "You know," I said, "when I tell those stories about the sacred mountain and crazy old men living in huts and caves?"

"Yeah."

"Like that."

"Wow. That is past Jersey."

"But I'm not there now. I'm here. And it is loud and smelly and no sky and no mountain except the hill in Central Park. But it isn't like I give up and stop practicing or start being an asshole or put my head under the pillow. This is where the practice gets hard."

"Hmm."

"You and me. We are in the advanced training. Do it in your room each night, then come out and keep trying during the day."

Jeffrey looks off at the ceiling. "Yep, enough assholes around here to keep me practicing a long time. Long time."

I Am a Sea

Patton Dodd

I am a sea!
I am a sea-aiche!
I am a sea-aiche are eye estee eye aye-en!

Everyone knows what is happening but me. I am sitting in a beige-colored folding chair, one of hundreds of such folding chairs in a long meeting hall on the Oklahoma State University campus. The month: July. My age: twelve. I should be riding my bicycle. I should be playing Nintendo. Instead, I am surrounded by hundreds of junior-high evangelical Christians who are clapping and swaying and laughing and sing-shouting strange words at the top of their evangelical lungs.

These kids are just like me. They go to church every Sunday. They live in the suburbs. They wear shorts and T-shirts and tennis shoes. They have youth pastors. They have too much gel in their hair.

Just like me, but different. They understand the words to the song.

And I have sea-aiche are eye estee in my aiche ee-aye are-
tee . . .

This is my first Christian summer camp. It will not be my last, and in time I will come to enjoy the sing-shouting—louder than mere singing, funnier than mere shouting. I will laugh and stomp and do the hand motions and hope that the girl next to me thinks I am being cute. But then I will know the words, while tonight I am utterly confused. I'm standing at the bottom of the Tower of Babel. I think they are shouting in tongues.

> . . . and I will el-eye vee-ee-ee tee-ee-are enay el el why!

Everyone knows what is happening, and within two full choruses—each of which is sung faster than the one before—I get it, too. It's a declaration. It's a joyful noise. It's a spelling game that forms a credo sung full and loud and silly.

> I am a C! I am a C-h! I am a C-h-r-i-s-t-i-a-n!
> And I have C-h-r-i-s-t in my h-e-a-r-t!
> And I will l-i-v-e e-t-e-r-n-a-l-l-y!

It's an initiation into youth group summer camp, a ritual I will perform excitedly through junior high and part of high school. Summer camp will involve games and Bible studies and flirtations and make-outs and pranks and the occasional threat to be sent home early, and it will also involve hours of sing-shouting. And nearly every night, we'll sing *I am a C*. For most people, "Kum Ba Ya" is the canonical Christian camp hymn, but every evangelical in America born after 1970 knows that nothing is as unforgettable—or inescapable—as *I am a C*.

At this particular youth group summer camp, called Crosspoint, every attendee picks a sport and practices it twice a day. The camp is built on the theme of running a good race in life, which was the Apostle Paul's favorite metaphor. Clearly a fan of the Olympiad, Paul knew a thing or two about running, and he said things like "I have fought the good fight, I have finished the race, I have kept the faith" and "Do you not know that in a race all the runners run, but only one gets the prize? Run in such a way as to get the prize." Such sayings are blazoned on banners and T-shirts and baseball caps at Crosspoint, where running a good race means several things: Loving God a lot. Reading your Bible. Not giving in to peer pressure by smoking, or cussing, or lying to your parents. Inviting your friends to church so they can hear about Jesus. Not just saying you are a Christian, but living like one.

But by far the most tiresome race I run at Crosspoint is each night's song service. Every night after supper, we filter into the huge meeting hall with the beige chairs where banners sway with Paul's race quotes. After a long day of fun and games, I anticipate the evening meetings with dread. I know that the meeting will begin with a solid half hour of sing-shouting. After that, a funny skit will be performed. Then a pastor will teach us about a Bible passage. I enjoy the skit, and the teaching is more or less bearable. But the half hour of singing is terrible. Every song is supposed to be goofy and funny and fun if you know the words and motions, but, for most of my first summer camp week, I feel uninitiated. When everyone else bends over I am standing. When I lean to the left everyone else leans right. I reach for the sky and wiggle my fingers; they grab a partner and turn around. I feel like everyone attended a Crosspoint sing-shouting orientation that I missed. Why do I not know this stuff? I was raised in Southern Baptist churches, too!

The problem is amplified by *I am a sea.* Even when I finally hear *I am a C,* I feel like an imbecile for not hearing it automatically. In my memory, it will become several minutes of not knowing, verse after verse of people spelling out the terms of faith and my head spinning at the abstract, foreign sounds. In reality, it is thirty seconds of confusion. But I feel each and every one of those thirty seconds like a reverberating gong.

I will feel those thirty seconds again and again throughout the years. I feel the terrible seconds with *I am a C* as a freshman in college, when I go back to church after a five-year hiatus, and again when I transfer to a Christian university and am literally surrounded by lifelong Christians, and again when I leave the Christian university for a state university and attend ministry meetings like Campus Crusade for Christ. I feel them with every group Bible study. I feel them with every conversation with a new kind of Christian—Baptist, Methodist, Lutheran, Pentecostal, Catholic, Episcopalian. I want these worlds to be familiar. I want to know my way around—and I should, for I have never been too far away from the evangelical world. But the cultural signage is consistently terrible, or, at least, I don't know how to follow it. "I was lost, but now I am found." But even when I feel found spiritually, I feel lost socially.

But I do learn the song and countless others, with the result that at Crosspoint and elsewhere in Evangelicaldom, I learn to shout my faith. I learn to wear it on my sleeve—at least while in the comfort of friends on beige folding chairs. *I am a C* is not merely a youth camp sing-shout. It is the very thrust of life. It is our duty to internalize *I am a C.* Finishing a race means hearing *I am a C* and declaring it at the top of my lungs. Being a Christian means banners and Bible studies and Christian rock music and not-drinking and not-partying and knowing in my heart of hearts that I will *l-i-v-e e-t-e-r-n-a-l-l-y.* Or, if not quite knowing it, then at least declaring it, spelling it out, hearing it and receiving it and believing it all at once, being part of a group that chants the entire content of our spiritual experience, learning that because we are *C*s we are different, but not different from one another, just different from the rest of the world who are not *C*s and do not have *C-h-r-i-s-t* in their *h-e-a-r-t-s.* The song is my leap of faith into a way of believing and living. My identity is forged in the fires of evangelical camp songs.

It takes me a long time to understand that shouting something does not mean that I believe it. Believing it is a whole other problem. Full-hearted assurance, if it exists at all, is motivated by something other than style of speech. Confessions of faith are always clothed in a particular expression, and for me, the particularity is the confession—and the obsession. Getting around that problem means getting around my whole experience of evangelical Christianity. Even when I am happy with the particular race I'm running, I feel like I've entered the wrong heat.

The language of Christendom, said Walker Percy, is worn out. He had high hopes that it would be revived by Christian novelists who could use the fallout of postmodernity (in his terminology: numbed consumers, hopeless autocrats) to point toward the heavenly kingdom. Percy was Catholic, but had he listened to the evangelicals he would have found that a new language had already been birthed: one consistent with the kind of evangelical belief that declares, that champions, that celebrates and thrusts hands in the air and claps and sways and knows for sure that it is Christian. But this would not have solved his problem; it would have intensified it, because the new evangelical language, in its sing-shouted confidence, was stillborn. *I am a C* rendered faith banal: loud and celebratory, to be sure, but overly familiar to the point of not signifying anything at all.

By the time I left Crosspoint, believing in Christ was like believing in blue jeans. There was nothing extraordinary about it. For much of the rest of my life, Christianity has been the strangest thing I can imagine, but rendered so normal in my memory and in regular evangelical experience that most of the time all I can do is poke at it, like an enormous, amorphous blob. Trying to see evangelical Christianity is like trying to see my own retina: it is that through which I perceive everything, whether I like it or not.

The difference between *I am a sea* and *I am a C* is not simply the difference between understanding a youth camp song and not understanding a youth camp song. It is the difference between hearing a song and hearing a symbolic phrase that renders intractable meaning to life. *I am a sea* is absurd, a singing game that I could happily play. But *I am a C* is a calling and a curse. It does not mean just being a Christian. It means being an evangelical Christian, being a cultural conservative, being all sorts of things that I did not—could not—choose. It means being immersed in a cultural form of faith that I may never quite be able to shake.

My Holy Ghost People

Ashley Makar

I don't understand Holy Ghost people, but I better believe them—every strange word. I'm a quarter Holy Ghost person myself: Pauline begat Judy and Barbara, and Barbara begat me.

I can't remember witnessing anybody speaking in tongues, but I must have heard the Word like that when my grandmother would take me to her Church of God when I was little. And I've heard from my mother what it's like: When people get worked up in church, somebody may break into what sounds like gibberish. And sometimes somebody will run whooping around the sanctuary, and some loudmouthed Sister so-and-so may interpret—it'll be something generic, like *Praise the Lord! Hallelujah!* They don't always interpret, though, and they don't speak in tongues at every service. It's supposed to be when the Spirit comes up on you, as they say, and when it does, they say something like *Ashundado ashundado kundai! Ashundado ashundado kundai!*

I can tell my mother's about to laugh when she imitates speaking in tongues, but she doesn't. She's not making fun of it, she'll tell me; she's just trying to demonstrate. But then a spooked look will come over the green eyes she got from her mother, and she'll say she doesn't understand it, but she's not going to criticize: the Bible says blaspheming the Holy Ghost is the only unforgivable sin.

My Aunt Judy spoke in tongues. Just after she was diagnosed with cancer three years ago, my mother heard her do it. Judy and Grandmother came straight from the oncology clinic to Mom's house, to tell her the bad news. Mom cried; Judy said, "Let's pray." They stood up and held hands in an almost circle and closed their eyes. Judy and Grandmother took turns praying out loud; Mom prayed to herself, still crying. Judy broke into tongues. I imagine a quiet change in her voice—as subtle as the way breath changes from awake to asleep. But Mom didn't describe the sounds of Judy's prayer in tongues. She just said *ashundado ashundado kundai* was part of it, and wondered aloud why it always sounds like that: Maybe that's what comes out when some people who've heard it all their lives get deep in prayer. Or maybe that's some phrase God uses whenever He gives a message in tongues. Mom knows it's supposed to be a gift, like prophecy, but she's afraid of the Holy Ghost.

When Aunt Judy almost died last fall, I was watching people speak in tongues in Peter Adair's documentary *Holy Ghost People*. She was getting resuscitated in a North Alabama emergency room, her blood sugar sky high, while I was getting high on taped testimonies—the quickening power of the Holy Ghost—in a New York film screening room. I watched at first in distant awe—the convulsive jerk of an Appalachian woman's head before she broke into tongues, a younger woman talking about the Lord dealing with her through a *twinglin'* in her stomach. But as I listened to these Holy Ghost people getting worked up, or the Lord working on them, as they put it, something like revelation came up on me: *my people are Holy Ghost people.* Their strange prayer is my Grandmother tongue—speaking sounds I know by the telling, stories I've heard all my life. It's in my blood, like cancer. And in the tube between my eardrum and the back of my throat, like swallowing.

I don't know tongues, but I know *how* Holy Ghost people talk to the Lord, by heart. I know how Grandmother prays, in a cadence like crickets, a tender drone—grieving and pleading and gracious all at once, swelling to that harsh stride that comes up on her when she's Cloroxing the tub with her hands, or when she used to whip her girls with a fly flap: *Whap! I* mean *you better straighten up and start actin' right, girl, or the devil's comin' after you,* she'd say, beating just as hard as she could, like she's in a trance, my mother's told me, over and over. Though I've never seen Grandmother whip like that, I heard her in a high-handed clap, on documentary tape. "Don't be ashamed to praise the Lord," the preacher called, *"repent of it."* The people shuddered, *heal us, Lord, help us, Lord,* yelled, *Yes, Lord,* and fell, *whap,* to the floor, back to the Lord.

"Have *you* got that kind of a Spirit?" The preacher's words haunt me. Or maybe that's the Lord working on me, wrenching my heart, where Jesus would be, if I'd just invite Him in to be my personal savior, like I was supposed to a long time ago. I've tried to get saved, but not "wholeheartfully," like the preacher says.

I don't know how much of her heart was in it, but my mother's asked Jesus in—"just in case," she says. She's willing to believe He's the Son of God, because that's what she was taught, and she wants to go to heaven. But she doesn't believe He's the *only* way, just because the Bible says so. She knows men wrote the gospels, and she knows how much stories depend on who's telling them.

When I tried to tell Mom all I'd learned in college about the scribe-altered scriptures and the ambiguities of Jesus's parables, she cut me off: "What's the point, if it's all up to interpretation?" I didn't talk back, about how mystery—even the strangeness of tongues—thrills me. I revel deep in metaphors, between the sense-making mind and the babble at the pit of the throat. My mother lives in black and white, truth and lie, real and unreal. She's my witness to the Holy Ghost–peopled world I inherited, but she doesn't tell me all I want to know.

I wonder why Grandmother says "the Lord" more than "Jesus" or "Christ," and "Holy Ghost" more than "Holy Spirit." Our Lord Jesus Christ is supposed to be one and the same with God the Father and the Holy Spirit, so maybe it doesn't matter what you call any of them. But God seems more cosmic to me, out there reigning over the whirling universe, and the Spirit more down to earth—blowing through everything in the world, sometimes hard and fast, stirring up even Jesus in the pillow of your heart. Jesus is the one who loves you no matter what, and He died for your sins, and He'll come again, so He's Christ too. But the Lord and His Ghost sound different and elsewhere to me. The Lord seems stern and strange, every time I hear his name, like far-off thunder; the Holy Ghost startles like the rumble, quaking louder and closer.

In Grandmother's prayer language, it's the Lord who gives and takes God's children. And the Lord willed not to take Judy, that time. Maybe because Grandmother prayed so hard, and I saw her do it. In an empty hospital hallway, I was the one who said, "Let's pray," and she held my hand and spoke—head snapped a little forward, eyes rolled up under her lowered lids, in a voice not quite her own, almost like crying, but strong and clear, in some strange stride: *Lord, we know she's one of your children, and she's been a faithful servant to you. Lord, you ask us to remind you of the Scriptures. And we remember that You gave Hezekiah fifteen years, and we're askin' you today for those fifteen years and more. Lord, we know it's accordin' to your will, but we're askin' you to relieve her sufferin', to heal her body, in Jesus's name. Amen.*

My mother believes God could heal Judy completely if He wanted to, she told me. She doesn't understand why He hasn't yet—Judy's spent her whole life serving the Lord. Maybe because people wouldn't believe it was Him if He did it before she got so sick: maybe people need to see suffering, or miracles, to believe.

Judy's got cancer all over her abdomen; not long to live, the doctors say. But Grandmother remembers aloud: "They didn't give Mother but three months. And she left that hospital to go home and pray—took three days alone with the Lord, and she lived six years."

Even I prayed over Aunt Judy, alone while she was asleep in her hospital bed. I laid on my hand like I've seen Grandmother do, palm to forehead. And I asked the Lord to heal her, half believing He would, maybe completely, if I completely believed. But I hardly ever believe everlastingly. A lot of the time, I forget the Lord. I've only let Him work on me in heart pangs. And the pangs come when I hear people pouring out to Him, and I remember: that healing-mercy-wrath in one *Lord, God*; that chorus of hand, heart, and hell on Grandmother's fly flap, in her prayers. And it sounds like going back to where I was from.

God Is Electric,
Jesus Electrochemical
Michael Allen Potter

The rifle rests on my lap, solidly bridging the gap between my knees as I listen to St. Mark (not his real name) pontificate about the Church. He goes on and on about solace, comfort, and our Lord. I feign attentiveness, but really my focus is directed at jamming the striker back into the bolt. Oblivious, he prattles on about choices, decisions, and faith. We are alone in the basement of our high school, sitting on the floor. It is a bright Sunday morning. There is not another soul in the building.

He is convinced that the Holy Spirit will be the panacea for my problems at home. Will quiet my cerebral rage. Will banish my teen angst forever if I will just open my heart. St. Mark's expression is earnest and serene, and I am silent and respectful while he urges me "not to cultivate this anger, to let go," but all I want to do is change the subject.

I have issues. I listen to speed metal constantly.

I have been pushed through the phases of Catholic family farming: baptism, Sunday school, first communion, and confession. I have come out on the other end mangled and dubious.

I grab another gun from the wall, stand, and push the heavy stocks against my hips. The Sabbath sunlight catches the corner of my eye and I squint, like Eastwood. Gingerly, I press the sights of both Enfields against St. Mark's temples and implore him to "shut the fuck up." He complies.

* * *

St. Mark and I are cadets at a military academy in upstate New York and I am simply grateful to be out of my house for an extended period of time. But St. Mark, I know, has conversion on his mind as we drive out of the city and into suburbs I am not familiar with. He's been lobbying for this moment for four years and he has simply worn me down. I've agreed to attend a single charismatic mass, and I hope to put an end to his missionary work, once and for all, this afternoon.

I do my best to be invisible once we arrive.

The church itself is modern, with angular, unadorned, yet highly polished rows of pews. Unfinished crossbeams span the ceiling and lend a Fisher-Price-barn-like quality to the space. The altar looks like an outdated Danish conference room. The congregation is completely white, with a neo-hippie aesthetic.

I refuse to sing, despite the guitars and tambourines. My heart rate triples when I'm forced to hold hands with strangers and pretend to pray. I am not nearly this social by nature. I am not a joiner. Still, the overall tone of the mass is different from the fire and brimstone of the traditional Catholic programming that I am forced to endure weekly.

St. Mark smiles at me at the end of the service like a dental assistant after a root canal, and then he urges me out into the aisle. I try to indicate to him, discreetly, that I am going nowhere except back out to the car, but I am navigated by this alleged friend, wide eyed, into a line of devout Christians waiting to be "prayed over."

After the members of Emmett Otter's Jug Band have finally silenced their instruments, I end up in front of the altar standing before a person who tells me not to be afraid. He promises that the man behind me will catch my fall. I begin to explain that that won't be necessary. But he places his hands on my head and starts to pray gently, insistently.

I fall to the floor.

I feel like I've been sucker punched, but without the actual blow. My body is flooded with a sensation similar to when your foot falls asleep, tingly and numb. As if my spine is Jell-O and the rest of me is liquefied. Until everything is suddenly reconstituted on the cold marble floor.

When I returned to the orphanage where I spent a great deal of my early childhood, I was warned about the possibility of "flashbacks," but none occurred. I had no movie-of-the-week freak-out, but I did become newly aware of certain memories.

I remembered how, as a child, I felt quiet and withdrawn whenever I passed the brick building, how I focused my attention on the statue of the Virgin Mary above the front entrance. I remembered that my school friends made fun of me for this, asked what my problem was, and that I had no idea.

But it was different when I returned to the place. I finally understood the fascination when I walked beneath her virtuous stone feet for the first time as an adult. This is where I spent the first years of my life, a fact that I learned over twenty-five years after the fact.

Nancy Drew (also not her real name) and I entered the building together, with twenty years of friendship between us, looking for anything that might lead me to my family. We were first struck by the silence, the absolutely oppressive silence of the interior of the building. Part of me was expecting packs of wild orphans running in the halls, but there were no voices, just two elderly volunteers staring at us from behind a desk.

Nancy Drew spoke to them privately for a moment and then they both grinned from ear to ear and watched as she took my hand and led me out of the foyer, in pursuit of records, files, and some sort of vague accountability. But we were waylaid by photography and portraiture.

All along the hallways, bishops and cardinals watched us pass with suspicion and disapproval. They looked miserable, each and every one of them, but their vestments were rendered in expensive, supple oils, the most vibrant purples and reds. These men glowed.

And then we saw the children. Hundreds of them, mostly in black-and-white, in archival photos on the upper floors near the administrative offices. Many of the photographs showed white nuns and nurses holding black babies against the backdrop of rows and rows of pristine hospital beds. Some of them were taken the day that a child was adopted or placed with a foster family. Everyone was smiling, except for a few children who seemed to know that they were merchandise, from a sort of Salvation Army.

The color photographs almost stopped my heart when I realized that one of them might contain an image of me, of the former me, of me before my identity was completely erased. Nancy Drew held my hand tightly as we walked slowly past these pictures like we had done a hundred times, in museums and galleries all over the Northeast.

It took us a while to figure out why everyone that we passed in those creepy, fluorescent hallways smiled so sheepishly at us. It took us a while to understand that we looked the part, like potential customers. All of the people we passed were simply acknowledging our Christian hearts, so full of love that we were ready to open our home to an unfortunate, unwanted child. Their sanctimonious stares made me furious.

After a session with a secular caseworker (sympathetic eyes, children of her own, net result: absolute zero), we found ourselves in front of a twentysomething blond receptionist. I explained to her that I was looking for some information about my own adoption.

To which she replied, "You want to be adopted?"

After we helped her over this mental speed bump, by explaining that I was a former resident of this institution and not some sort of confused volunteer, she dialed an extension for Sister Mary SomethingOrOther and we sat down so I could regain my composure.

Sister Mary SomethingOrOther had been the head nun during my tenure at the orphanage, and I wondered if there would be an instantaneous recognition on her part, if she might embrace me and regale Nancy Drew with stories about my Little Rascals-esque behavior during those first few years.

I wondered if she might be the trigger for the aforementioned flashback and if I would soon be escorted out of the building by some sort of Catholic Rent-A-Cop who'd been hired, ultimately, because of his uncanny resemblance to St. Paul.

All I really wanted was a picture of my father or my mother. All I wanted was my sister's address or my brother's phone number. Something. I wanted my fucking family back.

The receptionist held the receiver slightly away from her ear and her eyebrows were almost touching her hairline. She said, "Yes, Sister," into the receiver before dropping the phone like a piece of rotten fruit. Then she said to us, by way of apology, "Sister Mary keeps her secrets well."

We were refused an audience with Her Majesty because orphans aren't supposed to come back. So we left.

The first time that my mother met Jesus Christ was in a redwood forest near a pond of brilliant blue water. She was impressed by His stunning robes, but deeply disappointed with His lack of white wings. The first question that my mother thought to ask the Son of God was whether or not she could keep smoking. He said that He didn't care.

The first time that I met my mother, at the age of thirty, I was able to shed the Irish Catholicism of my adolescence after learning about the Norwegian Lutheranism of my biological family. Until that day, I lived my entire life without any knowledge whatsoever of my background or heritage. My legal and "official" birth certificate is postdated a full decade.

She asked me if I remembered being strapped to the bed in the orphanage, if I remembered the beatings, if I remembered the spinal taps.

My mother is a paranoid schizophrenic who rarely leaves the house due to acute agoraphobia. She listens to religious broadcasting 24/7 on an old AM radio and chain-smokes generic cigarettes at her lopsided kitchen table. Weeks before our reunion, she sent me *365 Read-Aloud Bedtime Bible Stories* with this inscription: "What I would of read to you early in Life." Statistically, I have roughly a 50 percent chance of developing schizophrenia at some point in my life.

I am so generically and incredibly Caucasian that my skin throbs a deep crimson soon after it is exposed to natural light, and this fact seems to have been the only criterion used to determine my placement in foster care. I am certain that Sister Mary SomethingOr-Other signed my release papers fully convinced of the righteousness of the decisions she was somehow authorized to make on my behalf. But I also believe her hand was guided by the Devil Himself when she wrote my name across form after notarized form for various state agencies, because those forms, after receiving approval from blind administrators and stamps from zealous automatons, released me into the custody of abusive strangers.

My mother overdosed shortly after I was born and arrived, supine, at the gates of heaven on a hospital stretcher. Jesus refused her entrance and told her to go back down into the world to spread the Good News.

When I went to visit my mother for the second time in my life, she gave me a list, a chronicle of all the visions she had experienced since the late 1960s. She also gave me a letter addressed to Oral Roberts. I stood in the snow outside of her apartment, around the corner from where I had once lived in college, and debated whether or not to put the envelope into the mailbox.

Her particular brand of paranoia manifests itself as a kind of ultra-religiousness. She talks about God constantly. Every card and every letter that I receive from her has a long closing salutation that, she hopes, will bring me into the light of God's love. The strange and fascinating thing about certain symptoms of schizophrenia, particularly my mother's devotion to "Our Lord Jesus Christ," is that they are culturally specific; paranoid schizophrenics in other parts of the world display different psychoses. Because of my mother's own religious background, her entire adult life has been spent chasing angels and waiting for miracles.

Do I believe in God? No. Do I believe that God exists? Yes. God exists in the electrical storms and irregular dopamine levels of my mother's frontal lobes, limbic pathway, and cerebral cortex.

Do I have faith, give thanks and praise, and worship the Lord Jesus Christ? No. The Church has given up on me and I have given up on the Church. St. Mark gave up on me as soon as I told him that I was gay. The disdain is now quite mutual.

Because of my mother's condition, I know that her Christianity is simply the institutionalized misunderstanding of mental illness. Each time God appears to Abraham in Genesis, and to Moses in Exodus, and when John has a vision of Christ in Revelation, I am convinced that what they all truly experienced were separate and distinct undiagnosed psychotic episodes. These were self-reported, recorded by others, and then made the transition from oral history to gospel truth. We all suffer to this day.

I did mail the check to Oral Roberts before catching my flight back to California. Not because I am a believer myself, but because I love an old woman who has faith, gives thanks and praise, and worships the Lord Jesus Christ. She is my own, personal savior.

Everybody Has a Mother, and They All Die

Jeff Sharlet

1. *Mothers*

Everybody has a mother, and they all die. Mine did; yours will too. When she does—if she hasn't already—you'll be sorely tempted to make sense of what has happened. Ten years ago, a few years after my mother died, I asked my grandmother for some of my mother's letters so I could write about her life. A book-loving woman, my grandmother nonetheless frowned. "Oh, I see," she said, her lips curling inward in what I recognized as quiet fury. "You want to make a story of it."

But I didn't. Stories require faith, and I don't have any.

My mother raised me unreligious in as many churches as we had friends. We went to Methodist to hear Roger the bachelor sing, to Episcopal to listen to Shersti the Swede sing, to Dutch Reformed to watch our neighbor, Mr. Nelson, direct bell ringers, and to St. John the Evangelist Cathedral across the river for Christmas Eve Midnight Mass. Since my father is Jewish but didn't know much about it and lived somewhere else besides, my mother took the Jewish holidays as her own as well. For a year when I was little she let a Buddhist named Veena live in the attic, and near the end of her life she invited charismatic Christians in to pray. Around that time my granny drove up from Tennessee to take care of her dying daughter, and she brought her own gods, as many as would fit in her Buick: the Pentecostal Holiness god of her childhood, the singular Knoxville, Tennessee, Christ's Church of her age, and the spirits of the books she held dear, Dostoyevsky's pagan Russian Orthodox, Thomas Merton's meditative lord, the bending willows of the Tao Te Ching.

Surrounded by faiths, I had none at all. When my mother was diagnosed with breast cancer, when she was forty-four and I was thirteen, I sat mute in the churches we attended with increasing frequency. I didn't know how to pray, not even for my mother's life. By the time I began to learn, it was too late. All I could think to pray for was an end to the pain, hers and mine.

Before she died, while she was dying—disappearing for long spells to have her skin drawn on like parchment and blasted with radiation, to cling to an IV as if it were a burning rope and she a drowning woman, to have the marrow of her bones sucked out by long needles and replaced with fresh cells that quickly withered —I'd lie in my bedroom and follow the yellow vines adorning the wallpaper up to the blank ceiling and stare, trying to see God.

"Please," I'd say. "Let my mother die."

The summer after she died, I sorted through the boxes of her papers she left behind: her half-finished stories, her abandoned novels, her never-sent letters, her journals, her poems, her patched-together prayers, thinking I might find the beginning of faith there. Instead I found fragments such as these:

Undated, from a letter about her treatment:

For about two days I was disoriented. No sense of time, no distinction between reality and fantasy. And I would clutch at the cloth on the bed, thinking it was my skin and wondering why it was so rough.

Three months before she died:

This body, bound in skin and downy hair, is shuddering, weeping. It breathes and whispers a thank you with each breath. It likes to walk fast and break into a run. It likes to be giddy. It likes the mysterious warm tingle of red wine on a dark winter night, the startle of fragrance when an orange is cut. It likes the smack of cold winter air. It likes to sweat. It likes to float in the water then dive, pretending it is a porpoise. It likes to dance until it is the music.

*   *   *

My mother drowned lying in her own bed. She died in her room on the second floor of the house in which I'd always lived and that she and I shared alone for the last year of her life. She was forty-eight, I was sixteen. Her last breath was of water—fluid had filled her lungs, to which her cancer had spread from her breast and her skin.

My last glimpse of her I stole from my granny, who that morning, while we waited for the hearse, forbade me from looking at her daughter's corpse, her sweet Nancy now gone. But out of duty and to repent for wishing her dead I snuck upstairs to the room she had died in and closed the door behind me. She lay in her bed, half covered by blankets. It was quiet, my quiet and hers, so calm I couldn't bring myself to say good-bye.

She wouldn't have heard. Not because she was dead, but because, Jesus, she died hard: her mouth open and dark, her lips pale and curved in to cover her teeth, her thick cheekbones worn thin like knives about to tear through her skin. Her eyelids had been shut by my granny's hand, but what they hid I couldn't guess, there was nothing under them, as if her eyes had sunk deep down into her in one last bid to not see death.

When those prayer ladies came to save her before she died, I thought, *she tricked them. They said, "pray for your soul," but she made them pray for her life. They prayed. She died.*

Her spine arched up like she'd have jolted out of bed if weren't for her arms, thick and shapeless, swelled to bursting from radiation. I wanted to slip my own skinny arms beneath her and lift her up high as the morning light, coming on white and soft through the winter clouds. But the longer I looked the darker it got. *That's not my mother,* I thought, and a second later I knew I'd betrayed her more thinking those words than I had wishing her dead. But all I saw was her mouth, gaping: filled with darkness, an empty universe within a corpse.

"That's my mother," I said.

I believe in my mother's body—her corpse—more surely than I believe in God. Of course, it's not exactly original to build a theology on a dead body. The Christianity my mother fled from and was drawn to is at its heart morbid: alive, and transfixed by death. The Christian savior redeems his followers with the flow of his own blood. Catholics celebrate their redemption by eating his flesh. Less inclined to beat around the bush, a small tribe in Central Africa used to believe in eating the dead bodies of their beloved. Otherwise, they thought, the corpses would cause them to mourn forever.

We buried my mother a few miles from home. A somewhat soulless cemetery, ecumenical, well mowed, each grave capped by a stone of uniform shape and size. Hers is several yards up a hill from a landscaped stream. A modest rectangle set flat in the ground. I stare at it, looking not for her body but for the world it once contained. But that's the tricky thing about the stones we set over graves—only once a millennium do they get rolled away. For the rest of us, they're walls between now and then. Now: undeniable belief. Death will happen. Then: incomprehensible love. How could it end?

For answers, you have to look somewhere in between.

Years after my mother died, I decided to read her medical records. There I thought I'd find the most precise evocation of her fate: the facts of her death, the hows and whys that stand independent of stories and dreams. So I asked my sister, Jocelyn, who'd been named executor of the estate, to obtain them for me.

Doing so wasn't easy. At first my mother's doctor's office fell back on confidentiality. That such facts were secrets presented a clue: a sign that they were not facts at all, but forbidden knowledge, stories none but a doctor could understand. Still, I grew more determined to have the records, which in my mind had metamorphosed into a manuscript. I must have underestimated the power of such details. The records would reveal not only results but also calculations: dosages of medicines multiplied by careful counts of red blood cells; the tumors that killed her known not only by names but by measurements; the width and depth of her disease a record of its age, a number discerned by peeling back layers of exponential growth to its origin, then tracing it back into the present. One mutant cell gives birth to two daughters, the two are mother to four, the four become forgotten ancestors of billions, a world born within my mother's breast.

Not only did the records contain secrets of the disease's beginnings and my mother's condition—really my mother's secrets—but also secrets that in all fairness belonged to the doctors: their estimations of the future. The prognosis, the prophecy—the story of her death laid out before its event. We wouldn't understand such stories, the doctors warned, and would unjustly turn against those who told them. We would sue. We would sue, and we would lose, because before the law the doctors would read aloud the records in voices of reason while we'd sputter with rage. The doctors would with authority refer to the "spirometry" record of August 21, 1987, observe that eight months earlier there had been no palpable lymphadenopathy, and that the white count on that day had been 6,000. Spilling papers onto the floor as we struggled to find the same page, we the plaintiffs would desperately counter that on December 8, 1986, you, Dr. G., wrote "Lungs are clear and the heart has a regular rhythm without murmur."

How can a dying heart not murmur? Yes, of course, we understood that the murmurs of medicine are not the same as those of emotion, but given such clean and lovely words, "the lungs are clear, the heart has a regular rhythm," how is it that the woman in possession of such virtues would drown in the fluid of those once-clear lungs, while her heart, calmed by morphine, did not even murmur in its own defense?

Here the doctors must sigh. Turn, then, to the pathology report recorded by Dr. C. on March 20, 1986, for SHARLET, Nancy, born June 28, 1941:

> Submitted for examination: Two specimens.
>
> 1. The specimen . . . consists of a . . . tissue mass measuring approximately 2 cm. in diameter. On sections approximately half of the parenchyma is represented by ill-circumscribed, firm, pink-tan tumor. . . .
>
> 2. Received is an elongated piece of skin measuring approximately 1.3 x 0.3 cm. DIAGNOSIS: 1. Infiltrating duct carcinoma of breast (left). 2. Fragment of skin showing multiple foci of dermal lymphatic invasion by breast carcinoma. [Her skin burned with cancer.]

Obviously, we obtained the records. The doctors relented and sent them to my sister, but the odd thing was that I then forgot. I forgot for months that I'd wanted them, forgot they even existed. And I only remembered while crouching on the floor of a library, looking for what I don't remember, when my eye fell on a book about fortune-telling. It was a dusty old hardcover. On its spine, embossed in gold, a campy, cartoon gypsy woman wrapped in scarves peered into a crystal ball, and for no conscious reason the fact of the medical records that I'd imagined into being a manuscript came rushing back to me so hard that I literally fell down. With a thud I rolled off my toes and onto my seat, and then I slapped my forehead, my mouth open in a comic O. Shit. I'd forgotten to read the book of secret things. At the very same moment, I saw in my mind my mother with her green scarf hiding her baldness, my mother the gypsy fortune-teller searching for the number of her days.

When I finally received the documents—not a manuscript at all, just a thick stack of doctors' reports, nurses' reports, radiologists' reports, records of physical exams—I cried at the modesty of the pages. In their letters to one another about possible treatments, her caretakers write cautiously and without clear vision, hopeful but uncertain. They turned out not to be priests meditating on life and death while my mother was consumed, but technicians with a homely concern for a nice woman with whom their trades had brought them into acquaintance. "A pleasant lady," observed Dr. G., her primary physician, on her first meeting with my mother. "She is very intelligent and she is also very scared."

My mother's doctors prescribed several cycles of a chemotherapy regimen called CAF, a combination of three drugs: cyclophosphamide, adriamycin, and 5-fluoricil. Sometimes the drugs made my mother nauseous; sometimes just thinking about them would make her want to vomit. She had frequent sore throats, and feared that they signaled the spread of cancer cells into her neck and throughout her body. Then she woke up one morning and found her thick red hair coming out in bunches on her pillow. If this upset her, she didn't let it show. Instead, she bought herself silk scarves, gold, green, red, purple, and turquoise. She also bought a wig of tight red curls.

I saw the wig for the first time when, at age fourteen, I came home from a friend's one Saturday afternoon and found it on the dining room table. At first I didn't realize what it was. I picked up the mass of red curls as if I'd discovered a new species of animal. Then I laughed; I was holding a wig! "Mom," I shouted, not connecting it to her, "look what I found!" My mother came down the stairs wearing a green scarf wrapped tightly around her head. She took one look at me holding the wig in the air with a grin on my face and barked a sharp "Jeffrey!" My name boomed through the house, summoning my sister and snapping my eyes open to the purpose of what I held in my hands. Jocelyn ran into the room just as our mother demanded the wig. "Oh, you idiot!" Jocelyn hissed. But our mother had regained her composure. She stepped into the kitchen for a moment, then reappeared wearing the red curls atop her head as naturally as the long wavy hair she'd had most of her life. That's when she announced her nickname to us: "I," she said, "am Curly." Cautiously I smiled, then Jocelyn relented from her angry face and smiled too. I grinned, our mother laughed.

"I'm not calling you 'Curly,'" I said.

"That's all right," our mother decided. "Because I just am."

From notes kept by her doctor:

February 17, 1988: "Today the patient has a subcutaneous nodule at the angle of her left jaw."

May 9, 1988: "The right breast is entirely replaced by tumor. She continues to have multiple erythema, one in a necklace distribution."

November 8, 1988: "necrotic"

November 21, 1988: "She is severely short of breath with any exertion, including just speaking."

From a letter to one of her doctors: "I tend to pray in the style that I imagine others have prayed. For some reason I don't find it necessary to be exclusive. I concentrate on Buddhist meditation and Christian prayer. And sometimes a phrase comes to me that seems addressed to the Great Spirit. This morning: please keep Nancy-Body together longer. Let me make a larger pattern."

And early on the morning of January 2, 1989, as I've said, she drowned. Her lungs had filled with fluid and her doctors had emptied them and they'd filled again, been emptied again, filled again. And she died.

After I'd seen the body, I walked downstairs. My granny was in the kitchen trying to explain to my grandfather what had happened. He was far into Alzheimer's then, but that morning was for him one of the worst in the course of his disease. Every fifteen minutes his daughter died anew. "Oh," he'd say each time, a word so soft when he said it that it fell from his lips like snow. Then he'd forget again, and amble up to someone to ask, "Say, who's that hearse out here for?"

I heard Granny in the kitchen—"Charles. Nancy is dead. Nancy our daughter"—and turned away, into the living room, where my father was standing. "I saw," I said, but before he could respond the undertakers were at the door, in the hall, at the foot of the stairs, their bodies between ours and the dead one on the second floor, their condolences stringing a tasteful curtain behind which they could do their work. They carried her down on a stretcher, out the door that my father held, and past my granny, who whispered, "Good-bye, Nancy." Then Nancy was gone. My grandfather saw me crying and asked me what was wrong; I told him my mother had died. He thought that was sad, even though he didn't know who I was, because it's a shame when anyone loses a mother.

"Her name was Nancy," I said.

"I have a daughter named Nancy, too," he said, glad to make a connection between us.

"That's who died," I told him.

"Oh," he said, and his mouth dropped open. In the flash of darkness within it before he forgot again and closed it and smiled, I saw the emptiness of my mother's body's face, so pained and so quiet. "Oh—" I said, because even though her body had gone, there it lay for a moment before me, still lingering in my grandfather's eyes despite his now-amiable smile.

When at the funeral I explained to him a dozen times who the woman in the casket was I saw her a dozen times over, each time more the body in the bedroom than that which I saw in the coffin with its reconstructed face, its lips pressed together, its eyes brushed shut beneath perfect mascara.

From her journal, undated:

> *You can, if necessary, keep warm with memory. In the darkness it gives off silent sparks like a star that falls slowly and disappears. When you have seen what you need, your sleep will be dreamless. In the morning, you can start something new.*

*   *   *

The really crazy thing is not that some people believe in resurrection, in Christ rising from the grave; it's that anyone doesn't. Not the Christian resurrection exclusively, but any faith's concept of continuity. Hindu and Buddhist reincarnation, Jewish sparks of the soul, the insanity of the rapture, when, according to born-agains, the dead will rise from the grave *just as they were*. I remember, during the months after my mother died, going to sleep on a given night with peace in my heart and the belief that at last I'd learned to live with her absence, only to awake in the morning with, as my first thought, an incredible frustration: "Wait—she's *still* gone? I thought that was yesterday."

Once my mother went on a vacation and wrote a friend a postcard, which she forgot to send. But she told him about it, and at her funeral, he told me. "She said she would have liked it if I could have been on vacation too, so she wrote me a postcard that said, 'Wish you were there, and you are.'" My mother's friend laughed. "Then she wrote, 'See how powerful I am?'"

This is how powerful she was:

One Sunday the summer before she died she took my sister, my friend Andrew, and me on a picnic. We went to Thatcher Park, a strip of grassland with a mountain rising above it and a cliff dropping from its edge. While the three of us ate, my mother sat against a white pine with her eyes closed. When I asked her what she was doing she said, "Smelling." So I sniffed the air too: pine needles and tree sap, burgers grilling and farmland far below. Then she opened her eyes. "Let's go to the waterfall," she said.

We walked with her down a series of metal staircases—each step for her a jarring bolt of pain—to a trail along the base of the cliff. Andrew and I ran ahead, looking for caves. Jocelyn stayed with our mother. Our mother had always moved slowly on hikes, but once she'd gone from each curious stop to the next with giant steps and swinging arms, her long hair flicked from her eyes. Now she strolled, an elegance to her gait that disguised the necessity of its caution. Even as she paused to inspect a mushroom or a gnarled root and declare it especially interesting, she used the moment to gather her wind; the deep draughts of air she'd taken under the pine had turned shallow. But as labored as her movement was, it was a pace, and her progress satisfied her. She gave Jocelyn leave to go ahead, and despite the red in her face when she joined us at the waterfall she grinned. We groaned, embarrassed but pleased, as she held her tired arms in the air like a marathon winner.

By then we'd all taken showers, perched on rocks beneath the thundering column, our heads bowed laughing, our arms held before us, our palms turned up to gather the rushing water. When she saw us my mother rolled her eyes and called us foolish, but then she ventured closer. Leaving the safety of the cliff, she stepped onto a boulder, then sat down and rested. Restored, she stretched a leg down to the next one, and with her hands behind her, she pushed herself farther. Like a crab she made her way down until she reached the point of contact between the waterfall and the stone, where the roar and spray and overpowering smell of nitrogen-positive ions, if you believed my mother, confused all the senses; where you couldn't tell what was up and what was down, whether the water fell from the sky or shot up from the center of the earth. Shoulders bunched to give herself strength, she poked her finger into the water.

I knew she couldn't stand under the waterfall, but I wondered, if she could have, what she would have made of the water cold as creation washing over her brittle bones. I didn't think about faith then, and I don't have one now. And yet: I still wonder what my mother might have told us when she emerged from the stream, a dying woman granted a glimpse of a moment not frozen, forever recurring anew; what she might have told us about a place where water meets stone.

2. Fathers

It's Yom Kippur, a good day for writing, and besides I've a letter demanding an answer. It's from my friend Sue, who has gone home to Lancaster County, Pennsylvania, to watch her father die. He is, or maybe now was, a self-made millionaire, a maverick Mennonite, a builder of hard, bony houses, and a shooter of animals on land and in water, which is saying something, since you must draw a long bead to shoot a fish. Her father is, writes Sue, "guns and sweat and beer."

When the ten years dying of his cancer began to accelerate last spring, he called Sue and her sister to tell them that when the time came, they would find his body in the hollow in which he lived, his head gone on to Heaven by way of his shotgun. He is, writes Sue, a man to be feared, not for violence toward others—none of that— but for competence plus disdain plus the dumb beast arrogance of any pretty man who can make women swoon. These virtues made him a twice-abandoned husband and an ignorer of daughters. The daughters have nonetheless returned to the house he built to ease his dying.

His oldest daughter, my friend Sue, is a scratch over five feet tall, her body taut and muscled and disciplined in youth to the easy use of a hammer and a gun and alcohol. I imagine she could handle all three at the same time. She cooks, too, and gardens, and sews, and if she thinks a man's brilliant she writes him a check from her meager salary—she's a college bureaucrat—and asks for nothing in return. She learned early on that men take, and take, and take, until they die.

When she was a kid she got out of Lancaster pretty fast and married I don't know how many times, taking from each husband a name she added to her own like a pearl on a necklace she never wears: I knew her months before I learned how many names she currently owns (five). She is shy of forty, a woman with a past and now yet another husband, plus another lover for good measure. She goes by only her latest surname, borrowed from a neurasthenic German architect, a pale, lovely guy who lives separately from her and stops by from time to time for conversation or for food. This is fair, she says, because he was a finalist in a very important architectural competition; he needs his space.

Sue's space, meanwhile, is in Bushwick, Brooklyn, where she is the white girl on a street of poor Puerto Ricans. She lives in a tired old flop of a building, the back wall of which bows outwards like the hips of a cello. The German told me that soon it will curl, like a wave falling, and bring the back of the building crashing down.

I call Sue a redhead, but she says she's blond. Her face is red, white, and blue: lipstick, pale, freckled skin, and blue eyes. She has bouncy toes. She was born to box. You can see this even when she wears her emerald-green, ankle-length, beltless tunic, which would be a burqa were it not for the fact that it's just about see-through. No naughty details to report, just the silhouette of a body given by God for the sake of combat. She is, in fact, a kung fu fighter, and also a surfer and a rock climber, but what she'd really like to be is a poet. She writes poems and then she hides them. Or she loses them, or gets the computer or the briefcase or the trunk they're in stolen—whichever doesn't matter, just so long as nobody reads them. Still, I have read a few. They're good. What would happen if she published one?

I think I understand her fear. I'm from a town not much bigger than Sue's, and every writer who has grown up in a small and rough place and then left it behind knows that the first published word is a declaration of independence, as irrevocable as it is thrilling. "Putting on airs" is an announcement of singular voice. Small places tell stories with "we," the sound of a first-person plural that is royal only in the fealty it demands of all within its tiny fiefdom.

Consider the version of her own childhood that Sue can hear for the cost of a Bud at any bar within an easy drive of her father's hand-built castle, from men who worked for him or drank with him or lost women to him: "Beer was on tap in our fridge, pigs were roasted, firewood split, flannels worn," she writes. "This is the myth, still believed and retold." She hears it repeated like a prayer, on bar stools and by her father's deathbed. "They"—the "we" of Sue's origins—"come from miles around to bear gifts and to pay homage, to this wisest of all men, self-made, prosperous, most capable man."

But, she asks, "How much does he really know when you take him from his kingdom?" That this will not happen does not prevent her from dreaming of her father dislocated, of her own dislocation transposed onto his "Marlboro Man," cancer-ridden frame.

Fat chance. Dislocation is a kind of doubling, the self where it is recalling the self where it used to be, neither self certain of where it currently belongs. Dislocation is a kind of splitting, a double consciousness. One half smiles, curtsies, says, "thank you" to those who hurt it. The other half rages, says "fuck you," plots vengeance, or escape, or, most romantically, redemption: the New Testament ideal, all that is split—knowledge and wisdom, body and mind, humanity and the divine—made whole.

But redemption is not a real option, and dislocation is a half-life. All of us who embrace it persuade ourselves that it is chosen, that it is a strategy. If we are in academe we call this idea a "site of resistance." If we are in the workaday world we call this half-assed approach "getting by."

The term "half-life," of course, refers most accurately not to a strategy, nor a plan. It is a simple, stark description of radioactive decay.

"Beer was on tap in our fridge, pigs were roasted." Now the old man is dying and all the lives Sue has constructed to leverage herself away from him—Sue in California, Sue in Berlin, Sue in Manhattan; Sue-as-surfer, Sue-as-poet, Sue-as-not-redneck-royalty—have collapsed back into the hollow from whence she came.

The myth of the hollow has its dark side. True to fairytale tradition, it's feminine: Sue's mother was the "local town whore," she writes, who bore her father two daughters and then left them. Good-bye. She was replaced by a wicked stepmother who dunked Sue's head in a toilet, held it there, beat her bloody. Sue's father didn't notice. Wicked Stepmom left, too, taking half of Sue's father's self-made fortune with her. Good-bye. There was one more attempt at a mother, another ex-Mennonite, but Sue's father kept this woman at a distance—bought her a house of her own miles away—and Sue barely knows her. She came around to help him die, but then she saw his wasted body in the bed they had occasionally shared and she packed quickly. Good-bye.

There is a story there, or least an *Oprah* discussion, but Sue won't indulge in such tales more fully told than in her letters. Her mother left her father, and her father left the Mennonite church, and Sue left the hollow, but that does not give her the authority to break free from anything. Thinking of her father's wavering on the question of suicide—not because of fear, but because his respect for the God he does not believe in restrains him—she writes, "ask God's blessing or thumb your nose at him, he still cuts the thread around here."

"You won't want to hear it," I write Sue in an e-mail promising her this essay in lieu of a proper letter, "but all this dying is giving you some fine sentences. 'Ask God's blessing or thumb your nose at him, he still cuts the thread around here' is just one of them. I'm entitled to make such seemingly ghoulish remarks because I've made stories from my own dead mother."

She died of breast cancer when she was forty-eight and I was sixteen; years later I published this chapter's first half, called "The Many Times My Mother Died," which began—glibly or brutally or honestly, depending on your imagination and your mother's health —with a sentence given to me by the Jewish novelist Melvin Jules Bukiet: "Everybody has a mother, and they all die."

I wrote the first draft of that essay when I was twenty-one. It began with something pretty about "memory" and continued on through medical reports, my mother's diary entries, my own recollections of her dying. Thereafter, I slept with sympathetic readers for the next several years. That essay also won me a literary agent, who in turn made for me a writing career. Thanks, Mom.

This was all before Melvin's observation of suffering's simplicity, an essential distillation of fact from "memory" that made of the essay a blunt object no longer easily turned toward the service of my various ambitions. I wrote it again; but you already know that by now.

We must work with what we have. Sue has a dying father; I have her letters. "I hear crickets," she writes, "an airplane, the wind in the acres of leaves, almost like the sound of rain, the brusque shift of this little shack on its supports." She is in a tree house built by her father on a section of land overlooking the Susquehanna. It's a complete outfit—bed, stove, TV, even, everything but a phone, and it's there that Sue retreats to write her letters.

She might miss his dying.

"A turkey vulture just soared so nearby I could see his eye"— Sue would wince if she knew I was reproducing her unintentional rhyme—"and hear his feathers rustle like a taffeta skirt."

I'd like to hear that myself, and so here I am, telling Sue. Save that sound, Sue, consider it a gift of your father's dying. He seems like the kind of man who might appreciate the thought that even in death he can be productive. Use all the parts, Sue. There will be nothing to spare. That's the trouble with half-lives, biographies split between one story and another, identities bisected. It's tempting to declare of yourself that you're one thing or another—your father's daughter or an independent woman, a redneck up a tree or a poet from Brooklyn, a dusty corner of someone else's myth or free of the past, down on the ground or high in the branches—but you can't. Despite the infinite decay suggested by the term "half-life," there is never enough to go around.

My mother was a hillbilly from Tennessee by way of Indiana, my father was and is a Jew from Schenectady. I'm not sure I'd have known I'd be forever split between gentile and Jew had they not divorced when I was two. Thereafter, I was a Jew on Tuesdays, Thursdays, and every other weekend, and my mother's the rest of the week. Jew days in my father's apartment, across the river from my mother's house in Scotia, meant SpaghettiOs, kosher salami on Triscuits, and, on holidays, chopped liver at my Aunt Roslyn's. It seems to me now that the rest of the time we went to the movies, although I can only remember two, *Excalibur* and *Hair*.

My goyish mother also took us to the movies. She found a job baking cookies and brownies for a concession stand at our town's movie theater, rehabilitated by a band of hippies who didn't want to peddle corporate candy. My fourth summer, while my mother baked, I played in the theater. On the sunniest of days, I sat in the dark eating warm cookies and watching reverently as the hippies threaded the two movies they owned through the projector, over and over: Woody Allen's *Sleeper* and *Harold and Maude*. This accounts for my Jewish education.

I was a pale child. Nobody cut my hair, so I went off to kindergarten like a little chubby Ramone, hidden behind a thick brown curtain that hung down to my eyes in front and my shoulders in back. The other kids asked me if I was a boy or a girl. This struck me as reductive. I refused to answer. Around December, I tried to explain my complicated-yet-clearly-superior holiday situation. While the other kids would receive presents on Christmas only, I'd be getting gifts for *nine* days (Hanukkah plus December 25), although, given the Tuesday/Thursday schedule, several of those days would have to be crammed into a few evenings, between SpaghettiOs and R-rated movies.

This was a lot for my classmates to absorb. My hair was unkempt and my clothes were dirty (I insisted on sleeping in them) and my mother sometimes dropped me off at school in a belching, rusty blue Plymouth that looked like a rotten blueberry. So, obviously, I was poor, maybe even poorer than them. But nine days of presents? Was I a liar? Were my parents thieves?

My parents provided another conceptual dilemma. There were a few kids whose fathers had simply left, but at the time, not a single one of my twenty-five classmates had parents who *split* them, mothers with whom they watched *Little House on the Prairie* on Monday and fathers with whom they watched *The Paper Chase* on Tuesday.

Plus, I was "Jewish."

Or so I claimed. For the fall of my first year of schooling this ancestry provided me with minor celebrity, until it came time for Christmas vacation. On one of the last days of school that December, Mrs. Augusta asked a student to volunteer to explain Christmas. A girl named Heather shot her hand up and told us about the baby Jesus and Santa Claus while the rest of us stewed, since this was an answer we all knew, and we wanted Mrs. Augusta to love us. When she asked if anyone could explain the Jewish holiday of Hanukkah, I raised my hand and she smiled, since the question, of course, had been meant for me alone. I stood. "On Hanukkah," I declared, "I get extra presents."

Mrs. Augusta kept smiling. "Why?" she asked.

"I'm Jewish."

"Yes," she said, "and what does that mean?"

"What does that mean?"

"Judaism."

I had never heard of "Judaism."

My classmates, until this day free of that ancient sentiment which, I'd later learn, had prompted whispers and unhappiness when my Jew father had moved onto Washington Road, began to giggle.

Mrs. Augusta tried to help. "What else do you do on Hanukkah?" she asked.

I beamed. I knew this one: "I eat gelt and chopped liver!"

Giggles grew into guffaws, as kids parroted me, special emphasis on "gelt." It was a stupid word they had never heard before. "Gelt!" "Gult!" "Ga!"

Oh, Mrs. Augusta! She tried.

"Now, now. Doesn't anyone have a question for Jeffrey?" Silence. "About being Jewish?"

Bob Hunt raised his hand. This would not be good. He had actually flunked kindergarten, so this was his second time through, and he was older, dangerous. For Halloween, he'd been Gene Simmons, of Kiss. If only I had known then what I know now about the American Jewish tradition of "Who's a Jew?," a campy little game that is, in truth, a self-defense training maneuver intended to prepare you for encounters with goyish hostiles such as Bob Hunt. Who's a Jew? Gene Simmons, for one. Han Solo, Fonzie, yer mother.

Bob's question: "Yo. Sharlet. What's 'gelt'?"

"Gold coins?" I tried.

"Jews eat gold?" (And thus the endless cycle of anti-Semitism keeps on turning.)

"I mean, chocolate?"

Mrs. Augusta frowned. She had expected Maccabees and dreidels. Instead she was getting gelt, which she had never heard of. I was making a mockery of "Judaism." "Which is it?" she asked. "Chocolate or gold? It has to be one or the other, Jeffrey. It can't be both, can it?"

How to say that it can?

Like this: "It . . . it comes in a golden net," I said.

"I think he means *candy*," Mrs. Augusta fake-whispered to the class, winning their laughter.

I sat down. Mrs. Augusta decided to smooth things over with a song, "Jingle Bells."

Bob Hunt leaned toward me, fake-whispered just like our teacher: "Candy-*ass*."

I didn't know what this meant, but it was clearly two things at once, and not good at all. Thereafter, I resolved to be halfsies. I could not be fully both Jeffrey and Jew, chocolate and gold. If anyone asked, I decided, I was half-Jewish, on my father's side, and he didn't live with us anymore.

Sue's father died a few weeks before Christmas. We drove down to Lancaster County for the memorial, a double pig roast in a hunting club perched above the hollow, a ragged American flag limp above the mud and bullet-riddled refrigerators and dead cars sleeping in the fields. Sue wore black pants and a black shirt and as a belt one of the ties her father rarely ever tied. There were men in camouflage and women in tight things and one old gray-beard in a dirty red Santa suit he wears all year round, an excuse to pinch the cheeks, lower, of girls who've been naughty. That included Sue and the ex-Mennonite, Katy, who was for all purposes the grieving widow. They didn't mind, not really. It was a day for drinking—beer at the memorial, and more beer, plus whiskey, at the house afterward. The house Sue's dad built is made of flat stones—carried one by one up from the stream by little kid Sue and her sister—mortared into a hall big as Valhalla, capped with the great wooden beams of a barn he scavenged, adorned with the skins of deer he killed. Their hooves are now coat racks and door handles. He was a man who used all the parts.

We gathered round a giant wood stove in the basement, shoveling in logs and gulping down beer and caw-cawing like crows about Sue's dad's adventures. It wasn't one of those crazy-funny grief kind of evenings, just a good and drunken one. We had left over several aluminum vats of pork and roasted potatoes, and somewhere in the evening a proposal was floated—perhaps by the man who'd inherited the title of "Mayor of the Hollow" from Sue's father, or maybe from the man whose daughter had moved to the big city to become a roller derby champion—for a roast potato battle, shirts and skins. Ladies topless, of course. A few potatoes splatted but the blouses stayed on. The men made the snow yellow. Citified, I went looking for a bathroom. Along the way I found Sue's dad's bedroom, now Sue's; on the nightstand there was a copy of *The Brothers Karamazov,* an eight-hundred-page novel about a disastrous father and his broken children. "*The Brothers Karamazov?*" I said to Sue when I returned. "Are you *trying* to kill yourself?"

"Beats *Lear,*" she said. She'd read that while she sat next to him, "140 pounds of man," she'd written, "about to be dust."

"Cordelia's my sister's middle name," I said. Lear's good daughter.

"Insurance," Sue nodded. She understood why a parent might try to name a child into loving devotion. "My father could have used some." She thought she'd failed him. After a vigil four months long, Sue's father croaked his last in the five minutes she stepped out of his hospital room to get a soda. The old man didn't even thank her. Never told her he loved her. Good-bye.

I read *Karamazov* after my mom died, too, only I was sixteen, and I was so damn dumb I thought it was a Jewish novel. My Jewish father took my sister and me on a grief trip, a long, gray boat ride to Nova

Scotia, which to us was nowhere, which was why we went there. I sat on the deck of the boat spotting cold gray North Atlantic dolphins and trying to read the book, which is really fucking long, fingering the pages I'd put behind me on the assumption that consumption counted as comprehension and that comprehension led to transformation. I thought Dostoyevsky, a Russian, must be like Torah, filled with secrets about what's right and what's wrong and how to be a whole person. A total Jew.

With my mother gone, what were the options? I took a look at my father, with whom I now lived, with whom I now ate not SpaghettiOs every night but whatever I felt like ordering at the Brandywine Diner, or the Olympic, or Son of the Olympic, and I thought, Here is a man, and now I'm one, too. A big, grown-up Jew. Watching death and eating at diners were my rites of passage, my bar mitzvah.

I don't count Dostoyevsky because I figured out halfway to Nova Scotia that a Russian surname does not a Jew make, no sir, not by a long shot. Raised among goyish wolves and by a hippie Christian mom, even I could tell, eventually, that all this crap about the smell or lack thereof attending to the body of a dead monk did not make for a Jewish novel. I was confused. I'd seen *Fiddler,* the movie, danced to it in my socks, knew the words to "If I Were a Rich Man," understood the movie's essential lesson: there are two kinds of people in Russia, Cossacks and Jews. Translated to America, there was Bob Hunt and me. So who was this weird Alyosha Karamazov, this stupid saint who didn't seem to understand that sometimes, death really is the end?

"What gives?" I asked my father, but he wasn't talking at the time and he didn't answer. "What gives?" I asked my sister, but she was stuck on the idea that *Madame Bovary* was the solution to a dead mother, to being split in half. If only my father had possessed the good sense to book Bob Hunt a passage to Nova Scotia with us, I could have asked him. "Bob, what gives? This book, it weighs like two pounds and it's boring, and what good is it going to do me now? My mom's dead and my dad's a Jew and look, man, I've got to pick a side and I thought this would do the job, but it won't, it doesn't seem to mean anything. It's not even Jewish to begin with."

"I know it's not," sing-songs Bob, at eighteen tall and feral, topped by a mop of the Gene Simmons Jew-locks he'd always dreamed of, "*you* are."

What a liar.

"Fuck Hunt," as the half-Jew and his band of weak and/or incomplete comrades said when we were thirteen.

"Douche" was another insult we liked. Also "Pussy." These were not bold vulgarities, but whispered truths. My Masada-dad had told me to fight if anybody crossed me, but what did he know? It was *him* who'd crossed me. I was a pale, chubby, half-Jew kid from half a family, son of the "kike-dyke" of Washington Road, as Bob Hunt christened my mother, with double inaccuracy. But he had caught the essence of the thing: even dumb punk kids understand that it's all about where you came from.

Europe's most organized people, the Germans, grasped this, and so do the Jews. It is both glib and brutal to point out that Germany and Israel are the only two nations with blood laws, and it's downright ugly to note that Israel's nonexistence notwithstanding, the Jews beat the Germans to the concept by half a millennium. Yes, only half; the matrilineal rule really came into being during the Middle Ages, when Christians raping Jews was such a common occurrence that Jews started counting bloodlines through mothers instead of fathers, lest they be cursed by generations of halfsies unto erasure.

Once I went up to a table of young Lubavitchers on the hunt for strayed Jews and told them I was interested. Not that I was really a Jew, I said, not that I went to temple, you understand, not that I really knew anything about it—

"You're a Jew," said the middle one, a tall redhead with a face full of pimples crammed between his beard and his black hat.

"Great," I said. "What do I do now?"

"You'll come to Shabbes dinner this Friday," Red told me, "and here's some literature." He handed me a pile of pamphlets as thick as a book. Then one of his companions, a very short, narrow-shouldered man, tugged on Red's sleeve and rattled off a few sentences of Yiddish. Red nodded judiciously and passed the message on to the third man, who nodded and drew a box from beneath the table. From the box he took two smaller boxes, with black leather straps dangling from them. These he proposed to tie onto me.

I'd seen them before. Tefillin, or phylacteries. You bind one to your arm, one to your forehead. They contain scripture that, as far as I knew at the time, was supposed to osmose into your bloodstream. It seemed an easy way to learn, so I stuck out my right arm. The Lubavitchers stopped and glanced at one another. Wrong arm. I stuck out my left. "I was never bar mitzvah," I explained. They took it in stride, with raised eyebrows but firm purpose. The leather straps wound around my arm. "I was raised by my mother," I went on, "and she isn't—wasn't—Jewish."

The Lubavitchers froze.

"Is something wrong?" I asked.

Red and Number 3 stared at one another, then turned to Narrow Shoulders, who shrugged what little he had. "What is there to do?" he said. Number 3 started unwinding the straps.

"Am I done?" I asked. "That's it?"

"I'm sorry," said Red, turning away. "We cannot help you after all. Perhaps a Reform rabbi might, could, I don't know . . ."

Make me a Jew in Red's eyes? I don't think so, no more than he could unwind his leather fast enough to erase *dos pintele yid*—my fragment of a Jewish soul—that had provoked the binding. Identity is a con like that, one eye winks, then the other. It's not just blood, either.

Look at my friend Sue, a pale wisp of a woman after the long months of her father's dying, a whiskey in one hand and a beer in the other, a cigarette between her lips and a hurled roast potato skidding past her into the snow.

She's standing in front of the house her father built with the stones she brought him, among the men and women she grew up with and the men and women she found elsewhere. Tomorrow, we'll all leave. It'll be Sue and the woodstove and the deerskins. Two mothers gone and one dad dead and the only one who ever told Sue she loved her was the stepmom who hanged her, yes, actually hanged her, in the garage. She still sends cards. She even showed up at the memorial. "What a hoot," says Sue.

Sue can't stay in this house—neither she nor Dostoyevsky belongs here—and she has no particular place to go. She's quit her job in the city and given away her apartment to someone who can deal with its collapse and written her German architect husband a fat check from her inheritance—good-bye and good luck—and tucked away all her secret poems. She's ready to move. She's in her late thirties, freed of her latest marriage, childless, jobless, only her memory of the hollow to sustain her. That, and her ex-Mennonite father's industrious millions. Or million, singular. Or at least a couple hundred thousand. The myth may have been bigger than the reality, but there's enough to keep her in Triscuits and SpaghettiOs for a long while. Her plan, in the making since the old man began his dying, is "travel," itself a glamorous destination, so unlike the stones from the stream across the road with which her father built the bony house she won't live in. She won't come back to the hollow, she won't come back to the city, and who knows when I'll see her again?

More important, what book will she take to start off her grief vacation? Not *Karamazov*. Enough already, we both agree. To hell with the fathers and the saints and all the other myths of purity. It's not that Sue hates the hollow (she loves it) or that I'm not a Jew (I am, a yid-and-a-half divided by three quarters), it's just that we're bound to stories that don't so much resolve as unravel, not unlike this one. The dead leave without saying good-bye, the past fails to provide an adequate explanation, and you *can* go home again but why the hell would you want to? The house Sue's dad built looks like it will stand forever, but the memory of it is already breaking down. This is, I suspect, as it should be. Half-life, nuclear decay, all the little parts of a thing moving on and becoming something other. Were it not so, what would we build from?

I have the perfect traveling book for Sue. Before her dad died, she wrote that she wanted *My Ántonia,* by Willa Cather, a great Jewish novel. Of course, I wouldn't think this was a very Jewish book if it wasn't for Colin Powell. Normally, I'm not one to admire generals, but Colin Powell is an exception. Forget politics: what counts is that he speaks Yiddish and his favorite novel is *My Ántonia.*

When Colin Powell was a kid, growing up in Harlem, a West Indian and thus not quite an American, he got a job working in a Jewish furniture store, which is where he learned the Yiddish. The owners taught him so he could listen in on the calculations of young Jewish couples figuring what they could spend, figuring the black boy couldn't understand them. Thus, the general spake Jewish.

As for *My Ántonia?*

Sue offers a theory: "I wanted to read the Pavel and Peter story again," she writes, "about throwing the bride and the groom to the dogs." No reason, she wrote. "Just because."

Sue's dad once shot a crow from his front porch and grilled it up and ate it, just because he wanted to know if the caw-caws tasted as bad as they sound. Apparently, they do. They're not good eating, but that's identity for you: greasy, without much meat on its bones, fit for the dogs.

Sue, the book is in the mail. Use all the parts; get lost; good-bye.

To Pardon All Our Fucking Iniquities

Laurel Snyder

In a world awash with human evil, some are guilty, but all are implicated.

Ismar Schorsh, chancellor,
Jewish Theological Seminary

Until I was seven, there were certain words I was not supposed to say. Although I regularly heard my parents muttering things like "damn," "hell," and "Jesus Christ," I understood that if I ever said any of the really bad words ("bitch," "shit," the horrendous F word) I could expect to have my mouth washed out with my mother's green medicinal soap in about two seconds flat.

And for the sin we committed against thee by offensive speech . . .

But then my parents got divorced, and when that happened, everything changed, including the words I wasn't supposed to say. Because, until I was seven, my Catholic mother and my Jewish father were both pretty unobservant. They were hippies, poor, in their early twenties, and very suddenly parents.

My father was a socialist, so religion was not the biggest concern of the day. If it wasn't the opiate of the masses, it was at least a kettle of fish better left alone. I did go to Hebrew school on Sundays, but only because it made my grandparents happy. That was religion.

After the divorce, my mom started going to church, and she

also started muttering "shit" and "fuck" instead of "hell" and "damn." When I once happened to say "Oh, Jesus!" my mom got really upset.

"I don't want to hear you taking the name of the Lord in vain!"

For the sin we have committed against thee by defaming thy name . . .

Which was confusing, because I hadn't. He wasn't the Lord. At least, not at my Hebrew school. Very suddenly, the rules of the game had changed.

From that point on, a lot of things were different. My father found himself a new synagogue, a *real* one. His kitchen became kosher and he started wearing hats. He made new friends. And my mother became the head of the liturgy committee at her church. In the summers she went away to a Trappist monastery for two weeks and painted watercolors in silence. When she remarried, she married a Catholic man. And that was all fine.

But as I got older, I had to make up my own rules. I was raised in a leftist community but bat mitzvahed at a massive Reform congregation (where I could find no signs of any political conscience), and a lot of the pieces didn't fit together very well. My best friend (who was Catholic) got involved with Catholic Worker activities, but I couldn't seem to find a young Jewish world that resembled the radical Catholic movement. In high school, I just ignored the problem. I pushed away from religion and embraced politics instead.

For the sin we have committed in thy sight by scoffing . . .

I protested against animal testing and the Gulf War. I demonstrated for gun control, abortion rights, and divestment in South Africa. I gave up meat, joined Earth First, stuffed envelopes, donated my allowance to Greenpeace and Amnesty International, and boycotted green grapes, Coca-Cola, and Hormel. I wrote terrible poems.

And for the sin we have committed against thee in passing judgment . . .

And then I was in college, and I took a few religious studies classes. I discovered that whatever else religion was, it was most of all *interesting*. I discovered my own ability to shape a Judaism that made sense of my political interests and my aesthetic. I went to Israel and Rome. I read a lot of books. I considered critically. I argued with everything, and I loved it.

Now, through a strange stroke of fate, I work at Hillel on the University of Iowa campus, and I find myself surrounded by other Jews for the first time in my life. I work in a building full of Jewish books and I live by the Jewish calendar. And I live in it the best way I know how, by examining and analyzing and arguing.

Which brings me to this season of awe—to Yom Kippur, the Day of Atonement. And here I am, trying to find a way to put my own sensibilities to work in this Jewish place. Trying to understand the texts, customs, and catchphrases. Trying to read this strange book called the Torah, to make it matter in my life.

My childlike understanding of this holiday has always been that Yom Kippur is about forgiveness. I have always known that during this season, we ask forgiveness from those we've harmed, and that on Yom Kippur the Book of Life is sealed. But I haven't always seen an obvious awareness of the holiday in the people around me, the ones who look more comfortable than me in their Jewish shoes.

They say the words, fast, maybe even avoid wearing leather. They bang their chests and chant the rhetoric of a Hebrew they can read and can't understand. Do they know what they're saying at all? I know that no member of my family, no Jewish friend of mine, no professor, has ever asked me for forgiveness. Nor, I realize, have I asked them.

For the sin we committed by contempt for parents or teachers . . .

But I'm interested in this chest banging, this physical prayer, this rhetoric of forgiveness. So I've been asking around, trying to uncover the reason for this custom. It's called the Vidui. The Vidui is said in unison, standing, during the Yom Kippur service. While we recite the Vidui, we bang our chests. Really, the Vidui is a list of sins for which we ask forgiveness, and it's notable that the Vidui is recited in alphabetical order, from aleph to tav, because "language, the very instrument used by God to create grandeur out of chaos, can be misused by us to revert the world back to chaos" (Ismar Schorsh).

Even more interesting than the alphabetization is that we say the Vidui aloud, in *first person plural*. We drum on our bodies and chant it as a community, because the Vidui is not a litany of individual sins, but rather a list of communal sins. Judaism recognizes that most of us haven't committed these particular sins, but that if one of us has committed any one of them, then we are culpable and we must all ask forgiveness for the community.

For the sin we have committed in thy sight by casting off responsibility . . .

And it seems especially important in these days of war and economic hard times. The Vidui should remind us that we all have a shared responsibility for the sins of our community. We are all culpable for the mistakes made by the administration we elect, the choices made by our religious leaders, the products our economy produces (*For the sin we committed in thy sight by oppressing a fellow man . . .*), along with the products our economy neglects to produce. Because the Vidui is not only a list of positive sins, crimes we've committed by collusion. The Vidui (like the list of 613 Jewish commandments) also begs forgiveness for our other sins, the crimes we've committed by omission and accident.

And this is what I'm really interested in—intention. The Vidui is a string around the finger—a symbolic reminder that this New Year is a time to look carefully at all the missed opportunities, the things we meant to do but didn't do in the year we are leaving behind.

And for the sin we committed in thy sight unintentionally . . .

The Vidui offers a chance to cop to all the mistakes we've made as individuals and as a community. It gives us a day to beat our chests, to apologize to others, ourselves, and also (if we like) to God for our mistakes and our missed chances. And then, the Vidui offers forgiveness. Because on Yom Kippur, if you ask your sister (or anyone else for that matter) for forgiveness three times and she refuses you, it's as if she forgave you anyway. That's the rule. No matter what. It's the proverbial new leaf. The clean slate. Which is nice. Right?

Because you can forgive yourself the same way, or at least I think I can. If I examine my life, and I'm honest with myself about the mistakes I made last year, and I resolve to do better, and I ask forgiveness for myself and my community, than I get a do-over—if I bother to ask.

David thy servant said to thee: "Who can discern his own errors? Of unconscious faults hold me guiltless."

Bible Porn

Erik Hanson

Once, when I was eight, I knelt down at my bed alongside my mother, admitted I was a sinner, and asked Jesus Christ into my heart. Once, when I was eleven, I stood up at a Bible campfire and promised my peers and elders that I would earnestly strive to bring my unsaved friend to church. And once when I was twenty-two, among ten high school boys whose souls had been entrusted to me for a week, I sat down on the carpet and read them, for their edification, Bible porn.

"Judges 19:29–30: When he reached home, he took a knife and cut up his concubine, limb by limb, into twelve parts and sent them into all the areas of Israel. Everyone who saw it said, 'Such a thing has never been seen or done, not since the day the Israelites came up out of Egypt. Think about it! Consider it! Tell us what to do!'"

These high school boys were members of what I have in the past called "My People," a term that referred sometimes to those who accepted that a salad was to consist of, and only of, iceberg lettuce, tomato wedges, Thousand Island dressing, and Bac-Os. Sometimes the term referred to midwesterners, sometimes to Swedish American immigrants, sometimes to evangelicals. But mostly "My People" meant the Evangelical Covenant Church of America.

Created by a pietistic offshoot of the Swedish State Lutheran church in the nineteenth century, the Evangelical Covenant Church is a denomination of about 100,000 members. Although they are now found in almost every state of the nation, My People cluster predominantly around Chicago and Minneapolis. Leaving the dry, empty formalism of state churches in Sweden for something more real, My People are Scandinavians with a heart for Jesus. Born-again Swedes. They are evangelical enough to think that a heartfelt conversion experience is necessary to ensure your spot in the Kingdom of Heaven, but Swedish enough to not make a big fuss over it.

Migrating to the United States, Covenanteers found greater religious freedom, but greater competition as well. Unable to simply baptize their infants into the state church before the kids even knew what was happening, My People now had to wait until some age of accountability and then let their kids make their own decisions. From every side—from charismatics to archaeologists to MTV—forces threatened to take Covenant kids from the faith of their fathers.

Hence the creation of CHIC. Once standing for Covenant HIgh Congress, now, like KFC or FedEx, CHIC stands for nothing but itself. Every three or four summers, CHIC calls every thirteen- to seventeen-year-old Covenant Kid from across the country to a big college campus where for a week they are bombarded with so much high-power Christian fun and high-volume Christian rock, and so many high-impact Christian speakers, that they have no choice but to dedicate their lives to Jesus Christ.

I attended CHIC in 1984, but because my mom had gone and gotten me saved seven years before, all I could do was get "recommitted." And I had already been recommitted nineteen times. So during the altar calls, while gospel music played softly and the speaker asked people to cast off their sins, come on down, and accept Jesus Christ as their personal Lord and Savior, I sat and felt guilty for feeling nothing at all.

On the one hand it made perfect sense for me to sign up as a counselor for the 1991 CHIC held at Indiana University. Family connections plus regular Covenant camp attendance plus having just graduated from the denomination's college, North Park, plus coordinating Covenant volunteer groups through my job with Habitat for Humanity meant that I probably already knew three hundred of the three thousand kids and counselors in attendance, and the others were probably only separated by a single degree. These were My People, after all. Not to go would have been like ditching a big family reunion. But on the other hand, signing up made as much sense as shaving my head and passing out the Bhagavad Gita at airports, because I didn't really want anybody to have a conversion experience. I went to be a counselor at CHIC to save the children from being saved.

The CHIC counselor application asked for a statement of belief. I knew that the right answer was something like "Once I felt tempted to go to a party where alcohol was being served" or "Once my friends' parents got divorced and I was feeling really down and I didn't know where God was in all of this." Then I would relate how I turned to a favorite passage of scripture and how it made me realize that Christ indeed was alive and relevant for my life today.

But I had no such simple heartfelt story of Christ's presence in my life. I stayed away from all the traditional Christian events at my Christian college and instead hid away in the library and struggled through deep thoughts and hard texts trying to make God and Jesus and the world as a whole make some sort of sense to me. From Kierkegaard I knew that "Truth is subjectivity," from Nietzsche that Christians were pop Platonists, and from René Girard that the New Testament revealed the scapegoat mechanism secretly present in all other myths. I knew Christianity, like life, was something far more complex and messy and hard and weird than you could explain to teens in a week. And I knew that it was condescending and wrong to make teens feel dysfunctional if they did not have a Jesus experience in just the way CHIC had preordained for them.

I still considered myself a Christian, but I had no statement of belief. I wasn't even sure if belief itself was very Christlike. So, I wrote down on the application the Apostles' Creed: "I believe in God the Father Almighty, Maker of Heaven and Earth, and in Jesus Christ, His Only Son . . ." Look, I said, I just believe what everybody else believes; please don't make me personalize my belief the way that everybody else personalizes their belief. I knew it wasn't at all what they were looking for, but I figured if I quoted a central Christian creed they couldn't keep me out.

So it was that on a warm August afternoon in 1991 I was sitting in a circle on the carpet with the ten high school CHIC boys whom I would "counsel." The first activity we were to undertake together was a scripture lesson. The official CHIC scripture lesson was from Matthew 14, in which Peter starts to walk toward Jesus on the water, but then the disciple starts to sink. CHIC had provided brightly colored xeroxed papers with "hip" clip art and with questions for me to give to each of my charges: "Have you ever felt like you were sinking and called out to Jesus?" "What risks might Jesus like you to take this week?"

I put away the sheets and asked my kids to turn to Judges 19. Judges 19 tells a tale less popular in evangelical circles. It tells the story of a Levite man who goes off to Bethlehem to track down his unfaithful concubine. On the way back, the Levite and his retrieved concubine stop to sleep in the town square at Gibeah. A Gibeahan offers to let the two travelers stay at his house instead. But then the men of the town come and ask to have sex with the Levite. So then the Gibeahan host goes out and says, "No, my friends, don't be so vile. Since this man is my guest, don't do this disgraceful thing. Look, here is my virgin daughter, and his concubine. I will bring them out to you now, and you can use them and do to them whatever you wish." They rape and abuse the two women, who then come crawling back to the house at dawn. What happens to the concubine next I mentioned at the start of this story.

After reading the passage to the kids that I was supposed to be turning on to the love of Jesus, I asked them what they thought. One kid from Alaska just got up and walked away. (He got himself assigned to another group and I didn't talk to him again.) I don't know what kind of reaction I was hoping for from the kids. Maybe "Oh my God! This Bible-Christianity thing isn't as straightforward as I thought! I'm going to run away from my namby-pamby Covenant home, smoke unfiltered cigarettes, and read about Kierkegaard and despair in a poorly lit coffeehouse!" But instead, they just lounged there in their brightly colored beach shorts and played with their sunglasses. One said something like "So that's in the Bible. Huh." Then another one asked if they could go to the mall.

Every evening at CHIC, everyone gathered in the gym for the main event of the day. The nights started out with some fun and/ or raucous songs, gradually shifting into softer, more meaningful numbers before a speaker came out to talk to us about how Jesus was really hip and how Jesus would help us with sports, parents, dating, and fitting in at our school. I was still trying to balance my roles as responsible leader, cool counselor, caring adult, irreverent gadfly, and evangelical for existentialism. I made all my kids go to the service, but we sat in the very back row of the arena. I encouraged them to mock any and all parts of the service, teaching them alternative lyrics to well-known Christian classics. ("And they'll know we are Christians by our cars, by our cars . . ." "God is Dead-wo-ho-ho, God is Dead-clap-clap-clap.") I taught them how to sing like Bob Dylan and Neil Young. I let them start their own mini-waves at inappropriate times. They did not appreciate the full theological meaning of their actions, but they had fun.

Everything was going okay until one of the CHIC authorities, Dale, came up to quiet us down. For most of the year Dale was the youth pastor for the Johnson County Covenant Church, and I had worked with him the previous summer when he brought his church youth group to Habitat for Humanity. But this week Dale was the head of CHIC security, the Covenant's Top Cop. It was his job not only to keep the kids away from unsafe and illegal activities, but from sinful ones as well. He came up and asked me to keep my young ones in line. I explained to Dale that everything was okay because these youth were part of an experimental ministry project called "ARMMFART." ARMMFART stood for "Alternative Role Model Ministry For Apathetic and Reluctant Teens." My logic, as I explained it to Dale, was that not every kid at CHIC was going to connect with the rah-rah, happy, shiny form of evangelicalism. I felt that it was my role to reach out to these kids. And if it took a few shenanigans to win them for Jesus, I thought it was worth it. I don't really know if I believed any of this. But I had good Covenant credentials and it sounded good, so Dale let it ride.

The week flew by quickly. Others guys came to join our evening ARMMFART gatherings at the back of the arena and we developed a codified set of rules: "You can sing, but not in tune; you can clap, but not in rhythm; you can stand up, but not at the appropriate times." I drove my kids around in my car until one midnight, on our way to McDonald's for Happy Meals, I was caught by the CHIC authorities and told that kids weren't allowed out past curfew even with their counselor, and counselors were not allowed to drive kids in their cars. (I got around this one by letting Seth, who had his learner's permit, drive.) One midweek afternoon, Josh and some of my other kids told me about the plastic Barbie dolls that had come with their Happy Meals and the explosives they were going to use to blow them up. I told them, in a firm and responsible voice, to do it far away from others, in an open area where they would hurt no one but Barbie.

Bible porn continued. In place of the official CHIC lesson every night, I read to my campers about how Lot's daughters got him drunk and had sex with him, the sexual purity laws from Leviticus, how Noah got drunk and naked and his sons had to cover him up, and the place in Song of Songs where it talks about breasts. Again, the kids were amused, but mostly felt like they were getting to skip homework. The fact that the book the Covenant Church holds up as God's "only perfect rule for faith, doctrine and conduct" was full of smut made no apparent impression upon them. But slowly, I believed, my message, whatever that message might be, was sinking in.

The last night of CHIC was the big altar call. Everything that was told to them so far in the week was just softening them up for the final night. The softer meaningful songs went on longer than other nights, and the speaker didn't make as many wisecracks. No fire, no brimstone, but in a sweet, sincere voice, he made it clear that tonight was the night to give yourself to Jesus. Jesus loves you no matter what you've done and he wants you to start living for him today. Soft music played, whole rows of people put their arms around each other and swayed.

As emotionally wrought CHIC kids came up to accept Jesus Christ as their personal savior, tears began to stream down the eyes of everyone in the arena. Except for ARMMFART. I was nervous about desanctifying this, the most sacred point of CHIC and of many young people's lives. But ARMMFARTers were mocksobbing, loudly blowing their noses, hardly able to keep from busting out laughing.

Youth Pastor Cop Dale shot a glance back that let me know in no uncertain terms that THIS BEHAVIOR WAS NOT OKAY. But I only shrugged, helplessly, to let him know that this was now out of my control. He came up and whisperingly (so as not to disturb the mood) told the kids that they should be ashamed of themselves and to keep it down. Apparently he had given up any hope of their souls being reached.

The kids quieted down eventually, but I was distraught. I was distraught by the emotional manipulation being perpetrated by the CHIC leaders. I was distraught by my kids' not knowing where to draw the line. I was distraught by my inability to make sense of what I was doing there. The soft music played on, the preacher again asked the kids to make a decision for Jesus tonight. Should I be listening to him? What had my arrogant ways done but create a bunch of teenage hooligans?

That night, back at the dorm, in place of our usual Bible porn lesson, I asked my kids what they thought of the altar call. No one had been paying enough attention to even know what was being said. Disgusted, I went on to explain the whole program: just how and why CHIC had been trying to save them, and how I had been trying to save them from that. What I had been trying to teach them that week was that salvation isn't enough. You aren't altogether without merit before you accept Jesus and you certainly aren't altogether good once you do accept him. You can't judge others based on whether or not they call themselves Christian or if they've had some special experience where Jesus entered their life. I don't know what happens after you die, I told them, but if Jesus is up there separating the sheep from the goats based on whether or not they get all weepy when Amy Grant songs are played softly, I don't want anything to do with it. There's a lot of other stuff going on in the world. People get drunk. People have sex. There's brutality, there's rape and mayhem, and that's just in the goddamned Bible. There's a whole filthy, messy, complicated world out there and nothing you learn at CHIC or Bible camp or at church tells you the first damn thing about how to deal with it. Do you understand?

Josh turned over on his bunk, where he had been lying and listening, and scratched himself. Seth flipped through his motorcycle magazine. Some of the other kids started talking about which CHIC girls they thought were the best looking. I was ready to beat them all senseless for being so oblivious, for paying no attention at all to my theological message or to anyone else's. Then for a brief flashing moment, I saw them. I saw my kids. I saw the kids I counseled not as saved or unsaved, brainwashed or reflective, good or bad. I saw them as just boys in high school, each having his own life and thoughts, even if such thoughts were only about how to blow things up, how to get girls, how to drive cars. For a brief and shining moment, I saw them like me, fellow Covenanteers, fellow children of the earth, yet entirely unlike me and entirely unfathomable. It was like watching a pornographic movie and all of a sudden—instead of feeling desire or disgust or even amusement—seeing the real people behind the porn actor bodies and wondering who their mothers were, how their houses were decorated, what they had for lunch. I saw my kids, My People, for the first time in my life.

All week at CHIC, like my fellow counselors, I had been trying to convert my children to a program I did not really understand myself. Because it was too much, too much, to just let them lie there without categorization, without direction, without ultimate meaning. But the full reality of nine separate kids, all with their own lives, their own thoughts, their own experiences, their own being, lasted only for that moment. The godlike perspective was too overwhelming to bear. So we all packed into my car and Seth drove us to the Steak & Shake and we popped straws and ate fries and talked about girls and cars and exploding Barbies.

The Mucus

Mary Valle

My expectations of what a Catholic girls' school would be like were formed by repeated viewings of *The Trouble with Angels,* a sixties movie starring Hayley Mills as a rebellious girl who learns to stop being such a pain in the ass and love the Lord. Plaid skirts, long hallways, good-natured but strict nuns—the kind who will surprise you with a mean game of softball—green-and-white linoleum floors, red lipstick, snuck cigarettes, high jinks.

But my school, Carden, was something else entirely. It didn't have an overtly Catholic name. No nuns, save for one wrinkled old specimen who served as school mascot. We had Mass once a week, but only school counselors and goody-goodies went, so the school's living room was big enough. The school itself was a mansion and it was so absolutely, positively fancy and mansiony that it was frequently used as a film set. I remember ducking out of Spanish class one afternoon because of "cramps"—I wasn't above taking advantage of the all-female atmosphere—only to find Diane Keaton sprawled out on my chaise longue in the powder room. Argh! Ever since, I have been unpleasantly jolted out of the waking dream of many a film and TV show by recognizing the dreaded site of my gilded incarceration.

Two hundred of Southern California's finest young ladies attended this school, all outfitted in summer uniforms (the preferred pastel dresses) or winter (dorky tweed skirts), complete with rubber-soled shoes. We couldn't wear loafers because we might slip and fall on the marble floors. Because of the amounts of money involved, I think the school felt a certain, shall we say, liability to-ward the stakeholders.

There were other liabilities as well. To spell it out: girls who went to Carden didn't get pregnant. One girl left suddenly during our freshman year because of a rumored pregnancy, but it wasn't too shocking—her hair was all wrong, and her name was kind of countryish, and she seemed like one of the "organ people," as my friend Claire called them. You know, the kind of people who have an organ in their living room, and live in places like Downey. Where the Carpenters came from.

It's Not the Sex That's the Problem

There's a lot of don't-ask-don't-telling going on in the families of the rich and modern religious. It's not the sex that's the problem. The real trouble is when there's evidence. Perhaps your daughter is hav-ing sex, and perhaps you even know about it, although you won't acknowledge it, even to yourself—it doesn't really matter as long as there isn't an unfortunate occurrence. An accident. The kind of accident that requires her to suddenly go on a yearlong "trip to Eu-rope" and return pale, flabby, and shaken to a welcome-home party complete with a cake bearing miniature flags of many nations.

To avoid such horrors, Carden dished out forbidden knowledge on a regular basis in bio and chemistry. We handled diaphragms, birth control pills, condoms, sponges. The most detailed contracep-tion exposition happened one day in science class. The teacher, Mr. Smitson, perpetually sheepish (as are most male teachers afloat in a sea of teenage girls), vanished, only to reappear at the end of the period to remind us of an upcoming test.

Two of my more advanced classmates, Veronica Twohey and Lizzy Frayne, who actually volunteered at Planned Parenthood, marched to the front of the room. They were efficient, practiced, businesslike. They seemed much further ahead on the curve of womanhood than the rest of us, who were still giggly and coltish.

Veronica held up a condom in its little square package. It fairly glowed with mystery. We had touched the objects, but now it was time to see them in action. She and Lizzy were a practiced two-headed beast of contraceptive information. While Veronica explained the outside of the condom package (check expiration date, peel gently down the side), Lizzy was readying a canister and a plastic syringe.

This was something new: contraceptive foam. "It's kind of like mousse," she said, and squirted a little puff on her finger. She wiped it off with a tissue and produced a syringe-like plastic applicator while explaining the advantages of using both foam and a condom. Then, she inserted the nozzle of the foam into the tip of the applicator. "You just fill it up, like so," and it turned white with the foam inside, "and insert it right before you're going to have sex. If you have a hard time getting it in the vagina, you might want to use a little lubricant like K-Y." She held up a tube of jelly. K-Y? So that's what it was. An unknown thing previously glimpsed in medicine cabinets and inside adults' nightstand drawers.

Another mystery solved. The world was full of them.

Then, without hesitation, the girls launched into the main event. The sheathing of the mighty banana. Veronica gingerly liberated the quivering latex balloon from its foil prison. "It's important to make sure you unroll it the right way, and you can tell by the little ridge at the bottom, which you want to be facing up," said Veronica, holding it up and pointing with her index finger. "It's hard to see if you're in the dark, so you might want to practice this beforehand." There were a few giggles and Veronica cracked a smile, stepping out of her official role for a second.

Lizzy held the banana while Veronica unrolled the condom on it. Lizzy narrated: "Make sure it's completely unrolled, down to the base, and then pinch the tip so there's room for the ejaculate." She expertly did so, in a way that seemed almost cute. Those of us who had already done the deed probably picked up a few pointers that day, while those of us who had not ventured into the land of "It" looked on impassively. When the future reveals itself to you, you greet it calmly and respectfully.

Adult Christian Living

There was a price to be paid for such Dutch-style levelheadedness, and that price was a class called Adult Christian Living. This was a class about lifestyles—Christian lifestyles, and, specifically, Catholic lifestyles, your three choices being: religious (no sex); single (no sex); and married (sex, but). Becoming a nun seemed far off and perilous, the kind of thing that only women who got themselves killed in Latin America ever tried to attempt anymore. I had never seen a nun who wasn't old and gray. We didn't spend too much time on this, anyway, because the stakeholders wouldn't actually be pleased if their daughters got religion in a non-grandchildren-providing way.

There was a lot of discussion about the single lifestyle. Mainly about the fact that you couldn't have sex. And you also couldn't masturbate. We had to memorize a mantra about the shame of Onan that stated: "Masturbation is an inherently disordered act because our bodies were made to glorify God, and our precious sexuality can only be expressed in the full commitment of marriage." Repeat as necessary.

Another topic of singledom was infatuation versus "real" love, love that waits until after the wedding to get it on. Infatuation was merely lust, and lust was, you know, sinful and stuff. The teacher, Ms. Flather, who was herself a single lady, was forcefully cheerful about her own lifestyle—but certainly, she was protesting too much. I felt tired just thinking about her. How old was she? In her thirties? And still fending off the guys? You really just wanted to say: Oh, get it over with already, lady. There was a "discussion" about living together and a couple who came in to talk about how their relationship fell apart when they lived together. Then, once they moved out, started dating again, and quit doing the deed until they got married for real, things were just great. We were tested on them: "How did Bill and Patty's relationship change once they made a real commitment in the form of marriage?"

Each day of Adult Christian Living was a little more humiliating than the next. As we moved into the marriage unit, the contraceptives made a quick appearance, were passed around the circle once again, and quickly ushered out. We were going to learn about the only Church-approved form of birth control: natural family planning.

This lesson was presented by another religion teacher, Mr. Grapwell, and his wife, Cindy. Mr. Grapwell was the kind of teacher that you almost feel sorry for as you paint your nails in his class and he doesn't stop you, or turn in an original poem about Diet Coke for an assignment about being grateful to God, and he still gives you a B plus despite indicating it wasn't exactly what he was looking for. We called him Grappy.

Grappy and Mrs. Grappy came in and set up a large calendar on an easel. They began to tell us about the practice in a tag-team fashion. "It isn't the so-called rhythm method of yore."

"It's ninety-nine point nine percent accurate when practiced carefully."

"It's the only way to go if you want to limit your family size and still be a good Catholic, because you're merely abstaining from intercourse on days when the missus is fertile, not stopping a human life from being conceived."

"It really makes us both involved in the process."

"It's brought us even closer as a couple."

Mrs. Grappy began to explain the process of natural family planning: Every morning she shoved a thermometer under her tongue and made note of the temperature. Then she examined her vaginal mucus. As she said this, she rubbed her thumb against her index and middle fingers to indicate texture.

Mrs. Grappy's fingernails were varnished a metallic lilac, and way longer than you wanted them to be. We had to think about her fingernails going up there, and wince internally. Because we were sitting in a semicircle, there was no place to hide, no place to look away. All of our faces were blank with the sure and terrifying knowledge that she was going to continue and there wasn't a damn thing we could do about it.

Mrs. Grappy talked about the mucus. She talked about its color, fragrance, and consistency, and how it changed from day to day. Sometimes clear, sometimes cloudy. Sometimes sweet, sometimes mustardy. Sometimes sticky, sometimes elastic and ropy "like melted cheese." She kept rubbing her fingers together. Grappy stood alongside her, smiling in that way that people who are totally convinced that the Lord is on their side do.

She kept saying, "the mucus." Here was this woman, in a nondescript green dress, tan hose, and brown sandals, coming into our classroom and talking about her vaginal secretions. What could we do but cross our legs, hard, and hope that it would end soon?

Grappy soon got in on the act. He explained how he helped. On days when Mrs. Grappy wasn't fertile, he marked an X on the calendar with a pen. He demonstrated this. On days that temperature and texture (fingers again) indicated that conditions were favorable for conception, Grappy put a sticker of a baby on the calendar. He demonstrated this, and explained that although the egg is only present for three or four days, fertility extends to seven, because semen can wait it out in the hot and moist vaginal environs, hoping to get lucky. He put baby stickers on an entire week.

Grappy and Mrs. Grappy stood alongside their calendar, which, by now, was a map of Xs surrounding a week of pink babies. The stickers scared me the most. I felt them looking at me—all seven of them. The horror. The Grappys explained that they "abstained during Baby Week." Said Grappy, with a grin, "It really gives us some time to appreciate each other as people." A brave soul, Heather Wa-ters, who was herself put on the pill by her family doctor because of "cramps" and enjoyed its other benefits with her college boyfriend, raised her hand and asked why they couldn't just use condoms during that time.

Grappy chuckled. "You could," he said. "If you punched holes in it."

Frottage, Felching, Fisting, Whatever

Heather looked puzzled. "No, really," he said. "That's the Pope's opinion. You see, conception is the Lord's will, and we don't have the right to interfere in that process. Natural family planning is all about abstaining during certain times, so as to avoid conception. It's a nice break for both of us. But any kind of barrier would mean that we were putting our own pleasure above the Lord's will. So, no, you really couldn't do that." As if anticipating our thoughts, he added, "And you really have to be careful about fooling around. Did you know that you can get pregnant without even having sex? If ejaculate, or semen, is near the vaginal area—on the vulva, or even, in some cases, on the inner thigh area—and there's enough mucus present, it can swim up and into the vagina, and bingo! You're pregnant. You really can't be too careful with this stuff."

This was a whole other side of Mr. Grapwell that I never knew existed. He was loose, comfortable, authoritative. In his element. Calling the shots. The only man in a roomful of women, and talking about vaginal mucus like it was the most blessed topic in the world. Also, by implication, he was talking about his penis and its activities. We had never had to grapple, so to speak, with the thought of anything living in those corduroy trousers, but today, we were learning its schedule.

At such a time, I wanted scrawl a sign and hold it up, facing skyward, in case anyone was out there in the universe besides God: THIS WASN'T MY IDEA. What can a fertility-obsessed religion do in modern times, when the time between sexual maturity and marriage (if any) stretches into decades? It's important to hew to your beliefs, especially if you are the Catholic Church and holding steady at number one on the chart of Christendom. Rome hasn't forgotten that whole Reformation/Counter-Reformation episode, and the Protties, although certainly outnumbered, continue to nip at the One True Church's heels like a yippy little pagan dog that steadfastly insists a piece of bread is just a piece of bread. If the Catholic Church dilutes its signature issues, it risks becoming yet another denomination, instead of the only church in the world that rules from a unique city-state.

But when you have a school full of impregnable teenage girls, this is where theology breaks down. One has to be practical: the technical information at Carden, according to my public school peers, was far more detailed than anything they were ever taught. I admire the school for slipping us the info on the sly, but the counterprogramming had another effect entirely. Preaching abstinence is a popular approach in public schools these days; but, judging from the number of teenage girls I see pushing strollers, it really isn't working.

I'd like to suggest another approach: give the kids all the facts, and I mean all of the facts. Frottage, felching, fisting, whatever might possibly happen between young hormonally charged humans. Add dental dams, finger condoms, and latex gloves to the party pack. Tell them what it all means. Then, bring in the Grappys to put them off the idea for a few years, at least, when they will, with any luck, be more conscientious about using the equipment properly.

A few years ago, on the other side of the country, I met a man who had, as an adult, dated one of my classmates. "Oh, I know all about Carden," he said. He rubbed his fingers together. "The mucus."

Sects and the City

Elizabeth Frankenberger

I look upon [my] life as an adventure, full of danger and romance, and every privation as an amusing addition to my diary. . . . What I'm experiencing [now] is a good beginning to an interesting life, and that's the reason— the only reason—why I have to laugh at the humorous side of the most dangerous moments.

ANNE FRANK, 1944

When I first read Anne Frank's diary, I was not yet thirteen years old. I remember the book report I wrote, and the cover art I created with all its burning hearts and swastikas. I hole-punched the pages and bow-tied them together with bright green yarn. My Hebrew school teacher never graded or returned my project. I think it stood in a glass case in our synagogue with a few other works of juvenile art—a Lincoln Log menorah, maybe a hand-painted mezuzah or two—but I can't be sure. I took so much Dramamine back then, to stomach those long Sunday car trips to Temple Emanuel, that even my memory is a bit motion sick.

What I do recall is camping out in my home, in a cedar closet beneath the basement staircase, trying to simulate Anne's persecution. I made three visits to the site before going into hiding: first I delivered the provisions; next, my homework and a flashlight; and, finally, my cat. I think I lasted about one hour, and that probably included one trip to the bathroom and another to the refrigerator. Out of respect for Anne, though, I tried to be quiet and think about how lucky I was to be alive and well fed and Jewish and American and in

school with all my friends. But soon my imagination/claustropho-
bia took over, and I found myself fantasizing about Prince Charming, or at least Shaun Cassidy, coming bravely to my rescue.

I am not a religious person, and I do not believe in God. If asked
about my beliefs, I find myself uttering the same words I used to
address the congregation at my own bat mitzvah: "Being Jewish
is about family and history and matzo ball soup." Mine is a typical, American-bred brand of Judaism that involves two Holy Days
off from work in September, a Passover seder come April, and a
schmear of weddings, funerals, and other ark-opening activities per
calendar year. I am the shameful result of my ancestors' suffering. I
am Zionism's greatest foe.

I am also a thirty-year-old female looking for love in New York
City, which means that being Jewish is something that I *am,* even
if I'd never choose to call it out in a personals ad, and even though
I've never placed, or responded to, a personals ad in my entire life.
And there are many others like me out there—SJFs who don't go
shopping for brand-name religious labels; SJMs seeking a soulmate,
race/relig. unimpnt. (but pls. send foto!!!)—and we're either too
Jewish or too not-Jewish, too white-bread or too ethnic, too Billy
Joel or too Beastie Boy. How, then, are we ever supposed to find
kismet when kinship keeps getting in our way?

I wish I knew.

Religious affiliation is about as important to me as blood type
is to a shark, and my appetite for new flesh is far from being satisfied. So I keep on swimming, hoping, bobbing for a bite out of the
juicy Big Apple in which I live. Sometimes, I get lucky: a guy with a
like-minded attitude about religion and politics and music comes
along, and I am buoyed for a while, sated. But more often than not
I'm going about the daily business of urban life—working overtime,
going out overmuch, being cautious and caustic, dreaming up cre-

ative ways to be, and feel, connected—all the while trying to see that forest *and* those trees, reaching out for the one ripe apple among the rest in the rotten bunch.

Things have changed a lot since Anne Frank was holed up in her Secret Annex, stealing brief glimpses of the outside world from a broken windowpane in the attic, wondering when the war against her people—my people—would end, and literally dying to have a boyfriend. She knew that there were more miserable conditions beyond the confines of her own barren heart. "It's a wonder I haven't abandoned all my ideals, they seem so absurd and impractical," she wrote at age fifteen. "Still, I'm sentimental, I know. I'm despondent and foolish, I know that too. Oh, help me!"

Our circumstances were vastly different, but as a teenager I identified with Anne's oppression and longing all the same. I too believed that I lived in a cruel, anti-Semitic world; and I was convinced that my being Jewish automatically disqualified me from ever falling in love.

Maybe it was the long, bumped slope beneath my brow. Or my frizzy hair that I tied up in tight silk scarves every night, praying it would be straight by morning. It could have been my thirteen-letter last name, or the absent father to whom it was attributed. All of these things—these disgraceful, non-Aryan characteristics that kept me in the girls' bathroom during recess to ward off the guerrilla Darwinism of the schoolyard—contributed to a nascent preoccupation with my Jewishness. Indeed, it seemed as conspicuous to the male species as Hester Prynne's "A," or Anne's six-pointed star safety-pinned to the lapel of her winter coat.

Why did I attribute all the angst of adolescence to my being Jewish? My feminist mother certainly has her reasons, as do a host of psychologists, anthropologists, rabbis, and plastic surgeons around the globe. This shame—this textbook Jewish paranoia—has shadowed me all the way into adulthood. It still amazes me when a man tells me that I am beautiful, and even then I bite my tongue to keep myself from convincing him otherwise. For the young Jewish Girl of my past brews inside of me, begging for attention; she's in hiding on the dark side of the mirror, looking back at me with beady, berating eyes, reminding me that I will never appear, or be perceived as, "normal."

She also encourages me to fall back on my Jewishness as an excuse for my romantic dissatisfaction. And I, in turn, continue to rack up enough evidence to support her theories.

I'll call him David.

We all know this David, this creative-guy-behind-the-suit who walks the walk but falls flat on his face once the curtain's down. He's also Jewish, which raises the self-loathing bar to dangerous, seratonin-straining levels. David develops a movie-watching, dog-walking, let's-go-jeans-shopping relationship with me, the "one who really understands [him]," only to reserve his romantic interest for a girl we'll call Blake Cheever. This Blake is, as might be expected, something out of a Bret Easton Ellis novel, complete with trust fund, magazine job, and a propensity to speak in quiet, question-marked sentences? So she became the girlfriend, I remained the friend, and weeks later—after they broke up—I couldn't help but ask David: Why did you want to be "just friends" with me? "I don't have *just* friends," he told me. "I have *real* friends." In other words, I am real. I am familiar. I am family. I am Esther, Rachel, Aunt Sylvia, Cousin Meredith, the red-haired roommate on *Will & Grace.*

I am a Jewish Girl.

Of course, for every David there's an Amir, who could never take me seriously because his family spoke Farsi at the kosher Sabbath table while mine swore in Yiddish when the pepperoni pizza was delivered cold. And for every Amir there's a James, whose Irish Catholic mother cared enough to have me to attend a baby shower for her first grandchild, but refused to have me over for Easter dinner because I killed Christ.

There are lessons to be learned, to be sure. I've been kicked to the curb enough times to know that religion matters in a relationship. While I still have not come to any great conclusions about Modern Romance, what I am apt to do is tell my stories—just like Anne did. She may never have experienced a "happily ever after," but I still hope for that ending.

Agnostic Front

Ben Rutter

Imagine that the reasons for belief in a wise and benevolent God could be weighed, summed, and assigned a value. Call this A, and call B the value of views to the contrary; then compare the two. In this way, the mystery of faith arranges itself in a neat stack of possibilities: either A is greater, or B, or neither—the two are equal—or the question itself stands unsolved, the irrational ratio of two real numbers. We are either theists, that is, or atheists, or else parties to some more learned form of compromise. In general, questions of theology are unlike those found on math exams. And yet the problem of faith has long seemed to me to share with standardized testing the foursquare clarity of multiple choice. Only lately, in the course of certain conversations with my peers, have I begun to think otherwise.

There are those who feel that a properly modern world would be one rich in concepts, a world in which each sort of thought and each sort of thing bore its own proper name. Such a person, I imagine, was Thomas Huxley, the Darwinist and freethinker who gave us, toward the middle of the nineteenth century, the notion of agnosticism. The agnostic has heard talk of God in heaven, the truth of which he can neither confirm nor deny. Huxley was not, of course, the first to climb and sit this fence. Protagoras, the ancient rhetorician, had opened his treatise on theology with a crisp proviso: "Concerning the gods, I have no means of knowing whether they exist or not, or of what sort they may be."

What Huxley did, in giving this form of ignorance a name, was to suggest the possibility of its permanence. In this way, the interval between faithlessness and faith came to sponsor a theology of its own. Huxley's position has traditionally assumed one of two forms. The strong agnostic holds that the question of God's existence is unanswerable in principle. God is transcendent, humans are not, and that is that. A and B are equal in value. The weak agnostic, by contrast, considers the question undecided only at present, holding open the possibility that further evidence—boiling seas, say, or a bolt from the blue—may someday resolve the issue. The difference is perhaps one of temperament. Does the virtue of our ignorance lie in worldly resignation or does it lie in hope?

Americans have tended to view the agnostic compromise as an elevated sort of dodge, a scholar's disguise for ordinary moral yellowness. William James, for one, considered the notion the worst that "ever came out of the philosopher's workshop." Huxley's cause suffers, meanwhile, from the lack of an attractive spokesmodel. Protagoras was known not only for his balky faith but also for the extortionate fees he charged his students. Agnostic Front is not a group of concerned citizens but a loud and menacing rock band. In fact, the only avowed agnostic who has made the papers in recent years was Tim McVeigh, and even he chose, in the end, to receive last rites from a death-row priest. Nevertheless, it will surprise me if the mentioned percentage has not grown by the time the next survey is taken. It is not that the faith of the American public appears to be shifting toward indecision. Just the opposite: agnosticism itself is slowly being tugged toward faith.

When I ask my friends to describe for me the views of a religious agnostic, only a few seem to follow the definition commonly found in dictionaries. For the rest, the meaning of the term bears a different weight. An agnostic, they tell me, is a person who remains aloof from fixed religious identities while preserving at the same time a vague faith in some higher power. In this reconception, the hard edge of Huxley's skepticism is softened and something like intuition is given greater rein. Supposing, then, that this sense of the term has in fact grown common, it will make sense to expand by one the roster of answers to the problem of faith. This fifth position, call it New Agnosticism, seems to me sufficiently distinct. The deists of the eighteenth century shared with new agnostics a belief in a higher power. Deism, however, is the view that this power, though responsible for the design and creation of the world, is unable or unwilling to intervene in its established order. For the new agnostic, meanwhile, as for the theist, this higher power shares with human beings the basic features of agency. That is to say, it thinks; it collects its thoughts in plans; and in plans it gives shape to actions. At the core of this view is the idea that in spite of its giant silence the cosmos is not ultimately inhospitable to purposes.

I am the sort of person who thinks, with Huxley, that our local, human purposes are probably all we need to furnish life with the meaning it demands. They are surely as weird and as deep, at any rate, as those of old man universe. Now one such purpose, a marginal one, is that of excellence in lexicography. A language in possession of a well-defined concept, you might say—any one will do—is superior by some tiny degree to a language without it. So I admit that on first learning of the innovation in agnosticism a mild concern did set in. At such points, a count to five and a reflection upon the leafy vigor of language is usually just the thing. Old words will put forth new shoots and the botanists will be on hand to measure and record. What is worth asking, in the meantime, is why the meaning of the term began its drift in the first place.

Agnosticism holds a privileged place in the family of concepts to which it belongs. An intermediate point between atheism and belief, it has the appearance of a middle sibling, an agent of compromise perhaps. This position is by nature unstable. Contests are staged on neutral grounds and influence, as in chess, depends upon control of the middle. Even the devil will not lay siege to heaven but waits to meet its armies, instead, at a point halfway between. In a contest of ideas, the midway is often marked out by a tertium quid, a third concept or term, and the possibility of reconciliation may depend upon its discovery. Where this term is absent, the weather tends to gather heavily at the poles. This was the predicament, I recall, in which MC Hammer found himself in 1991 as he sought to explain how he could both support the troops and oppose the war. What we lack, then as now, is perhaps nothing more than the right word. Consider the enthusiasm, the palpable relief, with which a culture tormented by prejudice has embraced the notion of the metrosexual—officially elected, in fact, the best new word of 2003.

A third term of sufficient authority may prove indisputable, as was the case when Michael Jordan mounted the podium at the 1992 Barcelona Olympics to accept his gold medal. The Dream Team was sponsored by Reebok, Jordan by Nike, who would hear nothing of his international appearance in the hightops of a rival. Preternaturally self-assured, Jordan arrived for the ceremony robed in the tertium quid itself: a large, new American flag.

More often than not, however, the third term does not offer an immediate solution, but rather marks out the terrain on which the conflict is staged. Consider the intense semantic pressures levied in recent decades upon the notion of political liberalism. Conservatives, by definition, stand for tradition, progressives for change. What, then, is a liberal? A generation ago, Richard Nixon sought (not without cause) to reclaim the term for his own party. Democrats, after all, mooned over equality; it was the Republicans, then as now, who stood for freedom above all else. When Nixon failed to retake the term, his colleagues simply made it a slur. Either way, though, the word has shed none of its political charge.

Agnosticism retains an academic, half-familiar air. It is not often heard on television, and the pressures turned upon it have been less intense than those turned, say, on "liberal," or "fair and balanced," or "french fries." Still, if the shift in its meaning is as deep as I have suggested, the idea of agnosticism may have come to serve as a minor fulcrum, a point of balance in the wider debate between secular and religious America. It is worth recalling that the term was never intended as such. Huxley was an empiricist and a skeptic who took little interest in the nature of sin or the fate of his soul. Arguments were to be judged, in his view, on the basis of observation and experiment alone, and theism, by this reckoning, scarcely merited consideration. Atheism, meanwhile, remained a plausible but ultimately unprovable dogma. Huxley's turn toward agnosticism was motivated by the demands not of spiritual faction, but of intellectual hygiene. Many of his temper, in fact, have claimed their agnosticism in a spirit not of tolerance, but of polite disdain. The great French positivist Auguste Comte, for one, declined atheism on the grounds that to embrace it would be to take the very notion of God far too seriously.

Agnosticism, then, is in its origins the edited atheism of a fastidious mind. It is a slim concept, a sort of supplement. What has lately begun to happen, however, is that other, less fastidious minds have begun to grant it a more robust, more relevant sense. It is not unreasonable to assume, on the one hand, that a point of true compromise between faith and atheism cannot be found. Tolerance and ecumenism may gesture toward such a point. And yet their influence, in the end, may serve only to underscore the difference: that one either is or is not a person of faith.

Suppose, though, that such a compromise, a balsam for our partisan scars, were possible. Suppose the discovery of the tertium quid, the third spiritual thing. Agnosticism has been dislodged and its meaning lifted into flux. The forces behind this shift may derive from the need, felt dimly by those on either side, for something like a genuine middle ground. Where Huxley was circumspect, the New Agnosticism offers a generous welcome. It is ecumenism drawn out almost to the vanishing point. Any tradition, any myth, perhaps even a persistent sense of gratitude, will do. Can this be the properly modern form of faith?

Citizens of a plural world have natural difficulty honoring the magic and heroes of one tradition over those of another. And yet the alternative—life as the banging along of stuff—leaves many just as cold. Our lives, so far as we lead them, are saturated at each point with notions of purpose and aim. To concede this fact, to steadily pursue one's ends, and yet to view them all the while as cheerful fictions requires a rather blackened sense of humor. For those both called to belief and wary of that call, there is little refuge. The nearest point of contact in the Western tradition is perhaps Unitarian Universalism, a faith that emerges in response to the same fact of pluralism. And yet the Unitarian Universalists offer not the reconciliation but the studious avoidance of theologies. What unites their church is a shared moral vision, and this, in the end, has nothing to do with the existence or absence of higher powers. The new agnostic offers no description of this power save for its bare existence and its vague agency. Perhaps, though, this is virtually all that matters. A *is* greater than B. It is a claim that offers scarcely anything, and yet so much more than nothing.

Please Don't Feed the Prophet

Daniel S. Brenner

God is a sweater that you grew out of. God is an old book on Soviet politics lying in a thrift shop. God is a friend from college that you want to get rid of but can't. God is a souvenir. I read the magazines. Ninety-five percent of Americans believe in God? Bullshit. The only ones who believe in God are children or old people or those ethnic minorities, you know who I'm talking about, with their "God Loves You" vanity plates and T-shirts, their "All hail King Moshiach" billboards. Their "What Would Jesus Do?" key chains. Here's a dilemma for you: you're trapped in traffic behind a car with a "Honk If God Loves You" bumper sticker. Would you honk?

I don't know what kind of person you are, but maybe you don't believe that God loves you any more than Barney the purple dinosaur loves you. And I'll admit that God has a nasty track record. God sat by and watched the burning fires of Auschwitz and didn't lift a finger. God sits by and watches the burning fires every night on CNN and doesn't say a word.

But what if God did?

This is how it happens. You're sitting there, minding your own business, scrambling some eggs, when the phone starts to ring. You wait for the machine to pick up. The beep goes off. Then you hear the VOICE. It starts to call your name. It's like your mother calling you in for dinner. It's like a mob calling for your head. It's like a lover whispering in your ear—except the voice isn't coming from the answering machine. It's everywhere, the walls, the stove, the lights, the toaster, they are all calling you. It's like a dream but awake, as when you're dreaming and two things are the same thing, like

Winona Ryder is rubbing your leg, then you look up and it's your brother, except he's got hair all over his body and he's wearing a dog collar. And it's all true, all at the same time. And you wake up and your leg feels funny.

This is how it starts, the phone call, your name, like a dream. And then come the voices. But it's not what you think—I mean it's not in your head. It's what happens between you and things. You walk by a mailbox, and love letters, condolences, get-well-soons, a check made out to a relief organization in Tanzania, a letter to a recently divorced man from an old friend all call out to you. And at the same time you see the dark side: denied medical coverage and student loan bills, countless advertisements for unnecessary items, a letter informing an aging woman that her son's remains have yet to be found. It all happens at once. Redemption and despair. A phone booth is packed with emotional history, haunted so thick that you walk across the street to avoid it. A plastic bag hangs from a tree and it is both a bag and a face. Every object speaks. A hubcap is a roulette wheel is a saw blade is a coin given to a young boy as he travels across the ocean. You see things, all things. All possibilities at once.

After three days, if you can last that long without losing your mind, you start to see people this way.

It's like in this old folktale:

Once there was a great and pious rabbi who lived in a small town by a river. He spent his days in prayer and meditation, and each evening, students would come to him with their questions. It was said that the rabbi did not need to be told the questions, for he looked into the minds of his students and instantly knew all their troubles. Once a young student, Lev, came before him with a request. "Rabbi," he said, "will you teach me how to look into people's minds?" And so the rabbi began to teach Lev his secrets. Lev learned how to listen to the thoughts of the people in the house of study and in the marketplace.

After many months, the rabbi took Lev out into the streets to see how he could use his new wisdom. First Lev ran up to a stranger and said, "God bless you for the work that you do!" Then Lev saw another man. "Listen," Lev scolded him, "you must repent!"

Afterwards the rabbi sat Lev down and asked him what he saw. "In the first man's thoughts," Lev said, "I saw the holy words of Torah. In the second man's, I saw people engaged in sexual unions." The rabbi sat quietly for a moment. Then he spoke these words: "Lev, my beloved student, the man you blessed works in the local print shop, and he cheats his customers. The second man is the most righteous man in the town, the matchmaker, and the couples he brings together are the best of matches."

That's the folktale. But what you see in people's minds isn't like the story. You see the printer and the matchmaker in each soul. You see the righteous and wicked woman in all women. Man in all men. Every act of giving is an act of taking, every moment of sensitivity is a moment of calculation. And then come the words.

The words come like Cyrano below a moonlit window, fed to me like I'm a skinny child in grandma's kitchen. God my muse, clothed in a libretto. God the milk, me a bowl of Alpha-Bits cereal, overflowing.

But God? I mean, come on, God? A message for you from God? Because God is a made-up idea, a metaphor, an interpretation. God is a way the ancients devised to answer questions that they were too stupid to figure out. They did not have the *Science Times* every Tuesday. God is what would happen if Santa Claus made it with the Tooth Fairy. God is a clever advertisement for the overly self-righteous. God is a lame excuse for a day off from work. God is what men invented when they got old and couldn't get it up. God is pre-Viagra. Whatever God is, it certainly isn't real. And we only base life on that which is real. You know what real is? Life itself. Not just the science and substance, but the experience of it all.

And we crave experience. We want sensual delights and orgasm and bliss. I want this new shampoo! I want to fuck my shampoo! I want to be fucked by my shampoo! Bliss! Bliss! York Peppermint Patties! Take me away! And at the moment of pure ecstasy you hit this white light of bliss, of eternal fuzziness enveloping you in its brilliance, sucking you in, so there is no you. Our station has concluded today's programming. But then you wake up and the pleasure fades—and we are always coming off it, coming down from the high, hung over, ill, poisoned by desire.

Then we get depressed. And not a damn thing will break it. No pleasure seems to work anymore. It is the tale of every celebrity—adored by thousands, trusted by no one. They buy lavish homes, lock themselves inside, and begin to take out their rage on their bodies. And we love it! We want more celebrities to self-destruct! Overdose! Kill your wife! Get fat! Divorce! Assault somebody, please! Who is next? Where is the videotape footage at which luxury bleeds into shame? Because that's what we want, to see our pathetic self-destruction as beautiful, our private tragedy as great entertainment.

We are stuck in a spin cycle of desire and destruction. So now hear this: "The trial period is over!" Humans must step down from their throne! Eternal God, come on down, you are the next contestant on The Price Is Too Damn High!

The prophet speaks: A time will come when we no longer place our trust in humans or their machines and screens. We will trust only in our God, irresponsible, imperfect, mad at times, but still possessing compassion and mercy for a thousand generations. Welcome to the paradox. We were made in God's image and now God is in ours. So hold yourselves responsible!

And so I say: Repent! Repent! Repent all you sinners and I mean me, damn it! And you, too, especially you! Not because you've been bad, but because you think that being bad will somehow make you feel more alive, not for what you did, but for what you will do—because you will take the most wondrous things for granted and then fail to take responsibility for your actions. You want to blame God? Blame him! But blame yourself too! And fall to your knees! Repent! Repent!

I'm sorry, I should have never said this. I should have ignored the voices, pleaded insanity, moved to Iowa, and started a gun collection. But God opened my eyes. God asked me to speak. And I trust that. Now it's your turn. You be the prophet. Go ahead.

There was a child born whose mother did not give her milk. Nor did she give her love, nor think of her as a miracle as she lay in the cradle. A bitter woman, she was, a tormented woman; her mind had been warped by the selfishness of those around her and she saw her child only as a burden, a chain, an affliction. Yet, in spite of the mother's neglect, the child grew. For in her dreams each night an angel would come and feed her. First the angel fed her letters, all the letters of all the languages of the earth. And these letters nourished the child. And as she grew, the angel began to feed her words. And this was good. She grew more and soon the words grew into poems, and the poems begat songs, and the songs begat stories upon stories. Soon the child was grown up, and she walked the earth filled with the letters, words, poems, songs, and stories from the angel. And in small groups, people would gather to hear her. Some men wanted to hunt her down and kill her for her stories frightened them. Some women wanted to slit her throat from jealousy. Her stories spoke of the deep shame of life, the silent pain, the loneliness. And when she spoke, those who heard her felt a nourishment they had never felt, a mending of all that has been shattered. She roamed from place to place and spoke in her quiet way, a cross between whispers and lullabies. Where is she now, this child fed from the letters of angels? Where is she that we can lift her up, and carry her through the streets in celebration?

She has disappeared. Wandered off deep inside your soul, calling out to you right now to join her. She's getting ready to tell you a story.

You're Not in Oz Anymore

Velvet, as told to
Peter Manseau and Jeff Sharlet

We met Velvet at an annual gathering of a few thousand witches, druids, heathens, and magick-workers known as Heartland. Velvet was her magick name, and as such it was all we called her for the three days we spent with her and her coven on the campgrounds of Heartland. Heartland is in Kansas, an hour north of Kansas City, and despite the buzz of small-engine airplanes overhead—muggles with binoculars spying on naked pagans—the witches and the Christians and the Harley-Davidson bikers in the area all seemed to get along. Not so in the small town from whence Velvet came. Velvet was a young mother, but she hadn't been able to bring her daughter with her. The local judge had awarded custody to her born-again Christian aunt and uncle, on the grounds that Velvet was, in the court's view, a Satanist. Velvet scoffed. "As if I'd ever be a Luciferian," she said. "They're dirty."

In fact, Velvet was an "elf-witch." This is not to say that she was an elf, since, as she pointed out, elves are imaginary. We asked her to explain the difference.

I heard about elf witches and thought, yeah, right, this is just some Dungeons and Dragons freak's odd little idea. But the person who told me about it, I met her grandmother, who taught it to her and had a Book of Shadows from *her* great grandmother. So I studied druidic magick for two years, two years of shamanic magick, two years of Egyptian magick, two years of old Wiccan. Elf magick is different than a lot of what you see amongst ordinary Wiccans.

Instead of four elements, it has six, seven elements. It adds Shadow, Depth, and Reflection to the list of elements.

Is that the only difference?

Elven magick also has rules against ingesting processed food.

Because elves don't do that?

Yeah, *exactly.* No, I'm kidding. Elves are nature spirits. Theoretical elementals. You will never see the little guys with the pointy ears. Pointy ears are a genetic defect. I know people with them. I know people with very fine bone structure and pointy ears. They are not elven. Go to Denver, man! There's an entire little clan of people there who all claim they're elves and trolls. And you're goin'—"You're all cracked." I do elven magick. But I don't claim to be an *elf.* They don't either. They say they were "bred" from elves—those little nonexistent beings that run around? Well, mythical, I should say. I can't tell you if they exist or not. I have never personally seen an actual elf. I'll give that they *might* have existed, just like I'll give that unicorns existed and any other mythical, quote unquote, beast, dragons, may have existed. But if an elf walked up to me during a ritual, it wouldn't make my ritual any stronger or weaker. It would just be rather odd. Because I'd have an elf. Amusing, maybe, but not important. It's just a name. It seemed to connect me with everything more than what any of the other magicks I'd tried did. There's a list of elven gods this long, but I don't even worship 'em. I worship Hecate and Loki.

Hecate and Loki are both "dark deities." I hate that term. The deal is they teach really hard lessons. And, they're not lessons you want to learn. People want magick to be all set out in flowers and rainbows. And life is not all flowers and rainbows. I'm sorry. Neither is it all death and such, but people don't even want to face that. Loki has a tendency to teach by playing a trick, and once you pick up on it, you go, "You know, I should've known that. That was *stupid.*" Hecate is more of the opinion of "Smack, okay you're in this situation, now get out of it. Yup, you got out of it. Okay, you learned something, didn't'cha?"

The way I came to follow Loki in the first place was, I was in a ritual down at Herne's Hollow. A men's ritual. I bet one guy twenty bucks that Loki would show up when we called him even if I was down there. And I won twenty bucks. I also went to sleep down at Herne's Hollow, and I had this dream about a coyote coming and taking off this one ring I was wearing and leaving another ring. Well, I woke up and I found the exact same ring I saw in my dream sitting at my feet. Well, I switched it out with the one on my hand. I wore that ring for like six months. That was a *cracked* six months, lemme tell ya. Most people don't even know anything about Loki other than he's a trickster god. Which he is. But they don't know anything about it. After Ragnarok [Norse mythological apocalypse] he's going to be one of the two gods remaining.

The other is Odin. And he won't really be alive. Ragnarok repeats, unlike the [Christian] apocalypse, which happens only once. Ragnarok repeats itself. It's a renewal cycle. Odin will technically be dead but he can be brought back.

Doesn't Thor beat up on Loki a lot?

Yep. Thor has a big hammer. If I were Loki I'd be scared of that big hammer, too. But if you look at all that Thor thuggery, somebody learned something out of all that, too. Whap! Learn it. Talk to a worshipper of Thor. Those aren't subtle lessons.

We've seen some guys walking around with big hammers.

Thor worshippers.

What did Loki look like when you saw him?

He looked solid. You could reach out and touch him. Little old guy. Really skinny, hunched over. Long beard. I was just going, wow. A god. Like, manifested.

After six months of wearing that ring [from Loki], I'd start thinking about what I was doing before I'd do it. It made me a considerably better person. I don't have nearly as much tendency to yap when I shouldn't. I lost the ring, but I continue to worship him, because he taught me a lot. Hecate has been more of a long, ongoing thing. I've worshipped her on and off since I first started being pagan. She was the first goddess I ever had any interest in. She is the crone [senior] form of the triple goddess. Mother, Maiden, Crone. I am not a crone. I actually chose her because she's the only one I feel any connection to. The Maiden is too happy and innocent and bouncy. That's not me. It's me out here [at the pagan gathering], but it's not me in normal life. My normal life isn't happy and bouncy, and it just doesn't work to try to be that way. I'm a goth, ok? Goths are not happy, bouncy. That would be just disgusting and wrong. Funny, but disgusting and wrong.

[*Velvet takes us around the lake to see "The Venus Mound," a ritual area for female pagans.*] The goddess gathering happens here. Over at Herne's Hollow, it has a very male presence to it. This is a lighter, airier, female-type energy. It's an altar for the goddesses. Plus it's just a place females can come and sit. The men who are comfortable down here won't mess with the females. [*Velvet steps, barefoot, on a thorn.*] Of course, then we have the spiky tree next to the chair. Locust tree. Spikes fall off. I step on 'em all the time. There's some mythos that locust trees are acquainted with females, though I don't understand because usually this little pointy thing they have going on is not equated with females. [*Wind chimes chime, Velvet rolls her eyes.*] Females like wind chimes. They react with air. Air is a female element. Air and water are female, earth and fire are male—no, wrong. I'm talking elven. Wrooong mythos. Typical. Um, earth and air are female. Water and fire are male. I don't know why.

[*We walk up onto a small hill.*] There's a Venus statue. Venus the goddess. The hinges around it are offerings left. They don't necessarily have any particularly meaning to other than who left them. If you rummaged through the grass, you could probably find $1.50 worth of pennies. Because people that don't have a personal item to give will give just something. I personally don't like leaving money. I don't have a problem with the penny thing, but silver is tacky. I think it's like trying to buy off the goddess. I have an issue with that. I don't leave offerings to Venus. Venus is a goddess of love. It's just not my deal. I usually leave stuff over at the generic altar. Do I see anything I have left here in the past? I'm looking. There. My little beaded key chain. It was all I had on me. I wanted to leave something, and I had a sarong and a key chain. So Hecate got a piece of key chain. She couldn't have the whole key chain, because I would have had to take it off the key. And it was the key to my house. I wasn't asking anything. I generally leave offerings as, "Hey I still acknowledge you." Because I don't have a tendency to ask for much of anything from anybody.

People come up here and sit and talk to the goddesses for just hours. And say prayers. I've seen people do rituals up on the mound. I don't, because I'm of the opinion it ties up the mound, and I can pray to my goddess down there as well as I can up here. Pray to my goddess down there, leave my offering here, and go do whatever it is I'm doing that day. As far as I'm concerned an offering is an offering. Leaving an offering here, it makes people feel they're going to be recognized. I'm not of that opinion. I think if the goddess is going to care, she's going to care wherever you leave it. The only reason I come out here to leave offerings is I feel power here. Same with Herne's Hollow. I come out here and do a ritual to Hecate and go over there and do a ritual to Loki. It's what I do. I won't demonstrate now because I don't want Loki now. Nooo Loki.

[*A mouse runs over her foot, running in circles around us, like it's trying to tell us something.*]

Maybe it's Loki.

Nope. It's hawk food.

Cowboy for Christ

Quince Mountain

I came of age as a God-fearing transgendered horse wrangler, which is not as surprising as it may sound; we gender-variant folk often fling ourselves toward some semi-hostile, straight and narrow home-away-from-home. I was only seven or eight when I heard the tale of Grandmother's *Chicago Tribune* coworker, Nancy Hunt, who published her autobiography the year I was born. My grandmother told me how Nancy, a male-to-female transsexual formerly known as Ridgely Hunt, had joined the military to assert her masculinity. Ridgely's enlistment was a last-ditch effort to succeed as a male. It was a sort of once-and-for-all, make-or-break gender trial undertaken with the belief that Uncle Sam, if anyone, might be able to transform this feminine creature into a man.

I understand the principle. I remember my welding teacher towering over me as I placed my project—a lap joint: two pieces of metal stock welded one over the other—in his custom-made double vise. I watched the big man grin sadistically while using a foot pedal to increase pressure until the thick metal snapped in two. If the metal broke along one of the welded seams, I'd fail. If the metal broke elsewhere—not along the weld—I could proudly place the useless remnants of my project in the pocket of my leather apron and move on to the next assignment.

I think of young Private Hunt like that, shipping off to Korea with steely resolve, not knowing if he would manage to hold together his masculine image long enough to die at the hands of enemy soldiers—in which case he would have passed his gender trial.

His mother could proudly bury the remnants of his body under an American flag before she moved on to her next project.

Nestled awkwardly among the Heritage Series classics on my family's bookshelves was an inscribed copy of Nancy's transgender memoir, *Mirror Image*, published in 1978. On Saturday mornings, when my grandmother was in the garden and my grandfather was out garage-saling, I would carefully remove the book, glancing furtively down the hallway before ducking into the bathroom.

I returned to *Mirror Image* often, trying to soak up some of Nancy's transgender savvy. Her company offered great comfort, even when sought only in the solitude of the cold downstairs bathroom. And the bathroom seemed an appropriate as well as a discreet place to contemplate this tattered scripture. My grandmother claimed to have been one of the first women to use the facilities at the Tribune Tower alongside Nancy, asserting proudly that she just did not understand the inordinate discomfort felt by her coworkers. I often sat on the toilet for the greater part of the afternoon, emerging only when I heard my grandfather roll up the garage door, signaling he needed help unpacking his spoils.

It's difficult to say how conscious I was of my identification with Nancy Hunt. I remember feeling sympathy for her even while I was confident I would grow into an honorable if often-unshaven cowboy. I did not anticipate the betrayal that took place when I hit the double digits: not only the realization that I wouldn't get the rawhide man's body I had thought was my physical inheritance, but also an awareness of the widespread expectation that a feminine social orientation would come just as easily to me as to any tomboy-grown-older. Transgender theorist Jack Halberstam describes adolescence as the shrinking of her world. For me, that shrinking happened when my grandfather caught me reading *Mirror Image* in the bathroom and returned it to the shelf, where it would collect dust for the next decade.

Junior high school was, of course, hellacious. "Are you a boy or a girl?" kids would ask, sometimes jeering, sometimes in earnest. Try as I might to achieve a passable femininity—shaving my legs, wearing hoop earrings, keeping my hair long, clasping a useless bra across my flat chest—I knew as well as they did that I was a failure. The harder I tried the more obvious it became.

I began to work out, lifting weights and riding my trusty mountain bike twenty or thirty miles each day. I drank Ensure to gain weight and carried my grandfather's fishing knife, still hoping I'd become that rough-and-ready cowboy that I had grown old enough to realize I was not expected to be.

It was only at Christian camp that I found not just a way to trade my bike for a horse, but also a modicum of acceptance. It was my megachurch-going mother's idea to send me at age ten to the Wisconsin Northwoods for a summer of frolicking and fundamentalist indoctrination. For the counselors, I provided the ultimate Christian challenge. One may quite rightly suppose that getting ten-year-olds to raise their hands at revival meetings is not all that difficult. This is likely part of the reason the counselors did not declare their spiritual victory immediately after I repented of a decade of accumulated sin, accepting Jesus Christ as my *personal* Lord and Savior. Neither were they satisfied when I slipped backwards into the baptismal vault, dutifully if clumsily making a public proclamation of faith before Pastor Jim could manage the words "Father," "Son," and "Holy Spirit." From me—the illegitimate and masculine daughter of a woman who had not until midlife wrested free from the grip of Catholicism—the counselors' satisfaction demanded serious commitment to remedial education in the ways of the Good Book. They urged me to return to the camp annually as a volunteer member of the support staff, and I was promised personalized "discipleship training" in exchange for twelve daily hours of hard manual labor. This annual exodus from suburban life and commitment to camp ministry would provide evidence that the tree of my Christianity was indeed capable of bearing fruit.

Fearing above all else the dead faith decried by Jesus's brother long before I was even so much as a nervous twinkling in my unwed mother's eye, I entered the workforce the following summer as an unpaid eleven-year-old, quite willing to spend six days each week mucking horse stalls as a junior wrangler at the camp's North Star Stable. Of course, my desire for living faith might not have kept me returning for so many years had I been called to serve as a lifeguard or a dishwasher; but the Prince of Peace sometimes puts his beloved children in just the right places, and I looked ever to His service, feeling my oats as a Cowboy for Christ.

More than a few trannies have taken solace in the performance of bizarre religious rites before settling into their niches as misfits in the mainstream world. *Gender Outlaw* author Kate Bornstein, for example, won her stripes as a seafaring Scientologist aboard a salvaged navy vessel commissioned to transport L. Ron Hubbard safely to and from any land that would allow him ashore. Two decades later, I set out to earn my spurs as a citified Calvinist astride a narcoleptic Tennessee walking horse predestined to transport middle-aged midwestern women and their reluctant but submissive husbands safely back to the barnyard after a five-mile scenic loop through the Nicolet National Forest.

Indeed, I submitted easily to the discipleship training that was to seal the success of my conversion. After all, nobody was more invested in asserting my femininity than I was, and to that particular end the Christian counselors were my most faithful allies. Their lessons on Proverbs 31 Womanhood (*Who can find a virtuous woman? For her price is far above rubies . . .*) consisted in large part of practical feedback on personal grooming. Since wranglers were supposed to wear jeans and T-shirts, and since devout young ladies were not allowed makeup, perfume, or excessive jewelry, I had little difficulty following the dress code. Jesus did not adorn himself, and neither would I.

Overall, I found Bible camp femininity much less inhibiting than any suburban junior high school femininities I encountered. Charm is deceitful; beauty is vain—I could get my rope around that. In fact, I took so well to this code of feminine strength and honor that I felt a little self-righteous around my cabin mates as they struggled to look sexy without appearing immodest and to walk the fine godly line between frigidity and promiscuity during pizza dates at the canteen. I basked comfortably in this self-righteousness right up until I met my first girlfriend.

She had untamed red hair and an attitude to match. I was sitting on a soggy bale of hay, exchanging evening prayer requests with a friend next to an especially loud and hungry bonfire when Whitney Layne returned to camp from a summer spent spreading Christ's gospel in the Amazon basin. I had hardly noticed this girl the summer before, but I remember well when she emerged from the Oconto River astride her chestnut horse, Vindicator, and trampled my every Protestant hope. I didn't see her coming at all. And it's a good thing, because I might well have betrayed my terror with an unbecoming scream had I not been shocked into silence at the sight of this intense young creature bareback atop her small Arabian gelding, red ponytail and red horsetail trailing high as the two bounded over the hay bale next to me, clearing the hungry flames at my feet with a yard to spare before galloping into the twilit horizon. I don't know if I was in love, but I was certainly in awe of this mysterious missionary girl whose horse forded swift rivers and leapt over campfires.

My boyhood was gone as quickly as she said *this* and I said *yes* —my nights filled with kinky, clandestine sex. At the time, I managed to reconcile this fact with my belief in the New Testament as the God-breathed template for a healthy life. Yes, what Whit and I did was something I knew should be kept to ourselves, something

I knew the camp leaders wouldn't understand. Still, I somehow thought our behavior was not sin. This was not anything like the sex or the sin or the sadism I'd been so thoroughly warned against. Stay away from the boys, I'd been told—we'd all been told. No couples off alone, no double-bareback, and a Bible-width between you when you share a pew. I could do that. And so even as I spent my nights bunked up with a whip-wielding cowgirl, I still hoped I would one day blossom into a comfortable womanhood and walk gracefully down the aisle with a handsome and godly fellow.

Even if I had not been invested in the Proverbs 31 myth, however, I would not have been able to explain my experiences. I had heard kids at school joke about bondage, but I wouldn't have thought to apply the term to my summer camp hayloft antics with Whitney, who was my boss at the stables. I didn't think too hard about why, even while I tried my best to elude her, I thoroughly enjoyed being caught in the loop of my boss's lariat, knocked to the dirt, and secured to the wall of a box stall where, for as long as my precocious young dom deemed appropriate, I would thrash in vain, choking occasional requests for mercy through the dusty bandana wadded up in my mouth. Even while I was afraid, I appreciated being forcibly immersed in the water trough, or having my wrists bound with the leather straps we all kept handy, or receiving a crack on the ass with a riding crop or bullwhip, or—most of all—being derided for my incompetence around the barn.

Just like the cowbois in the more interesting queer porn mags, I wore leather chaps and carried a rope everywhere I went. These should have been clues, but I was oblivious to my slant. Perhaps many otherwise curious adults are too horrified to partake in such pleasures, are not ready to see in themselves what they've been told is perverted. I know I was spared for a long time from the need for self-effacement or self-denial largely because of my ignorance of such terms as "flogging," "caning," "BDSM," "power play," "Fem-Dom," and the like. I didn't know a schoolboy scene from a shoe fetish, and was thus free to engage in all manner of erotic indulgence.

Until one of the deacons caught me lavishing Whitney's bare and salty beltline as she leaned back against a pile of sweaty saddle blankets polishing leather in the tack room, I was quite free, indeed. During the ensuing interrogations, I publicly denied any kind of sexual interest in girls (*What?! She's like a sister to me—my sister in Christ!*). I recounted my devotion, my service, their lack of solid evidence. The director, who called me out on the back barn porch and addressed me with his arms crossed, could hardly prove a long-standing sexual relationship. Still, my welcome at Bible camp was clearly limited to the end of the summer at best.

Privately, I had to agree with the director. I held up my desires to the holy light of God's word and, yes, they were out of line with His will. I may have failed as a camp wrangler, but I could get right with God.

When Whit and I left the camp without plans to return, we didn't tell our friends we'd been caught getting it on in the barn. We cited frustration with transient staff and milky sermons. We said we wanted community; we craved meat and potatoes. So the following summer—after I finished high school and Whit dropped out of missionary school—we moved to Whit's hometown, where we joined an even more conservative church. That's what I needed in order to be the God-fearing woman I was meant to be: more rigidity, more support. Whit may not have been like-minded, but she didn't stop me.

We moved onto a chunk of abandoned farmland with hopes of establishing a community where we could live with our chosen family. After a summer of sleeping on World War II army cots in a broken-down dairy barn, we built a twelve-by-sixteen-foot home out of construction work-site leftovers and windows salvaged from the town dump. Eventually, we put up an outhouse and managed to convince an ornery electric pump to draw sandy brown water from the drying well twice each week, providing just enough for the horses to drink if the weather cooperated. Several former camp wranglers moved in, and we took turns working outside jobs to cover expenses. Those not working elsewhere would while away their hours gardening, gathering wild edibles, singing hymns, swapping stories, painting, building furniture, or lounging near the river. Twice each year, we hosted weekend-long drug- and alcohol-free gatherings, inviting believing and nonbelieving friends and family from all over the country. Artists and thinkers of all ages who couldn't attend the busy gatherings often stopped by to break up their travels for a few days. It was a lesbian-feminist paradise—without the sex.

For several years, we lived this relatively asexual life on our queer Christian farm amidst a community of suspecting townies. Our church friends recognized our devotion—I tried even harder at Proverbs 31, wore dresses every week, wanted nothing more than to marry a wispy future pastor named Darryl and have his biblically named babies. I could be a country preacher's wife, surveying fields, keeping my vineyard tight and my candle burning. I slept chastely alongside Whit every night, but it was Christ's body that kept me warm as I waited for Darryl to fall for me. It wasn't my job to rush things, the church women told me.

And Darryl did call, though I can't say whether he was into me. Who knows?—maybe it would've been different had Whitney not erased his phone messages, or had my peers supported the match. It would've taken a village for me to marry a Christian boy, and as helpful as my elders were, the other young singles saw something else in me. I didn't belong with this or probably any church boy.

"You'll make a good wife someday," my pastor said once as I gave him a ride down a back road. I could've melted to my truck seat. I can still, right now—after years of skin and submission and girls and women and fuck this and goddamn, years of firemen and pool games and pierced nipples and Times Square and porn and Anne McClintock and feminist critique and trans support groups and trans social groups and San Francisco and emergency rooms and years of every other un-Christlike thought and desire—feel molten just thinking about that moment. I remember exactly the back road, the direction of the morning headlights, the cold coffee, the certainty, the gravity of his words, the relief they provided, the relief he knew they provided, the smell of hay and shit in the cab, the trailer full of Tennessee walkers pulling the truck slightly into the shoulder. Was it the walkers, or was it—did I just hear him right?—yes, he said wife, he said good wife, he said someday. Yes— in this lifetime, a good wife.

Outside our tight circle of church friends, though, we were recognized as women living together and not dating men. Outside church, that meant dyke.

Until the fourth year of commune living, when I spent enough time off the farm to take a few college classes—enough time to fall for and hook up with a female instructor more than twice my age—I still thought the townies were wrong. I thought I had defeated my twisted longings. When the professor turned out to be too warped even for my tastes—consensual knifeplay is one thing; drunken gunplay quite another—I turned back to my redheaded domestic partner and acquiesced to her unspoken but ever-present request that we put the queer sex back in our queer relationship.

Which is how eventually my top dresser drawer came to contain a camouflage cock and how Darryl's sister, who was curious, and one of my Christian roommates, shocked Darryl away from me for good and how I finally gave up trying to conquer certain desires of the flesh. Some would call it *coming out,* or *liberation,* or *failure.*

What would I call it?

Ever the fundamentalist, I defer to the original text. I just couldn't do Proverbs 31. And back in the day, my lap joint broke along the welded seam ten times over and the shop teacher chucked my final attempt into a pail full of failed projects and turned away without saying a word. And eventually Nancy Hunt's welded seam came apart, too, and there was only the jagged remnant of the original stock. And though I never did learn to make a passable lap joint, I've noticed that it rarely matters.

Jesus Gonna Strip You Naked

Jeff Sharlet

The Greater Morning Star Pentecostal Church is on Dix Street in northeast Washington, D.C. On Sundays, the bishop Charles E. Johnson preaches to the true believers. The rest of the week Morning Star sends out roving teams of street preachers to sing, dance, and pray for the souls of passersby.

A few weeks ago, in Dupont Circle, a park in Washington, I stopped to listen to one of the Morning Star teams as they preached via a bullhorn to the crowd of lawyers and homeless chess players. First, a young man sang a song about Jesus. Then three women in long dresses jumped up and down and clapped and shook their hips—apparently, a dance about Jesus. And finally, a short, dark-skinned woman with chipmunk cheeks, angry eyes behind big glasses, and a voice that made her sound like the love child of Muhammad Ali and Janis Joplin took the bullhorn.

"The Lord," she boomed, "that is, Jes-us, Jes-us, Jes-us"—that much she said slowly. Then she ducked her head, took a big breath, and came up rapping:

> He got somethin better than money
> He got somethin better than yo honey
> He is out here to save you from money,
> The honey,
> and all damnation.
> Now lay yo money down!
> Lay yo money down!
> He gonna make you clean,

He gonna take yo cigarette,
He gonna take yo needle,
He took it from me,
He take it from you.
I know! I was a ho!
Yes, I worked these streets,
I stood out here with myself for sale,
Yes.
I had on the hot pants,
I had on the spike heels,
I had on the bi-kee-nee, showing my teeties
And I said I was for sale!
But Jesus wasn't buyin,
Jesus only savin.
I was a ho, I was a crack ho, and He took the smoke right
    out of my veins.
He took the cigarette from my lips,
He took the liquor from my tongue,
He stripped me naked,
And He gonna strip you naked too,
Jesus gonna make you clean.
You all come over here, we gonna tell you,
He gonna tell you.
He gonna shout it,
Jesus, He gonna whisper it,
Jesus is it,
We gonna whisper Jesus in yo ear,
We gonna strip you clean,
Clean for Jesus!
You think you clean in yo five-hundred-dollar suit,
You think you clean in yo armani-versace-ralph-
    karan-donna-lauren-tommy-hilfiger
thousand-dollar ni-ke clothes,

yo fancy shoes,
yo shiny car,
with a woman ain't yo own,
a man ain't yo own,
weeelllll
Jeeesus gonna tell you,
Jesus here today to tell you,
Jesus gonna tell you:
You ain't clean.
You ain't clean now.
He gonna clean you up.
You gotta let him help you.
I let him help me.
I was a ho.
You may be a ho too.
Jesus don't care.
Jesus love the hos,
Jesus loves you with the needle,
Jesus loves you with the five-hundred-dollar suit
Jesus loves you with yo honey,
And honey, Jesus love you too.
But He smell your perfume,
He don't like it.
Jesus see your suit,
He don't like it.
Jesus see yo green money,
He don't like it.
Jesus gonna help you!
You can cry for yo momma,
You can cry for yo daddy,
Bring 'em down.
Jesus help them too.
'Cause there ain't no help but Jesus,

Nothing you do is but Jesus,
You think you clean?
It's because o Jesus.
You take a shower, that's Jesus,
You button up your bright white shoe, that's Jesus
You tie your shiny black shoe, that's Jesus.
Jesus already there, you just gotta open up!
Everybody hear me now?
Open up!
Everybody hear me?
Open wide,
Stretch your heart wide,
Make it WIIIIDE!
Open yo window!
Jesus wants to come in.
You gotta let Him in,
Don't matter if you five, twenty-five, one hundred and
    twenty-five—
Jesus.
He comin' in.

She was still going strong, but my time was up; worldly concerns awaited me. So I crossed the street and asked for a pamphlet from Reverend Green, the man who'd sung the warm-up song. Instead he gave me a hug and told me to come down to Morning Star.

"Does she preach there?" I asked.

"Oh, yeah!" he said. "She ain't even preaching now. All that she's doin'? It's just mumblin'. That ain't nothin' but mumblin' 'bout the Lord."

The Joy of Dissent
(Or, Why I Miss Fundamentalism)

E.J. Park

> *Here's to the crazy ones.*
> *The misfits. The rebels. The troublemakers.*
> *The round pegs in the square holes.*
> *The ones who see things differently.*
> *They're not fond of rules.*
> *And they have no respect for the status quo.*
> *You can praise them, disagree with them,*
>   *quote them,*
> *disbelieve them, glorify or vilify them.*
> *About the only thing you can't do is ignore them.*
> *Because they change things.*
>
> ad for APPLE COMPUTER

It is a damp May day, and I'm sipping chai tea in Greenwich Village, thinking about Timothy McVeigh as I listen to Jessica's Marxist ranting. "Oh, I don't know. Maybe I'm just thinking too hard," she says. "I mean, okay, so maybe America is oppressive and unjust, but what about all the things I enjoy?" She giggles. "I love mocha Frappuccinos, and I'm not willing to give them up." What she really wants, she decides, is a revolution that goes well with her new Prada shoes.

"Look." Jessica holds up a plastic bag that has been resting next to her left ankle.

"Urban Outfitters," I reply.

She pulls out a small T-shirt with a Charlie's Angels decal on the front of it and a pair of black leather pants. "Aren't they awesome?" Tyler Durden would be proud. "I can't give up Starbucks, but the reign of Gap is officially over in my life."

I imagine McVeigh sepia-toned on the back of the *Atlantic Monthly,* the harshness of his rebellion filtered with a soft Gaussian blur. He leans, Brando-like, against a truck full of explosives, arms folded, brooding, a perfect vision of cool defiance. He is the Picasso, the Gandhi, the Einstein of the extreme Right. He thinks different.

"I'm going to change my taste in music," Jessica says. A year ago I was her. I bought two Bob Dylan CDs: *Highway 61 Revisited* and *Blonde on Blonde.* I ordered them from Amazon, along with Jack Kerouac's *On the Road.* I also got a tattoo. "I'm thinking Eminem and Limp Bizkit," she says halfheartedly.

I became a fundamentalist when I turned fifteen. I not only got my hair cut, but I refused to give out my Social Security number. I picketed abortion clinics and adult bookstores with an old lady named Marge who wore fuchsia lipstick. I once drove my friend past an adult bookstore while he shot marbles at a titty sign with his Trumark wrist-braced slingshot. We shrieked with delight when we heard the sound of glass breaking. Somewhere, teenage boys are gathered together in a cheaply paneled basement celebrating the fortitude of McVeigh. I know. He is Mel Gibson in their eyes. William Wallace. The Patriot. You may strap him in your torture chamber, but he will cry out *Freedom!*

"But, damn, if I don't love nicely packaged products." Jessica goes on to tell me about her recent obsession with Snapple's new drinks. They are expensive and taste awful, but the sleek bottles call out to her. How is a freshman girl supposed to resist the seduction of Diet Air? I used to think that awareness was the difference. If we were only more conscious about the ploys of marketing, more critical, more knowledgeable. I became a PhD student in media studies and learned from my professors that producing a marketable dissertation is all that really matters.

"I just feel so trapped, so surrounded, so overwhelmed." She looks at me, and my long hair, and my dad's short-sleeve dress shirt that's missing three buttons, and believes that I have an answer to her dilemma. "Is it even possible to transcend the market?" She has no idea that I used to be a right-wing, anti-government fundamentalist. I look too artsy. "I don't know," I say. "You could be like Timothy McVeigh." She giggles.

"Seriously."

"That's not funny," she says.

The fundamentalist church that I used to attend had its property seized by federal marshals this past February. For sixteen years the church refused to pay taxes as an employer. The leaders insisted that the church was not a corporation, that it had no responsibility to the state, that it had to obey God rather than man. The courts disagreed, ruling that the church had to pay $6 million in overdue taxes and fines, or be punished by the law. The congregation of balding men and big-haired women reveled in the tension. You can't serve two masters.

I realize now that McVeigh could never be an Apple icon. There is a fine line between fashionable rebellion and dogmatic rebellion. The former sells computers; the latter gets you killed, if you are lucky. McVeigh not only thought too differently but also believed too dogmatically, and God forbid that we should actually do either.

"You're right, Jessica. It's not funny."

I must admit that somewhere in the depths of my postmodern liberalized heart I secretly envy McVeigh's tenacity, even as I am appalled by his actions. When I read the news of my former church's persecution, I felt a tremendous urge to abandon my sense of grace and nuance and, once again, fight the good fight of faith. The truth is, I miss the genuine dissent of fundamentalism; I've grown weary of purchasing clever T-shirts that mock society. I want to believe arrogantly. I want to be more narrow-minded. I want to see in black and white. But I can't. So I buy, while others bomb.

God forbid.

She takes a drink of her mocha Frappuccino and giggles.

Here's to the crazy ones.

The Cross and the Color Line

Timothy B. Tyson

My experience of race began in 1967, when Oxford joined many other communities in North Carolina in "desegregating" its public schools. What this meant, specifically, was that two African American children, a boy and a girl, came to the previously all-white C. G. Credle Elementary. One black teacher described J. D. Adcock, the Granville County superintendent of schools, as "from the old ways—a cracker from his heart." Adcock intended only to comply minimally with the Supreme Court's edict—now thirteen years old—in order to evade any legal challenge that would compel wholesale integration. In principle, "freedom of choice" prevailed, in that parents were free to request that their children be assigned to any school of their choice. In practice, two carefully selected middle-class black children, a boy and a girl, enrolled at Credle. Everyone pretended they were not there.

My first memory of being in school with black children was standing behind the African American boy at the water fountain. I hadn't noticed him in the line, and suddenly there he was, bent over the stainless steel spout. Deep down, I did not want to drink after him. I did not know why. The world had kenneled a vicious lie in my brain, at its core a crucial silence, since there was no why. Black was filthy, black was bad. And even at that moment, because I had also been taught to know better, I knew that the revulsion was a lie, someone else's lie, and an evil lie at that. I did not turn away—I drank after him. But I succumbed slightly; when he moved, I took my turn and pressed the button down, but let the water run for a few seconds before I drank, bending over the arc of cool water but pausing for a moment before I touched my lips to it. I guess that made me a "moderate," since there were quite a few white children who turned away.

In Oxford, I made my first black friend, although we were not peers at all. Mrs. Roseanna Allen was a tall woman with chocolate-brown skin and moist, beautiful eyes. She kept house for our family so that my mother could continue to teach school. In her starched white work dresses and rubber-soled canvas shoes, Mrs. Allen was quite imposing. By 1966, I had two little sisters, Boo and Julie, and Julie hadn't started school yet. Mrs. Allen cleaned the house and washed the clothes and cooked our supper, while she took care of Julie.

Mrs. Allen revered my father for his well-known positions on racial issues. Reverend Tyson was *somebody* in her world, and she was intent on making certain that we understood why. "Your father believes in what is *right,*" she told us over and over again. She had full adult authority in our household; I remember her chasing me down the brick walkway in the morning, when she saw that I was wearing jeans with the knees kicked out. "Your mama is a teacher and your daddy is a preacher," she huffed, turning me around quite forcefully, "and you *ain't* going to school dressed like that."

Southern white boys from time immemorial have issued glowing encomiums of nostalgia for their beloved "mammy," hosannas flung practically in the same breath with their white supremacist diatribes. And thus I hesitate, really, to say how I felt about Mrs. Allen, for fear of falling into an embarrassing and perhaps unsavory cliché. But I loved her truly, and she was the object of great fascination for me.

It was not just that she was kind, although I can scarcely think of anyone outside my family who was kinder to me as a child. Roseanna was a matchless cook and rewarded my enthusiasm for her handiwork with great indulgence. If I wanted a chocolate pie, I knew how to get one. Detailed and specific praise was the key—

"How do you make that squash casserole so sweet?" or "I think that your chocolate brownie pie is even better than my grandmother's chocolate meringue pie." Her skill, her grace, and her good spirits made quite an impression on me, and I noticed how much my mother respected her abilities and her character.

And Mrs. Allen had what seemed to the Tyson children an exotic secret life. Her husband, Fred Allen, ran a taxicab service. If he got more than one call at a time, he might telephone Roseanna and ask her to pick up someone on the far side of town. She would trundle whatever children were in her care into her car, and off we would go. Since white people did not ride in "black" taxicabs, we were always off to pick up an African American who needed a ride from someplace we might never have seen otherwise to the hospital to visit a relative or to the post office to pick up a package. We saw the neighborhoods without sidewalks or pavement, the poor huddled in rundown houses. This was "Niggertown," as the children in our neighborhood called it.

The older boys and even some of the younger ones knew about "Niggertown," because they had visited uninvited many times. On warm nights, a gang of Oxford teenagers would pile into the back of a pickup truck and go "nigger-knocking." They filled the truck bed with Coca-Cola bottles and rocks and roared through the African American neighborhoods hurling them at pedestrians, windshields, and windows. I heard tales of these vicious adventures many times. And then one Christmas, when I saw my cousins from Laurinburg at my grandmother's house, they told me about some white high school boys near Maxton who had thrown a Miller High Life bottle out of a moving car and hit an elderly black man in the head, killing him. It seemed so awful, boys that young charged with manslaughter for what amounted to a senseless prank. But I knew exactly what had happened. I nearly whispered "nigger-knocking" under my breath when they told me the story, for I had known that one day those boys were going to hurt someone badly. It didn't matter that it wasn't our town or our boys who had killed someone; I knew even then that it was all part of the same evil somehow.

But until the day I heard about the murder, the sharpest memory of the color line that lingers in my mind is a spring day in 1968, when I was almost nine. Roseanna stood at the ironing board in between the twin beds where my brother and I slept, which she used as laundry tables on wash day. I remember the smell of starch and the hissing of steam, and then the sudden realization that Mrs. Allen was crying. Silent streams of tears trickled onto my father's white shirts. When I asked her what was wrong, she almost bellowed: "What's wrong? What's *wrong*?" She seemed desperate and almost out of control. "They gone and killed Martin Luther King, that's what's wrong!" She choked hard on her sobs and buried her face in the laundry.

I knew vaguely who Dr. King was, and I knew that my father admired him greatly, but I was too young to understand even a little of the magnitude of that murder in Memphis. All I knew was that I wanted to comfort my beloved Roseanna. Never had I seen a grown-up crying like that. And so I said the only thing I could think of to say: "Maybe it will be all right, Roseanna, maybe somehow it will work out for the best."

She lifted her head and almost roared at the obscenity of the thought. "Work out for the *best*? How could it possibly work out for the best?" Mrs. Allen's face, contorted with tears and anger, looked at me with a stunned expression of rage. "How could it work out for the best that the man that God lifted up to save my people has been shot down like a dog in the streets? Did it work out for the best that Hitler killed six million Jews? Would it work out for the best if somebody burned your house down to the ground? Did it work out for the best that they took King Jesus out and nailed him to the cross?" Her head pitched forward into the crook of her arm again, and once again she sobbed into the laundry.

Somehow I managed to whisper, "We think it did, don't we?"

"What?" she said, raising her red-rimmed eyes at me.

"We think it worked out for the best that they hung Jesus on the cross, don't we, Roseanna? Jesus died on the cross to save us all from sin, didn't he?" I asked her.

"Oh, child," she cried, crawling toward me on her knees. "Oh, sweet child." And before I could move she was kneeling in front of me, reduced to roughly my height by her kneeling, and she squeezed me tight, rocking me back and forth in a muttered mixture of tears and prayers, and she held on to me for a long, long time. Afterwards, she rounded up my brother and my sisters and gave everybody their own little bottle of Coca-Cola, and we took the thick green bottles out to the back steps, where we sat together for what seemed like the rest of the day. Mrs. Allen would wail and cry from time to time, and cling to us. When my father came home, I remember, he hugged her, which I had never seen before. It was a terrible, terrible day. How terrible it was I had no way to know at nine years old.

Another Man's Prayers

Stephen Prothero

Yes, I read the prayer Barack Obama left at Jerusalem's Western Wall.* I was angry it was stolen, and by a seminarian, no less. I was angry it was published. But I read it. I read it because I am a voyeur, too, because I am struggling with how to pray and wanted to see how someone with Obama's rhetorical skills might try to talk with God. I wasn't kidding myself. I knew this wasn't a truly private communication. In our age of celebrity nothing is truly private for those who would be president, so he must have known that the Wall might not be the only place it would be published. Still I wanted to listen in, take some measure of Obama the man. So, yes, I read the prayer he left at the Western Wall.

Last March I was in Jerusalem researching a new book on the world's religions. It was a business trip, tax deductible. But I felt drawn in a not-so-professional way to the *Kotel,* as locals call the Wall. On my first day in Jerusalem, a Jewish friend and I took in the plaza scene in the front of the Wall: black-hatted ultra-Orthodox men with their covered-up-and-silent wives; young modern Orthodox guys with colored yarmulkes and *tzitzit* (fringes) hanging out over their cargo pants; and Christian hajis from Korea and Nigeria and the United States. (You will know they are Christians by their name tags. Jews and Muslims rarely take guided tours of the Old City.)

On my way down to the Wall I donned a paper *kippa,* which kept getting blown off, as if the wind or the God stirring it knew I

*July 2008.

131

wasn't really Jewish. The real Jews were reading from prayer books, rocking back and forth, giving their plastic chairs (the kind you find at Kmart) a workout. My friend, a male convert from Trinidadian Presbyterianism whose circumcision is still ahead of him, asked me if I wanted to pray. "Not yet," I said, since I was desperate to pray but wanted to do so later, in private, away from his eyes.

On his recent trip to the Middle East, Obama arrived at the Wall shortly after 5 a.m. on Thursday, July 24. It was still dark. He wore a white skullcap under a clear moon. He listened to the Wall's official rabbi, Shmuel Rabinovich, read the 122nd Psalm: "Our feet are standing in your gates, O Jerusalem. . . . Pray for the peace of Jerusalem. May those who love you be secure." Then he approached the Wall, placed his hand on a stone, bowed his head, and placed his prayer in a crack.

The Wall is, in addition to a repository of prayers, a repository of stories. It is hard to imagine a more vulnerable place of power than this portion of the Jerusalem Temple, destroyed by the Romans in AD 70. I don't know if that is why I kept returning—to reckon with this odd combination of power and vulnerability. But I kept going back, every day of the week I was in Jerusalem.

Although I have largely forgotten how to pray—*because* I have largely forgotten how to pray, I wanted to pray at the Wall. I was intrigued by the bobbing and weaving of these people and their prayer books, the intimate orchestration of the solitary davener accompanied in his intimacies by others here and there until all seemed attuned to the same notes, rising to the same crescendos, falling into the same denouements. I wanted to find my own posture before God, my own voice.

On my last day in Jerusalem I felt ready. Unlike Obama, I didn't have to endure hecklers or paparazzi or seminarians intent on stealing my private prayer. I wandered from my hotel in East Jerusalem through the Damascus Gate into the Old City, down the Via Dolorosa, and then out of the Old City and up the Mount of Olives.

"Every place here has a story," a friend had told me on my first day in Jerusalem, and atop the Mount of Olives I took some of those stories in. The storytellers were Nigerian Pentecostals, and proud JPs (Jerusalem Pilgrims) all. Someone was filming them offering brief testimonies about their experiences in the Holy Land, their smiles wide with pride, their backs to the Church of the Holy Sepulcher of the Christians, the Temple Mount of the Muslims, and the Western Wall of the Jews. The woman I remember best looked into the camera with more conviction than I can ever remember mustering myself and said, "For my entire life I have heard stories about Jesus and Mary. Today I saw where Mary was born. I saw where Jesus was crucified. And now I know that each and every one of those stories is real."

I have no idea what sort of reality came over Barack Obama when he was standing at the Wall, preparing to give over to God a scrap of paper laden with his prayer and embossed with the logo of the swanky King David Hotel, but I find it hard to imagine that awe was not included in the mix. Yes, the place is segregated by sex. Yes, it is a tourist trap. And the mystic in me knows if God is anywhere then God is everywhere. But it is nonetheless an awesome place, testifying in blood and stone to the human propensity to colonize the unknown, populate it with words.

It is also a place that invites a reckoning—in words and actions—with our own admixture of power and vulnerability. To be human is to live between able and unable, to know (as that Serenity Prayer goes) that there are things you have the power to change and things you have the power only to accept. To be president, however, is to know that you live between bombing and getting bombed. This is not a knowledge I would wish upon anyone. But for those who possess it I am grateful for a place such as the Wall.

Like Obama, I prepared my prayer in advance, carried it with me up past the Garden of Gethsemane and down past what is reputed to be the oldest Jewish cemetery in the world. I wish I could say it was a prayer of gratitude. It was not. This might be my last visit to the Wall and there was no way I was not going to ask for something. So I gathered up the names of the thirteen most important women in my life. (Thirteen is my lucky number.) Mother and sister and daughters and ex. A woman who broke my heart. Another who taught me to dance. Yet another who taught me to be human. I asked for one thing (in one word) for each. I said these thirteen prayers quietly to myself. Breathed in a name, breathed out the hope that she would find hope or healing in whatever I was wishing upon her. Then I folded up the paper and tried to find a place for it in the wall. This is harder than you might imagine. Real estate is precious in the Old City, but none more so than at this location, where every crack seems to be preoccupied with a prayer not your own. But after some folding and shoving and refolding and more shoving I found a niche for whatever part of myself I was pressing into this prayer.

As I was leaving I saw a man sweeping up prayers expelled from the wall by wind or rain or the impress of gravity. There were hundreds of prayers exiled to his clear plastic bag—petitions in Arabic and Hebrew and English and other languages I cannot even recognize. And because I am a religious studies professor and a human being I was sorely tempted to reach in and pull out a few dozen or so, read them for signs of the times, or for their prurient delights. What unbearables do people bring to this place? What loves and losses, confidences and confessions? But I did not steal any prayers.

Which is why I will not say here what Obama prayed for. If you need to know that you can find it online, though I recommend you leave the prayer to itself, and Obama to his God. I will say that Obama did not pray for any of his ex-girlfriends. And that his prayer, at least to my ears, fell a bit flat. Reading it didn't teach me anything I didn't already know about Obama, or, for that matter, about praying.

My consolation is that what really happens at the Wall cannot be contained in the words put onto paper or into stone. It cannot be stolen by a seminarian or published by a newspaper. Even in our age of celebrity some things are not accessible to photographers or editors, or even writers such as myself.

If I were to return to the Wall today, I would leave a prayer for both Obama and John McCain. I would pray that each would listen to what the Wall has to say about power and vulnerability, and the delicate and dangerous dance between them. Some things are possible; some things are not. At least for me, that is what transcendence means: the significance of any human being, however large, is dwarfed by the mystery of the millions of things we will never fully understand, not least the practice of prayer itself.

I Was a Prepubescent Messiah

Irina Reyn

When my family left the Soviet Union for the United States in 1981, my parents decided that I would not lead the same godless existence they had led. Persecutions coupled with seventy years of communism created lots of Russian Jews like my parents. Their Russian passports had been marked "Jew," right below their name and birth date, but they'd never had any education as to what that might really mean. They were silently proud of their Jewishness, but they were completely ignorant of rituals, prayers, biblical stories. In America, when they went to synagogue on Yom Kippur, they held the prayer books in their hands carefully. But their eyes would stare vacantly at the text.

When we found ourselves in Queens, the first thing my parents did was send me to Hebrew day school to undertake the religious reeducation of my entire family. With this rather monumental burden on my shoulders, I shuffled off to the conservative Solomon Schechter School of Queens.

My grandfather, the only other member of my family who went to synagogue regularly, picked me up after school. Sometimes we would go to synagogue as soon as I got off the school bus. Upon walking out, I always asked him what he prayed for. For months he gave me mysterious looks and said, "It is something about you, Irochka."

One snowy December afternoon, after another round of pleading, he whispered, "I pray to God for you to live forever," and winked.

"What did God say?" I asked.

"He says you will," my grandfather said, pressing the tip of my nose with his finger.

My feelings of being an awkward bystander, out of sync in America, were finally validated. In Solomon Schechter, the day was divided evenly between English/general education and Hebrew/Bible sections. I was surrounded by American Jews and immigrants from Israel, all of whom seemed to negotiate their terrain with immeasurable confidence, but I felt neither American nor Jewish.

In school, we watched somber documentaries about the Maccabees, always moderated by Abba Eban, but I was memorizing vocabulary for English class. In Bible class, I read Hebrew without understanding the words, tracing the print with my fingers, right to left, reciting Macbeth's "Tomorrow, tomorrow and tomorrow" speech under my breath. I had realized that if I could never succeed in uniting the two parts of the day into a seamless whole, I would place my full concentration on the English side, to prevent a lifetime of wandering.

A deathly pale, raven-haired Mrs. Hacker, who eerily resembled the Russian witch Baba Yaga, taught us various portions of the Bible with a demonic somnolence. In her class, I wrote short stories, hidden beneath the Bible, until I felt The Hacker's black eyes boring into me and heard her frustrated sigh at my deliberate neglect. When she scanned the classroom for responses to particularly knotty Talmudic puzzles, she would skip over me automatically. But I had stopped feeling the faint ache of regret in my stomach, because I knew I had plenty of time—actually, an eternity—to ponder the Talmud.

This secret made the taunts wafting from the back of the bus and the black-inked scribblings of "Communist!" on my new blue notebook bearable. If I would never fully experience the unrestraint of American belonging, at least I could embrace my difference as mystical strength, the potential for a kind of universal knowledge.

A few months later, sitting in Rabbi Spiro's class, I woke up from my daydreams. Rabbi Spiro was a thin, aging man whom everyone respected. He held our attention not only with his quiet certainty, but also with his inability to move his neck, something we felt was probably a sign of great piety. He was talking about the Messiah, about how Jews everywhere yearned for his arrival and the preparatory measures we should all be taking for his imminent appearance. The leader of my tormentors, a gangly redheaded boy named Eedo, asked the rabbi, "But how do we know when he is coming?"

Rabbi Spiro smiled, shifting his body to look at Eedo. "Why, Eedo, do you think the Messiah is 'he'? In fact, it could be anyone at all, girl or boy, someone still growing up, not knowing who they are, what they will do later, saving the Jewish people." The rabbi paused, surveying the class with the eyes that rarely missed anything peripheral no matter which way his body was directed. "It could be one of you."

Was it my imagination, or was he looking at me? Granted, it was always difficult to tell with Rabbi Spiro, but now I understood the link between his words and my grandfather's promises of my immortality. I knew without a doubt that this was a sign to me, an indication of a definable, undeniable identity that was being revealed to me through this great man. *Rabbi Spiro knew that I was the Messiah.*

Well aware of how any messiah would be treated within the junior high school social hierarchy, I kept my mouth shut about my unique role in the world. That summer, my parents sent me to my relatives in San Diego, and in a halfhearted attempt to extend my religious upbringing to summer vacation, they enrolled me in Gan Israel camp. Apart from baking endless loaves of challah, and maniacally counting the few *mitzvot,* or good deeds, I had accomplished that year, I sang the official camp song every morning with the rest of the campers. "Gan Israel have no fear, *moshiach*"—Messiah— "will be here this year!" I watched everyone singing, some drawing out the word *moshiach,* others lingering on "this year."

Naturally, I felt I should be exempt from these songs, and tried to explain the situation very obliquely to the camp director, making every effort to give nothing away.

"You see, there is . . . um . . . no need for ME to sing. Well, it's just that . . . YOU know, I may know a few things about the *moshiach* . . . um, let's just say, these songs are stupid, for ME." She gazed at me blankly, shoved a cherry popsicle in my hand, and ushered me back in line to sing. I understood, with a sigh, that life for the *moshiach* would always be permeated with such mis- understandings and cold dismissals. Suddenly I wanted to be one of those joyous people, calling out to the *moshiach* innocently and communally, instead of marking myself with the loneliness of eter- nal solitude.

I came home a little wiser and sadder. "What's wrong?" my mother asked, between bites of a ham sandwich, as I somberly handed her my Gan Israel menorah, made out of red candle wax.

"I dunno, I just don't think I'm ever really going to belong, you know?"

"Well, you'll never be born here, if that's what you mean," she said. "But, after a few more years, you'll be a real American, you'll see."

I watched her carefully placing the crooked, beautiful red me- norah in the middle of our windowsill, and made a mental note to myself. The next time I go to synagogue with my grandfather, I will make sure he asks God if, maybe, instead of the *moshiach*, God can make me an American.

Dreading the Buzzer

Hasdai Westbrook

"Mrs. Westbrook!" the little man bellowed. His heavy leather shoes pounded the stairs, powering his way up—bull-mastiff head tilted forward, shoulders bunched tight, neck nowhere to be seen, chest parallel to the stairs, torso stuffed into a brown leather jacket and held rigid at an impossible angle to his legs. At the landing, he came to a sudden halt, switched his leather briefcase from one leather-gloved hand to the other, slicked back a wisp of hair, then brought the hand down to offer in greeting as his mouth spread into a giant feral grin. With his eyes almost hidden behind the tint of his aviator glasses, Mr. Wolf looked like some crooked relative from the old country—the kind who distributes boiled sweets to children and launders money for the Prague mafia.

Mr. Wolf came to us by way of a Viennese chocolatier. My mother had encountered the future confectioner as a teenager, as she hoarded Freud and Schiller and plotted her escape from Vienna's stifling huddle of displaced Jews. Soon enough she fled overseas to university, found an Englishman to marry, and ensconced herself in London. She had her passport changed from "D.P." to "U.K." and her nails done every week.

A manicurist was in love with a Jewish man. So much in love that she braved the conversion test, passing thanks to Mr. Wolf, whom she found through her fiancé's synagogue. Her new husband: none other than my mother's compatriot, who now slung fancy bon-bons for a living in London. My mother was already looking for someone to prepare me for my bar mitzvah when she heard the story. Mr. Wolf was called up.

It was my father who insisted on the lessons. When I was seven, he had taken a job in the States. Whenever he came back to London, he would take me to synagogue. It was boring and stuffy, with an endless succession of sittings and standings. My legs ached. Around us, rich North London businessman greeted each other with puffy-fingered handshakes. They set to davening, a flock of little birds pecking at the air. Next to me, my father davened mechanically, stopping each forward dip at precisely the same angle, as though cantilevered at the hip.

A drab Sunday afternoon, streaks of rain on the windows. Mr. Wolf was already seated when I walked in. He stayed silent as I took my place. We stared at each other across the circular living room table, our faces reflected in the polished wood. I pursed my lips, my eyes set on his. He peered at me through his twin visors, then flipped open the book lying next to him on the table.

"You shall not boil a kid in its mother's milk," he read aloud. He raised his head, magnified eyes meeting mine. "You know what kosher is?" he growled. I nodded. "When you eat, you have different plates for meat and for milk, and different knives and forks, yes?" I nodded again. He grinned. "So, show me," he commanded, twirling the book round so the text was in front of me. "Where does it say you have to do that?"

I stared dumbly down at the page. My forehead grew hot as the silence expanded.

"Nowhere," said Mr. Wolf suddenly. I looked up. "Why do you think Jews keep kosher?" he asked. Again, I was stuck.

"Because God wants us to," I offered weakly. Mr. Wolf's lips began to curl. "Is that what you think?" he asked. I shrugged. "But *this* is the word of God," he said, tapping the page. I stared blankly at him; I was getting irritated.

Mr. Wolf sat back and grinned. "Do you think God cares if I eat a ham sandwich?" he asked.

"Yes," I said distractedly, sinking my hands into my pockets.

"Why?"

"Because it's not kosher," I said, slouching back and picking out a spot on the wall to stare at.

"Hmm," said Mr. Wolf. "Well this is what I think. I think God couldn't care less." I stopped staring at the wall. His grin deepened.

"This rule was written by a man," he said. "God didn't write it. What, we're supposed to believe that God wants us to not eat the goat in its mother's milk, and to have separate kitchens for meat and milk like the religious? No, this is just what the rabbis say. You know the rabbis?" I nodded. "They take this one line in the Bible and they say, 'Oh, this means you can't have milk when you eat meat.' *They* make up all these rules."

He fixed his gaze on me. "I believe in God for one reason only," he said. A pause for effect, a great suck of breath through the nostrils; then he started in again: "I read in the paper about the Big Bang—you know what it is, everything starting from one big explosion with hot gasses and particles and so on. Scientists say this is the how the universe was created. This for me is not an explanation. Where did it come from?" He paused again. I had no answer. "The only reason I believe in God is because I cannot explain the existence of the universe *any other way.*" He tapped out the last three words in the air, then hunched forward. "But to say that because of this God cares if I eat milk and meat—this," he said, finger pricked to the heavens, "is bullshit."

So began Mr. Wolf's assault on piety. He was a marvel, a revelation, and I his acolyte.

Every Sunday that summer, he took me through another Bible story, reveling in its inconsistencies. Genesis had two creations —Adams and Eves with irreconcilable differences, man and seed swapping places in the birthing order. Moses ascended Mount Sinai, or Mount Horeb, depending on whether you were reading

Deuteronomy or Exodus. And of course Mr. Wolf's favorite—the riddle of Cain's wife, for which his brother had paid dearly.

"My brother was the most brilliant student in his class," Mr. Wolf said proudly. "One day the rabbi was reading, 'Adam knew his wife Eve and she begot Cain and Abel. And Cain knew his wife and she begot Enoch.' My brother put up his hand. 'Who was this wife?' he asked. 'How could there be another woman in the world unless Eve had daughters?'" Mr. Wolf bared his teeth. "Without a word, the rabbi took his heavy wooden walking stick and hit my brother on his back. His spine was crushed. He was a cripple for the rest of his life."

The rabbis were Mr. Wolf's nemeses. No lesson passed without his ridiculing them. Rashi the Frenchman, scratching away at his illuminations as he surveyed his vineyard. The great Maimonides and all the others straining at exegesis. They were fools as far as Mr. Wolf was concerned. So obsessed with what to obey, what the rules were, what precisely God wanted. They were like acrobats to him, tottering on the edge of the text, performing logical flips and linguistic contortions. He only waited for the moment when they tripped and tumbled, so he could pounce . . .

" . . . Then I will take My hand away and you will see My back; but My face must not be seen," Mr. Wolf read from Exodus—God speaking to Moses atop Mount Sinai. Moses had pleaded to behold God's presence. God had met him halfway.

"Now," said Mr. Wolf laying the book down, "The rabbis ask, 'What are we to suppose Moses saw?' Their answer: that God was wearing prayer phylacteries and had side locks growing on the sides of his head." He pulled off his glasses. The skin around his small black eyes crinkled with tiny lines. "Can you believe it?" Mr. Wolf exclaimed, growling baritone spiking as high as it could go. "This is bullshit!"

The lessons continued. Noah fell down drunk in his tent. Lot slept with his daughters. Mr. Wolf delighted in their debaucheries. God had delinquents on his hand. Do this, don't do that, because I say so. And still they acted up. It made "Him" seem rather hapless. Meanwhile Mr. Wolf stood on the rocks, suitcase in hand, gleefully parting a sea of nonsense. It was wonderful just to listen, to smile conspiratorially at the unraveling. We drifted through the summer like two Cheshire cats, grins floating in the ether.

Then one Sunday, Mr. Wolf snapped open his briefcase. He extracted a little Hebrew calendar and asked me when my birthday was. A few calculations later, my bar mitzvah date was set. He slid a cassette tape into a black handheld recorder and gave me a photocopied sheet of strange pen-scratches—dots and dashes in peculiar configurations, like the ink-dipped footprints of a drunken ant. "I have done everything for you," he said happily. "You will go down the notes and repeat after my voice on the tape." I stared at him. He told me it was simple and pressed "Play."

Yom Kippur fell on a Wednesday that year. The Day of Atonement, when the gates of heaven opened and you had your chance to be written in the Book of Life. My father's voice crackled on the transatlantic line. He wanted me to go to synagogue. I put on a shirt and tie and made my way to St. John's Wood.

The assembly hall was stifling hot. I sat down next to an old man with watery eyes, an ivory-handled cane between his legs. The service had already begun. Muttered prayers reverberated around us.

"You see all these fools here, you see them praying." The old man was speaking to me. "I was in Auschwitz. God was not there. Where was God in the camps?" I didn't respond. "I tell you it will happen again," the man said. "You cannot stop it. No one can. Praying won't help anything." The top of the old man's cane swung back and forth between his hands, constant as a metronome.

"I'm a little confused," I told Mr. Wolf on his next visit. Once more, he was eager to explain. The notes matched the syllables of the Hebrew words in my parasha, the Torah portion I was going to read at my bar mitzvah in a few months' time. Three times a week, Jews took the scrolls of the Torah out of the tabernacle and read another portion. When they finished the story, they started again. "And where does my portion fit in the story?" I asked.

"Ah, this is a very good question," said Mr. Wolf excitedly. And we were off again . . .

" . . . How far did you get?" Mr. Wolf asked me a few weeks after giving me the tape. I was half-smirking, slouched on the velvet-cushioned seat, shoulders slack, hands in pockets.

"Not as far as I would have liked," I said. His lips began curling into a smirk of his own, deep creases sinking into leathery cheeks. Laugh lines rippled over rising cheekbones.

"Hmm . . ." he said, then tipped his great mastiff head forward and slicked back his already slicked-back hair.

" . . . *Koo-mi U-ri Ki-va-a O-re-ech.*" The notes lurched up the register like an old man climbing stairs, a whining nasal lament. I shut off the tape and switched on the Super Nintendo, Street Fighter II already lodged in its cartridge slot. Tinny Nintendo music replaced Mr. Wolf's voice as I smacked the life out of a computerized sprite.

My mother began preparing for the event. She booked a hall in Vienna. My aunts and uncles called to ask what presents I wanted. I sat in front of the flickering television in my mother's bedroom, dreading the buzzer. The hour on Sunday before Mr. Wolf was scheduled to arrive now included a flurry of activity during commercial breaks in *Lost in Space* or televised showings of *20,000 Leagues Under the Sea*. These were spasms of homework, nervous twitches stored up from all the times when I was meant to be practicing.

"You know, I've never had a student fail with me," Mr. Wolf said in class. He scratched his forearm, fingers running through a straggly thatch of black-gray hair. Underneath them, thick lines of bluish-green ink formed a row of numbers above an inverted triangle. "I had one boy whose parents swore he would never do bar mitzvah. He couldn't read Hebrew, had never seen it in his life. And..."—a finger shot up from the table for emphasis—"...he had only six weeks to study. But with me, in less than a month he was ready and did a beautiful parasha." In my case, he said, there was nothing to worry about: I was smart; *that* boy had been an idiot.

In the following weeks, Mr. Wolf's list of miracle children grew longer. This one had suffered from stage fright. That one's first teacher had died before they even started preparing. Their time shrank: only two months, a month and a half, three weeks. No matter.

All had been saved by the tapes. Mr. Wolf made them for every student, happily dictating for hours on end. It was like having an ecstatic Czech genie trapped in a Sony Clear Voice, obeying only the command to stop or start singing. And when I pressed the Play button, all *I* had to do was obey, and Mr. Wolf would have another successful launch.

Months went by. And yet time didn't seem to matter because of his awesome powers. He and I carried on in a kind of alternate universe, where time had no relation to speed and the twelve-year-olds he'd salvaged seemed to float around us like dogs in Sputniks.

My father called and asked me how the preparations were coming. It was late at night, earlier for him. I told him things were going fine. He said he was glad. After he hung up, I stayed on the line, listening to the dial tone's empty hum. I squeezed my eyes closed and let the sound reverberate, certain that I was the only one there.

"You should really be paying more attention to all of this," my father huffed at the end of the service, folding his prayer shawl lengthways. He was back in London on his winter break. This time I'd been more sullen than ever. I'd refused a prayer book and spent the entire service staring out of the synagogue's one open window.

"Why," I said, my voice sticking in my throat. "Is God going to be angry with me?" Someone pushed past me through the door as I said this. I looked out to the cement parking lot, ready to do battle.

"God?" my father said quietly. "What's that got to do with anything? That's all nonsense." He rolled the prayer shawl into a bundle, then tucked it into the wooden bookshelf and made for the door.

Months passed and the tape never spooled past the first few notes. My progress stalled. One aunt told me she was giving me a CD player. Another said antique cuff links. My mother whisked me off to Savile Row to be decked in a beautiful blue suit that was astronomically expensive—a suit I'd wear once and grow out of within a year.

My mother asked me what kind of cake I wanted; the caterer could do a spaceship if I liked. Mr. Wolf kept repeating himself, my lack of preparation getting harder to ignore. The synagogue in Vienna was alerted to the date.

Once I saw a boy do his bar mitzvah there. He stepped up to the podium and warbled confidently from the open scroll. Above us in the balcony sweet wrappers began to rustle, the women pulling them from their bags. The rustling grew louder as the boy sang his bar mitzvah portion, louder as he sang the first blessing, and so loud as he sang the second that a few men turned their heads up, hissing admonishment.

The boy came to the last chord, the rabbi and cantor raising their voices in unison to sing with him. At that moment the synagogue burst into color, a kaleidoscope of sweets pelting down from the rafters. A rumble of "*Shkoi-ach*"—"well done"—went up from the men as the shower rained down on us, and small children scrambled between the pews to collect their booty. Outside, an Austrian soldier stood guard with a machine gun, laced-up army boots a shoulder length apart on the cobblestones.

It was hot that Sunday, early spring. Mr. Wolf was in short sleeves. He scratched his arm. "How far did you get?" he asked.

"Not as far as I would have liked," I said. I tipped back on my chair and gazed out of the window. Mr. Wolf didn't smile.

"You know, I've never had a student fail with me," he said. I turned my head back. We were coming close to a reproach. I felt my body grow warmer. If he said it outright, in full growl, I'd have to be defiant. I'd wrinkle my nose in a snarl and say nothing.

"But with you something is different," Mr. Wolf said softly. This was new. I froze in mid-tilt. "I had one student who knew no Hebrew. He was ready in less than a month. If you wanted to, you could do this. But you . . . you resist."

He sat pensively for a moment. Then he stood up and snapped his briefcase shut. I heard the other hangers clatter a little in the hallway as he took his coat down. We were only ten minutes into the lesson, forty minutes still left. I heard the front door slam shut; then silence. The rest of my Sunday was free.

Raised by Jews

Naomi Seidman

Forty-seventh Street, between Fifteenth and Sixteenth avenues, is the teeming Jewish heart of Boro Park in Brooklyn, bursting with kids in strollers, or hanging onto them, or pushing them, kids on Big Wheels and bicycles, on the stoops and leaning out the windows. Now, the pale-brick houses are packed together and built all the way out to the sidewalk, but when I was growing up on the block there were still some nice old-fashioned houses set back from the street, with glassed-in porches and driveways and big backyards where dilapidated sukkahs sagged year-round.

There must have been ten or twelve girls more or less my age on the block, but they were different from me, brash girls from enormous families (there were only four of us children) whose tall fathers and blond-wigged mothers had been born right here in America. A bachelor lived in the attic apartment, an oldish-youngish man whose pale-red eyelashes disappeared in the light. Next door, in the basement of the apartment building, was the super you called to relight the pilot light on *shabbes* if it had gone out. In the grocery on Sixteenth Avenue, the grocer pulled down boxes from the top shelf with a long stick that had a claw on the end. Across the avenue were the shadowy, crowded aisles of Mrs. Greenstein's toy store. Mrs. Greenstein had been in my mother's class in the Beis Yakov seminary in Czernowicz before the war, but that didn't stop my mother from once making my brother and me march right back to her store and tell Mrs. Greenstein to take back the BB gun she had sold us, since it wasn't coming into the house.

When I turned five, I started Beis Yakov myself, a squat beige-brick elementary school on Fourteenth Avenue where we sang a song about Sara Schnirer, who in a little town in Poland (actually, Krakow) took the stones her enemies threw at her and said, "From these stones will I build a school to teach girls Torah." Our backyard shared a fence with the main synagogue of the Bobover Hasidim, where once, in pursuit of a stray ball that had bounced down the concrete stairs of the basement of the shul, I stumbled into a steamy room filled with naked men, their shaven heads bare, shouting "*a maydl, a maydl.*" This fleeting and confused vision confirmed my suspicion that there was a hell that lurked just underneath the surface of our lives. Later, the pizza stores on Thirteenth Avenue opened, one after another—Amnon's, Tel Aviv, Masada—and we had our first taste of falafel, which my father jokingly called "*plopple,*" turning the exotic Middle Eastern spices into something Yiddish and familiar. These landmarks constituted the known limits of the world, beyond which lay dragons: Italian, across Sixtieth Street, and Puerto Rican, under the elevated subway tracks.

That there were Jews who weren't *frum,* Orthodox, was an unsubstantiated but intriguing rumor. Evidence of its truth turned up in my own house one afternoon when I was ten or so, in the form of three previously undisclosed cousins, sons of my Uncle Bushy, who was actually my father's *Amerikaner* cousin. The boys stood in our front hall, no doubt over their protests, huddled stiffly together against the strangeness pressing in on them. Shiny bar mitzvah yarmulkes, the folds still visible, perched on three thick heads of hair. The middle one, Barry, was perfect: sun-streaked hair down to broad shoulders, blue eyes and dark lashes against a tan acquired in circumstances outside my own experience. And what did they see when they looked at me? A blue skirt down past my knees, glasses, a braid. I was probably staring. Did they see *me?* Did they know that inside the blouse buttoned up to my neck, inside my scratchy tights, the blood surged with sudden lust and yearning?

What *did* I want so badly? Sometimes I thought it was Barry, but sometimes it seemed to me that it must be God, calling me for some special purpose beyond the ordinary pieties that occupied my life. For months at a time, I davened myself into a frenzy on the roof of the school or tried desperately to improve my character, to stop biting my nails on *shabbes,* to stop telling *loshn harah,* gossip, about girls in my class, to dedicate my life to being good. There must have been more, too, because I remember the principal of my school calling me into his office to inform me that I couldn't possibly be a prophet (What had I told him? What had he heard?), since prophecy had ceased among Israelites with the Destruction of the Temple.

But these zealous periods alternated with equally intense fits of agnosticism and alienation. I harbored the suspicion, all through sixth grade, that I was the subject of a secret experiment, in which a whole community had been recruited to perform the elaborate play that was Orthodox Judaism. The point of this exercise was to see whether repetition and unanimity alone could make someone— me, that is—believe the most incredible untruths. It wasn't God watching from behind some one-way mirror, but rather invisible scientists in lab coats. There was no way to resist the whole charade altogether, but it was important to signal as often as I could—if only for my own dignity—that I wasn't completely fooled.

The other side of my paranoia, my fear of being surrounded by spies and automatons, was the hope that somewhere beyond the streets of Boro Park were the real people, the people I should by all rights be part of. The library gave me a glimpse of them: Nancy Drew dressing for her prom, twirling for her father's approval, and the tomboy Georgie brushing down her pony; the whole crew of girl detectives camping under the stars. I lived in an apartment with the people who thought they were my parents, even though they were too old to be anyone's parents, and they spoke English with thick accents, and my room had a curtain instead of a door, but one day, my true family would figure out where I was being held captive and bring me home. Night after night I listened for the sound of an emissary from that world, the roar of an approaching motorcycle, the tink of a pebble on the windowpane, a soft call, the door as it creaked open and then shut again, finally, behind me. My own jeans were hidden behind the schoolbooks on my shelf; on Sunday afternoons, I perfected the quick-change from skirt to pants, and (less happily) back again, behind odorous pillars on subway platforms. On Friday evenings after the meal, when there was nowhere else to go, I would wait until the *shabbes* clock had ticked off and the lights gone out and write furiously and blindly in a notebook, as if I could scribble my way out of the suffocating darkness.

I began to look around for chinks in the walls that enclosed me, the tracks of others who had broken through earlier. There was, first of all, Uncle Bushy himself, who had apparently shared a childhood with my Orthodox uncles Motl and Anschel, but somehow emerged from it a Conservative rabbi with his trio of sturdy Jewish goyim. There were darker rumors, too, that the twin granddaughters of a great Torah sage (even now, the old taboo keeps me from sullying his name) had posed in a magazine, stark naked; that a daughter of Rabbi H. had married her professor, an Indian, no less. In my mother's hushed conversations with her sisters and friends, these scandals were tragic not only because they tore a family apart, but also because they saddled that family with a stigma that could never be made right. To leave when there were other children to be married off—this was a sign of the cruelest indifference to the brothers and sisters whose chances for a decent match were forever ruined. And when the girls in my class repeated these stories, they had another force: for us, the bearers of chaste Jewish blood, rumors of girls who had strayed were pieces of the puzzle of sex we were always trying to reconstruct, evidence of some provocative, terrifying power that was neither entirely inside nor outside us. For me, and maybe a few others, these scandals were also the signposts I was watching for, the arrows that marked the exit.

Conservative rabbis and Playboy bunnies. Like the signs on restroom doors, it was clear which of these was for boys and which for girls. A boy might conceivably become an *apikores*, a heretic, but transgression in a girl could only mean something sexual. The first few steps of the Beis Yakov girl gone bad were visible enough: I knew girls who sneaked out of camp to meet boys at pizza stores in the Catskills, who wore their denim skirts over the knee and hung posters of David Cassidy inside their closet doors. They were "bums," the term we used for the nail-polished and boy-crazy among us. I chose my friends from among these circles, but I myself aspired to something more dignified, something that signaled intellectual force rather than bodily weakness. I was a philosopher, I hoped, not a whore. At *shabbes* lunch, I would harass my parents by asking how they could bless the wine "after Auschwitz." My brother, caught in the turmoil of his own adolescence, would cover his ears and yell "*Shah! Apikores!*" Once, when he demanded that my parents throw me out of the house, my father asked him, softly, who it was that was paying the rent.

A generation or so earlier, the crisis might have been addressed through a rebbe or matchmaker. My parents turned instead to Jewish Family Services, where we were assigned family therapy with a staff psychologist, a burly Orthodox man with the circumspect, businesslike manner of a diamond merchant. When he asked each of us why we were there, my brother sullenly responded: "Because my sister's a bum." There was something curiously cheering for me in his straightforwardness.

The office lay in the shadow of the elevated tracks of the B train, and every few minutes a train would rumble by a few feet from the office window and the session would come to an awkward pause, since my father was hard of hearing. In fits and starts, though, we were beginning to learn the ritualized gestures of family therapy, the parallel airing of grievances, the alternating deference and complaint, tears and outrage, when the entire exercise was abruptly terminated. The psychologist opened our third session with the announcement that he would not be continuing to work with us, since "the main problem your family has is that you all want Naomi to be *frum* and she doesn't want to be." As far as he could see, he continued, that was a theological issue, not a psychological one. There would be no charge for this last session, he added, and he wished us all the best. It would be another year or two before I made my break, but those words, I think, were what finally set me free.

It wasn't until I was a graduate student at Berkeley that I finally discovered that my own break with tradition was itself part of a tradition, amply recorded in the first, dusty generations of modern Hebrew and Yiddish literature. For the other students, these nineteenth-century narratives were almost unreadable, with their gothic descriptions of cruel *melamdim* and overbearing mothers-in-law and their archaic prose style (as it turned out, this was exactly the sort of old-fashioned Hebrew my own education had prepared me for!). For me, this literature of the Haskalah, the Jewish enlightenment, was full of glamour and adventure: forbidden books hidden in the pages of the Talmud, heretical ideas discussed in heated whispers, the ritual of a Friday night smoke in the garret of a fellow freethinker, the divorce from a marriage arranged by mercenary parents, the move to a big city. I sensed a community of fellow outsiders in these long-dead men. In their bitter stories, I found language and shape for the hole in the middle of my own life.

But it was only a partial camaraderie. After all, I never belonged to an underground cell, never read Chernishevsky on free love or Marx on class warfare. My own story, it seemed to me, lacked collective resonance, historical shape, intellectual substance, the conviction of revolution. I left the traditional world not with a wave of heretics, but against a tide of once-secular Jews who had "returned" to "Torah-true Judaism," repackaged as the antidote to the hollow successes of the American-Jewish middle-class. The damning in-

dictments of traditional Jewish life as depicted in Haskalah literature had themselves become historical curios, relics of an outmoded
and forgotten past. Where would such Jewish rage come from, after
the Nazis had done their work? The parents I left sleeping in their
beds when I slipped out the door had seen that destruction, and
the home I left behind was their bid to salvage something from the
ruin. Whatever the accounts had been between those nineteenth-
century parents and their rebellious children, surely the debts had
shifted under the pressure of the history that had intervened.

My dreams of escape had always ended, in the hazy tradition of
the American road movie, with the roar of an engine, in a blast of
exhaust. But what was there, exactly, beyond that, in the vast indifference of the American continent that opened up before me? The
Hebrew and Yiddish writers I read in graduate school had left the
traditional world for the capitalized ideals of their time: Enlightenment, Freedom, Literature, Socialism, Palestine. The biggest thing
in my life, it sometimes seemed, was what I had left behind.

In those first heady days after I left home, it was transgression
that spiced every bite I tasted, every step I took, riding the subway
on Saturday—a whole new day of the week, a whole new city was
mine—or eating a *treif,* street-corner shish kebab. Even now, twenty
years later, carrying a heavy bag of groceries home to my family,
the Berkeley dusk is ripe with the expectancy of *erev shabbes,* as
if my childhood, a clock I'd long ago packed away and forgotten,
nevertheless continued to tick. Everything comes down to a before
and an after, between which there is no commerce, no common
language; but just because this is so, I live always in both. My father,
craning his craggy neck to knot his necktie in the mirror, would
catch my eye and say, "Old age, what a strange thing to happen to
a little boy." Stranger still, my father is gone, and I have a little boy
now whom I call "*tatele,*" little father. He bears his grandfather's
name, Hillel, the way secular American Jews carry the impossible
names of an earlier generation, as a middle name, tucked between

his two public names like a recessive gene, a secret message. He has a cousin Hillel born the same night as he was, my brother's ninth. They've never met.

Every summer, though, we fly into the sweltering city to visit my mother. She buzzes us in and stands at the top of the steep stairs beaming. She is smaller each time I see her, and I am larger. Every time, there's less excuse for what I've done. One of my two sisters allows her children to see me, and once each visit, they troop up the steps to meet their little cousin from California. The twins stand in their plaid school uniforms, turned in to each other like a pair of pigeon toes, staring at my son's improbably yellow curls under the oversized yarmulke I found in my father's nightstand drawer. I suppose I should know what they're thinking, but I don't.

The Only Truth That Mattered

Rebecca Donner

We were living in Los Angeles then, in an apartment complex a few blocks from the barrio. My twin brother and I were nine, and hadn't yet adopted the code of behavior that governed kids' conduct in the building: eat a pickle to hide the cigarette stench on your breath, use a Bic lighter instead of matches to set off the fire alarm at school, run like hell after you shoplift. The city government subsidized the stuffy, cramped apartments we all inhabited—we were Section 8 kids, the local lingua franca for poor kids, bad kids, although Erich and I were different from our friends in many respects. We weren't born here; we'd moved from Virginia. We didn't steal, or swear, or smoke. We had piles of books in our apartment, a piano, too. And, most exotic—we didn't go to church. In the eyes of our friends, we were sinners, damned to burn for eternity.

Our father meditated regularly, and on any given morning could be found in the living room performing some acrobatic yoga stance, face beet-red, veins pulsing at his temples, legs stretched high above his head. UCLA had offered him a professorship in their East Asian studies department, but he'd had a breakdown, and now we were living here, on welfare, our apartment suffused with the pungent smells of sandalwood incense and marijuana, which he smoked in a corncob pipe throughout the day. As a Zen Buddhist, he embraced the principle of the Middle Way, and sought to avoid the extremes of both self-indulgence and asceticism. He told our mother he'd worked out a system to ensure that he only got stoned in moderation: he'd lock his baggie of marijuana in a metal box, enclose the key in a stamped, self-addressed envelope, and drop the envelope in the corner mailbox. This way, he couldn't have access to his stash for at least three days, which was about as long as it took for the post office to deliver the key back to him.

He was fond of systems, and imposed order on an otherwise chaotic household by assigning each chore a point value ranging from one to five (one if he loved the chore, five if he detested it). Washing the dishes, for example, gave him three points, since he neither enjoyed nor hated performing the task. Each day he was required to earn ten points, and the incentives he'd built into his system encouraged him to complete chores he detested and limit the number of chores he preferred. If he vacuumed the living room (five points) and scrubbed the toilet (five points), for example, he could devote the rest of the day to reading, whereas if he made the coffee (one point) and fed the cats (one point) in the morning, and at night fed the cats again (one point), he'd still have seven more points to earn before going to sleep.

Our mother found a job as a social worker, but the $13,000 base salary was barely enough to cover the bills. Our father spent his days clipping coupons, and devised an elaborate filing system complete with numeric codes designating each coupon's category and subcategory.

Princeton offered him a teaching position, but he refused. He spoke seven languages and had spent a decade studying Buddhism, but he decided that he was through with academia. From now on, he told us, he was going to be a coupon-clipper.

It was raining, and our father walked out the front door with a pillow and a blanket tucked under his arm. He was spending the night in the Datsun again. Our mother watched him go, shaking her head, still crying a little. They had just had another one of their fights, which had been increasing in volume and frequency over the last few months.

In our bedroom, Erich laid two Hefty trash bags on his mattress. He'd started wetting the bed again, which he hadn't done since kindergarten.

I closed the door, sat on his bed, and cupped my hand to his ear. "I heard Mom say she wants a divorce," I whispered.

He peered at me crossly. "Nuh-uh," he said.

Our vacuum was one of those old kinds with the elongated, accordion hose, which could be disconnected from the machine. The hose stretched four feet or so, just long enough to insert one end over the tailpipe of the Datsun and the other end into the driver's window.

When we left for school that morning, our father was vacuuming the hallway. There was a PTA meeting scheduled later in the evening, and school let out one hour earlier than usual, which our father hadn't counted on when he devised his plan.

After school, Erich headed off to the arcade with his milk money, so I walked home alone. When I opened the front door, my father was on his way out, clutching the vacuum hose, a roll of duct tape, and a handful of old rags.

As he describes it, encountering his daughter en route to self-asphyxiation was enough to startle him to his senses. The next day, he moved out of the apartment and into a closet-sized studio at the Zen Center, deciding that Buddhism would be his salvation. He participated in the *sesshins* held there, extended periods of intense meditation and sutra services headed by the *roshi,* and by the time our mother filed the divorce papers he had become a monk, changing his name to Chi-Yu.

On weekends, we visited him at the Zen Center, taking a one-and-a-half-hour RTD bus trip to Koreatown, which bordered East L.A. The bus was usually empty, and we'd sit on the long bench in the back, stretching out our legs, and pretend that the bus was our private limousine. To pass the time, we made up new lyrics to the songs featured on *Schoolhouse Rock* cartoons, which we'd sing to our father when we arrived.

He met us at the bus stop at the bottom of the hill, between the pawn shop and the King Hua restaurant, standing barefoot on the hot asphalt and dressed in a long black robe. We'd sing our song quickly, before we reached the Zen Center compound, a block of residential buildings flanking a temple, where we'd have to lower our voices to a whisper. Other monks passed by on the sidewalk, arms folded under their robes, their faces placid as they nodded at us, wordlessly.

His studio was sparsely furnished, with a cot and a small chest of drawers at the far corner of the room. He'd make green tea for the three of us, heating up a pan of water on a hot plate. Erich and I sat on his cot with our cups, facing our father, who'd sit on the floor and quiz us on the tenets of Buddhism. Life is suffering, according to the First Noble Truth. There's a Second, and a Third, and a Fourth, and we learned them all, but the First was the one that resonated for me, back then, when I was nine, staring at the soles of our father's bare, blistered feet, where the skin hung off in filthy hunks.

Ooga Chaka Zen

Paul W. Morris

One day Gensha said, "In the deep mountains and inacces-
sible peaks where for one thousand years, for ten thousand
years, no man has ever trod, can we find Buddhism there
or not?"

A few hours north of New York City, tucked away into the valleys
and foothills that run along Interstate 87, there's an echo of an ancient tradition that can be heard coming down from the mountains.
It's said that in a few hundred years, the Catskills will resemble the
summits and ranges of eighth-century China, when a Buddhist
monastery capped almost every peak, populated by eccentric masters and crazy old hermits. Some of the classic Zen stories to come
out of this period relate the varied dynamic between teacher and
student.

These tales are called mondoes.

A monk said to Seppo, "The seeing into this nature of a Svra-
vaka is like gazing at the moon at night; a bodhisattva seeing
into his nature is like the sun in daytime. What is seeing your
nature like for you?" Seppo smacked him three times.

Unlike the more familiar koans, such as "What's the sound of
one hand clapping?" or "If a tree falls in a forest, does it make a
noise?" mondoes reveal a lighter side to Buddhism, a vibrancy that
is in stark contrast to the traditional grays and blacks of monastic
life. They're filled with tales of teachers disparaging students, her-

mits smacking monks, boys mocking elders, and little old ladies slapping them all, an entire genre of Chinese literature dealing with pratfalls, spittakes, and witty one-liners. They're nonsensical, individually tailored, and usually end in an insult or blow to the head, or just an obtuse reply. They sound more like the physical comedians of the early twentieth century than the great Zen masters of the T'ang Dynasty.

> *Seeing a monk, Hofunku struck the outside post of the temple; he then struck the head of the monk, who cried out with pain. Hofunku said, "Why doesn't the post feel pain?" The monk gave no answer.*

Gensha wasn't talking about the Borscht Belt when he asked, "Can we find Buddhism up in the mountains?" but it seemed like a good place to look for an answer.

The first guy I meet at the Buddhist monastery is a Phil Donahue look-alike named Smitty. He greets me at the base of the stairs outside the reception office with an extended hand and talk-show host enthusiasm. He's the kind of friendly that puts a displaced New Yorker just minutes off a Greyhound a little on edge.

"Smitty," he says, "nice to meetcha," and shakes my hand vigorously. As we walk upstairs, he tells me all about the history of the hundred-year-old monastery, talking a mile a minute about the Benedictine monks who inhabited the area for over half a century, and how the building we're in was refitted to suit a Zen community in the seventies. He comes up for air as we enter the dorm-style sleeping quarters. Scanning them quickly, I count four bunks, eight beds total, seven of which are already occupied. I've got ten minutes to unpack and get settled before Friday evening meditation begins.

"Hope you don't mind the snoring," Smitty says, thumbing at

his unfurled sleeping bag directly below my bed. His shoulders give a resigned "oh well" up and down. I'll soon learn the value of holding back when it comes to dealing with Smitty's nonstop chatter. He's got a self-proclaimed "gift for gab." That's what working as a cook in the navy will do to you. "Hadta keep up the banter in the mess hall, you know," he'll tell me, "never a dull moment down there." Smitty ends all his sentences with a shrug.

I make eye contact with some of the other dorm mates, middle-aged and twentysomething guys, all of us typical American Buddhists up in the country for a weekend of contemplative peace and quiet. We swap names with a nod. Then a disembodied head pops up from underneath one of the bunks.

"Hello, I am Jesus," says the head before it dives back down again. I turn to Smitty, who is leaning against the post at the foot of our bunk.

"He lost his wedding band," Smitty explains. "Have you told the monk downstairs?" he asks Jesus.

"Huh?" Jesus's forehead and eyes poke up over the bed frame.

"The monk at the desk, did you let him know?"

Jesus nods, and then he's gone again beneath another bed.

"Poor kid, he just flew in from Venezuela," Smitty tells me, "then had a rough drive over the George Washington Bridge, up Route 17. City traffic," he says derisively. "Now this. He's been looking for that ring for the last hour."

Jesus crawls out into the open and stands up. He's a young guy, short and stocky, with big, sad eyes. He looks around, a little dismayed. "My wife's gonna kill me," he says. Smitty looks at me and shrugs. He walks over to Jesus and places a hand on his shoulder. "C'mon. Maybe you left it in the car." They head off together, with Smitty offering to help tell the monk all about it when they get downstairs.

*　*　*

One day Joshu fell down in the snow and called out, "Help me up! Help me up!" A monk came and lay down beside him. Joshu picked himself up and ran away.

The majority of the weekend is spent in the meditation hall, a huge space that can accommodate 250 people. It's all very formal, from the bowing to the chanting to the actual meditation. There are correct postures for sitting on the mats and even a special way to hold the sutra books. A strict vow of silence is observed in the hall. No one is allowed to speak except for the head monk. This comes a little harder for some than others, and for Smitty it's a constant struggle. He has to be told "Shhh!" several times early on, after which he communicates with a series of shrugs and gesticulations that I'm unable to fathom.

We wake up at 4:30 a.m. to meditate for two hours before morning service. After sitting for a half hour, everyone gets up off their mats to engage in walking meditation. This isn't a time to stretch or limber up, it's just a different type of meditation—a slow, deliberate walking in unison that snakes throughout the hall. No matter how incrementally slow the steps, though, it's a welcome reprieve, especially after sitting upright and still, back stiff, legs twisted into a knot, a little sore, or else a lot numb.

When Smitty stands up, he immediately falls down. As he tumbles, he tackles Mike in an effort to stay standing, and they both hit the floor in front of me with a thud. I should have toppled next and knocked over Jesus in the process, then Scott and so on and so on, like dominoes falling in a chain reaction—monks and laypeople falling bald head over socked foot in a kind of living embodiment of cause and effect, Buddhist style. But when Smitty takes out Mike, I'm sitting on my cushion, still massaging my leg, which has fallen asleep.

I've learned my lesson over the years. Whenever I sit for long stretches of time, whether on a cushion or in a cramped seat, one of my legs invariably falls asleep. Stand up too soon, and I have to reach spastically for support or else fall flat on my face. One time, I was hauled up onstage during the audience participation segment of a Shakespearean comedy routine. I had just stepped onto the stage when my leg gave out. That's when I heard with dread what the nature of my role would be: as Ophelia's Ego I was supposed to run back and forth repeatedly between two columns as her Id and Superego, played by two other audience members, reenacted her suicide scene from *Hamlet*.

"My leg's asleep," I whispered to the actor who had chosen me, teetering in a kind of halfhearted Karate Kid pose. He smiled reassuringly and announced in a mock-Elizabethan accent, "Ladies and gentlemen . . . the Ego's leg has . . . fallen asleep!!!" The explosion of laughter got the blood flowing, and my leg suddenly came alive. I ran like the wind, as any healthy ego would, and stopped only after Ophelia lay dead in the water.

On the cushion, I'm reliving this incident over in my mind as the circulation returns to my foot. In Buddhism, the ego is referred to as "monkey mind" because of its inability to stay at rest; it hops from one thought to the next like a primate in the treetops, always racing into the future or replaying the past. It is the goal of meditation to quiet this ego, to coax the monkey into falling asleep. Smitty, Mike, and I eventually manage to rise to our feet, tentatively at first, still a little wobbly, and we fall in behind a gray-robed monk for a round of walking meditation. Wending our way around the hall, we try to quiet our minds, taking it one step at a time.

*   *   *

A monk asked Chokoman, "What is this sword that will cut a single strand of hair?" Chokoman said, "You can't touch it." The monk asked, "How about a person who uses it?" "His bones and body are smashed to smithereens," said Chokoman. "Then," the monk said, "it's a jolly good thing we're not able to touch it!" Chokoman smacked him.

The afternoon is reserved for work practice, the period when each person is assigned a task to be carried out in silence. The idea, we're told, is that Zen practice isn't just about meditating or walking slowly; it's to be experienced in the everyday moment of tasks and chores and errands. It sounds like a fine idea, but when some people are instructed to clean the grout in the bathtubs or move the compost heap up the hill, sitting on the cushion with a leg full of pins and needles doesn't seem so bad.

I'm given the task of cutting office paper down to size. A young laywoman leads me over to a table where a half dozen reams of eleven-by-seventeen-inch paper are stacked neatly in two piles. Next to them rests an old, small paper cutter with a thin blade. "Someone donated this paper to the monastery," she explains, "but we can't use this size in our office. It all needs to be cut in half."

I do some quick math: six reams, five hundred papers per ream, if I cut 33.3 sheets per minute, I'll be done just as the hour-and-a-half period comes to an end. But the paper is large and cumbersome, and fitting a small wad of it into the cutter becomes a lesson in patience itself. The papers won't slide through the fitter, so I take some out. Then I take some more out until I'm able to fit only about fifteen pieces in. I need to readjust my calculations.

Then I discover that the old blade is dull, and when I bring the lever down to cut the sheets in two, it gets about halfway through before giving in to the bulk of the paper, making a ragged tear off to the side. This happens repeatedly before I realize no amount of force or finesse is going to help. And it occurs to me that I'm ruining their donated paper. I hide the mutilated stack and try it with just five or six pieces. The blade cuts into it neatly, offering up the crisp sound of a freshly sharpened blade at work. That's more like it, I think, and fall into a groove of swift and effortless slicing.

Standing at the table, alone in the silence, I pull out the paper, stack it flush, align it against the ruler, and bring the blade lever down in a decisive cut.

CHONK.

Pull out. Stack flush. Align right. Slice off.

CHONK.

Repeat.

Marathon runners often describe how songs get stuck in their heads during the long stretches of time their bodies spend rhythmically pounding the asphalt. Apparently, the most frequent song they cite is the Iron Butterfly classic, "In-A-Gadda-Da-Vida," a song so monotonous and plodding that its seemingly never-ending drum solos and refrains perfectly match the rhythm and posture that long-distance runners fall into. I'm a ream into the job, making some headway, when a melody begins to dance in the margins of my awareness.

Ooga chaka

And I bring the blade down.

CHONK.

Ooga chaka

CHONK.

It happens subliminally at first, slowly. *Ooga chaka ooga ooga.* CHONK. Then faster still, until I realize those words have been lurking around in the back of my head ever since breakfast.

Earlier that morning, I had been assigned to KP after mealtime. I was running dried dishes and utensils from the sink and putting them in their proper places. Except that I didn't know where anything went. Every time I picked up a new item, I had to ask someone where it belonged. In the kitchen, the concept of silence was thrown out with the dishwater; people were talking and laughing and singing, everyone relaxed and working in a din of motion. Trying to fit in, I would approach a different person with each item in question. When I asked a young monk drying a colander where an oversized spoon should go, he replied in a Keanu Reeves voice, "There is no spoon, dude." It was a pretty good imitation, and I laughed at the reference to *The Matrix,* a much-quoted line among Buddhists who hear lessons on emptiness peppered throughout the movie's hyperviolent story.

A little while later, it was the same monk who started singing it, that infectious "Hooked on a Feeling" song about a guy's desire for a girl, the taste of her candylike lips, the comfort of her reassuring embrace, which he admits is a kind of happy addiction, a sickness that gets him high—about as perfect an analogy for the Buddha's Second Noble Truth as you can get: "Attachment is the cause of suffering." A saccharine pop song, to be sure, made all the more silly and sweet by the litany of "ooga chaka ooga ooga" pulsing underneath the primary lyrics like a heartbeat.

The monk singing in the kitchen had a great voice, you could tell he loved to really belt it out. His whole face lit up when he hit the high notes—"I'm high on believing!"—though he probably didn't get a chance to sing much around the monastery. He kept with it and those who knew the words joined in while those who didn't backed him up with a steady chant of ooga chakas.

"Anybody know what that's from?" he asked when we'd all finished.

"*Ally McBeal!*" Judy squealed.

"Nope. It's from *Reservoir Dogs* first. Know who wrote it?"

"Yeah, it was Blue Swede," another monk said.

"Nope, they covered it. B.J. Thomas performed it first, in 1969." He paused thoughtfully. "Hmmm, actually, I think Neil Diamond did a rendition, too, but I like Blue Swede's rendition best, they added those weird 'ooga chakas.'" The conversation quickly trailed off into a discussion of the films of Quentin Tarantino and I asked somebody where the chafing dishes went.

Back at the cutting table, the Blue Swede/B.J. Thomas tune fills my head with its infectiousness. It goes from a whisper to a full-blown pop concert with backup singers and everything. I'm keeping the beat, my slicing synchronized perfectly with the song as I cut more and more paper, racing against the clock.

Ooga chaka ooga ooga. CHONK. *Ooga chaka ooga ooga.* CHONK.

I've cut through only half the paper as the work practice period nears its end. Smitty wanders into the office, already talking, joking, making fun of the pile of mangled sheets I tried to hide. He says that when he was in the navy, paper was a limited commodity and he'd have to decide whether he was going to write to his wife or wipe his ass with the amount he'd been rationed. His voice is loud and gruff, and I laugh louder than I mean to. Before I know it, the abbot of the monastery, the head honcho around the office, is by my side. He looks directly at me, his eyes like two still pools of water, and says calmly, softly, "We're supposed to practice this work in silence, to really achieve a deeper understanding of our mind at work."

I nod okay, a little humbled, a little embarrassed, but what I really want to tell him is "It's not me, it's him! It's his fault! Tell it to Smitty! He's the one with the gift for gab." But with a whole chorus of "oogas" and "chakas" resounding in my skull, I begin to understand how noise has its origin in the mind and not in the mouth.

* * *

Joshu asked an old woman with a basket, "Where are you off to?" "I am going to steal your bamboo shoots," she replied.

Joshu said, "Suppose you run into me afterward, what then?"
The old woman slapped his face. Joshu shrugged and walked
away.

Gensha asks, "Can we find Buddhism up in the mountains? Yes or no?" It turns out to be a trick question. Either reply could warrant a smack in the face, or maybe just a slap on the wrist. The mountains are full of mondoes; new ones are being told all the time. Who knows, maybe in a few hundred years, in response to Gensha's question, they'll quote from "The Smitty Sutra" or tell the one about "Jesus's Lost Ring." By then, they may have forgotten all about one hand clapping and the noise a falling tree makes. That's how strong the rhythm could be.

Hunger Is God's Food

Jesse Maceo Vega-Frey

By nine o'clock I thought I had gone insane. I was consumed by my desire to consume. Orange juice, café con leche, bread, water. Fucking *water*. Who in this country fantasizes about water? But there I was, four hours into a monthlong fast and I was fantasizing about streams of cool clear fluid moving through my body like raindrops flowing through soil to the roots.

I wasn't even hungry, not really. The hunger I was feeling wasn't the result of an empty stomach—it was desire. And it was obvious, even to me, that I felt it so strongly only because I knew I wasn't going to eat again until after the sun had set that night. It must be so much worse when Ramadan is in the summer. But knowing that didn't matter.

That morning I'd woken up at five. As far as I could remember, I hadn't been up that early in years. *Maybe* for some road trip or something—I liked to think that if I had to get up before dawn then it should be for devilment, mischief. Instead, there I was in the cold darkness of my mother's house preparing for an act of religious piety, of submission to God, of profound internal discipline: things completely foreign to me. And yet there I was, making my breakfast in the dark.

When I first stumbled into the kitchen, I decided against my usual habit of turning on the radio. The silence felt encouraging. Instead, I turned up the dial on the thermostat and, as I heard the furnace pop on, I felt instantly warmer even without the warmth— just the anticipation of heat was enough.

Click click click whooomp: The burner on the stove flowered a thick blue flame. I filled a metal saucer with milk, put it on the burner, and watched beads of water form on the outside as the flames wrapped around the cool aluminum. Quickly, they evaporated. I placed a pot of water on another burner to boil. As I put two slices of bread in the toaster I stopped to look at the stars outside through my kitchen window. It was still legitimately nighttime.

After a few minutes the water came to a boil and I dropped two eggs into the pot. One cracked a little as it hit the bottom and thin streams of egg white swirled around in the boiling water like heavy smoke. I sat and waited for them to cook.

I could get into this, I thought to myself. It was peaceful. I rarely paid much attention to my breakfast. It felt good to be so mindful. When the eggs were done I brought them to the sink, cracked them gently on the tile, and peeled them under cold running water. As I went to grab my toast I noticed the sky was changing color. There was a bright shot of blue behind the houses across the street and it moved slowly through the treetops. Time had been moving faster than me. Still, I ate slowly. Mixed my coffee into the hot milk. *I only eat hardboiled eggs on Easter,* I realized. *They're dope. I should eat them more often.* My breakfast was simple and perfect. After eating, I drank a glass of OJ and downed three more glasses of water. Once the sun came up, that was it: there would be no food or water until the sun had set.

Each night at work I broke fast with a glass of water. I had come to look forward to the feeling of the coldness rushing down my throat and into my stomach, where it was instantly absorbed into my body. As I stood there in the dark appreciating the sensation, my supervisor came into the kitchen and, realizing that my fast was over for the day, clasped her hands and graced me with a gentle bow. She asked me how it was going, how I was processing the fast spiritually, where I was orienting myself in relation to the Divine.

I could barely even fucking think straight, never mind start talking spirituality and metaphysics. She talked about my spirit as if it were a tool I had some idea how to use. I just listened and poured myself another glass. I recognized the disconnect, but I didn't understand it. It was about the water and it was about my soul. There was a relationship between them that I was trying to bring into focus. I was honest with her. I had very little sense of the Divine or of what my spirit consisted, never mind in what direction it was oriented. This path that I had found myself on was new to me, and I was learning how to walk.

She told me about a three-week-long fast she had done once in Holland or Austria or somewhere. The first week was just water. The second week, she was allowed to drink goat's milk. The third week she could eat yogurt. It sounded intense. There were a few obvious ways in which it was a lot different from what I was doing. First, she could relax all day in nature and just chill and meditate and read and write. Plus, she wasn't starting and stopping every day—it was a prolonged, slow fast that began severely but gradually brought her back.

There is something about the flux of Ramadan that might make it more psychologically debilitating than a straight fast. At least different. As my supervisor explained it, in a complete fast your subconscious has time to catch up with your mind. Your whole being slows down. You start to become more aware of and in tune with your inner clock, your internal way of understanding time that seems so foreign to us as we measure our days and weeks by mechanical devices. For her, the sensation was deeply moving. It must be pretty amazing, I thought, to reconnect with this lost sense of time, our innate sense of "real time."

But Ramadan didn't seem to be about that. The fast during Ramadan begins and ends according to completely external factors. It reminds me of that game you play in gym class in elementary school: red light, green light. You run toward the teacher when she yells, "Green light!" and you stop when she turns around and yells,

"Red light!" If you don't stop at that instant you're fucking out of the game. It's all about someone else's clock.

Now, Allah is thought to be a lot more merciful and forgiving than your gym teacher, but the point is the same: Ramadan messes with you. There's something about the stop-and-go of it that's just debilitating to the psyche. The fast gets physically easier as the month goes on, but for me it became more difficult to commit to.

After a few more glasses of water, I left work and it was completely dark. Though I was exhausted, the air was cold and energizing. I didn't feel hungry, just calm. As I waited for the cars to pass before crossing the street, I happened to look up to the sky. There was the moon right above me, dangling, half glowing, half invisible. As I watched it I got hit with this wild realization. I realized I could follow the progress of my fast by keeping an eye on the moon every night. Ramadan starts when the first sliver of moon is seen and ends at the first sign of the next sliver. Here I could see I was about a quarter of the way through. For one of the only times in my life, I felt connected to the *Big Clock*. Not the internal clock that my supervisor was telling me about, but the kind of time that moves in giant tectonic sweeps, manifested in the impenetrable mechanics of gravity and light, of space and stars. And not only did I notice it, I was connected to it. I was doing something I had never consciously done before: basing my actions on the motions of planetary objects, on the motions of the heavens. How sad, I thought, that this was the first time.

Boss was supportive but realistic when I told him I was going to fast for Ramadan.

"You know, Vega," he told me, "maybe you should fast only the first two weeks. For your first time, one month is a lot. Even the toughest cannot go too much past one month. Even the toughest, they break. One month: It is the breaking point. You suffer and you suffer and you suffer, then at that last minute, right before you break, Allah lets you eat again and drink. Oh, He is merciful!"

He told me maybe I should not fast completely. Maybe I should drink water or even juice for the month. "This way you don't suffer too much."

He was fucking with me, but still his warnings made me feel good. I had no intention of drinking juice or water. If I was going to do it, I wanted to commit to the whole shebang.

Two weeks into the fast, though, I told him I was thinking about starting to drink water on the third week. It was getting pretty rough.

"Pussy," he said, "only the pussies drink water during Ramadan. Vega, are you a pussy?"

Whoa, I thought, *Boss called me a pussy.* Boss was good at making you realize the tough things about yourself. I decided to stick with it, not just 'cause I didn't want to be a pussy but because he made me realize I was tricking myself into quitting. Boss was good like that. The tough part is when his honesty isn't consistent. His opinion changes all the time so one day he tells you to drink juice and the next day you're a pussy for drinking water. But by now I've come to learn that's what's great about him: it's not about the water, it's about the honesty.

"To be totally honest, it seems kind of silly," another friend was saying to me, "I mean, why are you doing it? Are you just trying to prove that you can?"

I was a little offended. I was also a little disturbed because I felt there was an element of truth in it. But no, I realized that wasn't even true: I knew I *could* do it. I wanted to see if I *would* do it.

"No," I said, "I'm doing it 'cause it's a worthwhile spiritual endeavor." That was becoming my line, and I was getting tired of repeating it. "Fasting makes sense to me and I've never done it and

I've always wanted to. It's pretty simple: ever since I worked for Boss I wanted to fast during Ramadan but I wasn't in a place where it seemed feasible. Now I'm in a position where I can. Plus"—I was feeling defensive—"there's like more than a *billion* Muslims in the world, you know? One-fifth of the goddamn planet. And they're all doing this. Why wouldn't I, no—how *couldn't* I try it once in my life?"

My friend wasn't really hearing me, so I went on:

"People are willing to try all kinds of stupid shit all the time: crack, skydiving, whatever. Trying to have new experiences. But those things don't take any kind of commitment. You're not making any sacrifices when you have those experiences. They're easy. No effort. This is a commitment. Why is it strange that I would commit to an experience?"

"Why don't you fast for Yom Kippur?" he asked sort of snidely. He was Jewish.

"Maybe I'll do it next year," I said. "Anyway, I got fucking *circumcised.* Isn't that enough of a commitment to one religion for a lifetime?"

"Yom Kippur?!" Boss scoffed as I recounted the story to him that night. "*One* day! Big fucking deal! And the Christians are even *worse,*" he said. "Jesus Christ died and *rose from the dead* to save these fucking people, sacrificed his own life, and what do they do to celebrate? They go and buy all kinds of junk, they go and buy clothes and remote-control cars and all this bullshit and then they eat and drink all day long till they're drunk and fat and sick to their stomachs. . . . Fucking cocksucker motherfucking white people."

"Well, you know they're supposed to give up their favorite thing for Lent, that's like forty days—"

"So what?" He wasn't cutting them any slack. "Some fat old lady gives up chocolate for one month. Big deal. Americans don't know about suffering. They don't know about sacrifice."

"Well, they don't need to."

"And you know why? You know why, Vega?"

"No, why?"

"Because Allah *loves* America," he said. I laughed, but he went on: "My wife tells me I'm crazy"—Boss's wife is an American, non-Muslim—"but it even says so in the Koran."

"It says 'Allah loves America' in the Koran?" I asked.

"It says: 'Allah shall bless the people and the countries he loves.' Look at America. How many jobs, how much opportunity. Allah *loves* America. Vega, go to Algeria, and ask anyone on the street if they have ever heard of a place where it *rains in the summer!* Do you understand that, Vega? Nowhere back home, in all of Africa or the Middle East, does it rain in the summer. All of Africa!" Of course, he was exaggerating. "Vega, do you know how people think about water back home? What they would do for water in the summer? Do you know what it means to them?"

I was thinking about my fast. That is, in fact, part of the point of Ramadan. Many feel that when we deprive ourselves of food and water we come to an understanding of the needy and live in allegiance with them for some time. We experience suffering by intention, and through that we come to better understand the nature of suffering. In general, Islam puts a great emphasis on alms and giving, respect and offerings for the poor. Here was another way to respect it—not through charity but through direct experience.

"I don't know," I answered, and I thought of the words of the Prophet Muhammad, peace be upon him: *Hunger is God's food whereby He revives the bodies of the sincere ones.*

"Maybe I have some idea," I said.

"Aaahhh," Boss whispered knowingly. "Maybe now you know!"

Revelation Road

Peter Manseau

From three thousand loudspeakers affixed to the city's three thousand minarets, the canned wailing of muezzins rings out the call to prayer just as the sun puts the first hints of color in the sky over the Bosporus. Istanbul has been a Muslim city for five hundred years, and yet still there seems to be no coordination when it comes to scheduling this most basic of Islamic customs. With each chorus of *allahu akbar* beginning imprecisely at sunrise, it's pretty much every mosque for itself. Some start ten seconds early, some ten seconds late; at least one seems to wait until the coast is clear so that its *adhan* will have the air all to itself. The effect is devotional chaos, the ear-rattling racket of competing voices shouting the same holy words not quite simultaneously from every corner of the city, five times every day.

"That's nothing," a Turkish friend would tell me later. "You should hear this place on Atatürk's birthday. You ever been in a city of ten million when every car honks its horn at once?"

Before six o'clock on a summer morning, the cacophonous call to prayer is as close as I ever want to get. Inescapable, intense, it sounds to my lapsed Catholic ears like a rosary recitation mashed up with an air raid alarm.

Turkey at the time is bracing itself for an election that in its outcome will serve as a good reminder of all the ways it's easy to get fumbled up when talking about "religion" and other words with meanings that are hard to pin down. The defeat of so-called "secular" forces by "religious" ones would seem by the usual use of the words to be very bad news for liberally inclined people. Yet Turkey's secularism has long been as religious in its own way as the Islamic elements the secular establishment so fears. After all, this is a country whose supposedly secular fealty to Mustafa Kemal Atatürk, the founder of modern Turkey, surpasses even American genuflections to the Founding Fathers. It is illegal to defame Atatürk, for example, and every year on his birthday, the country stops. No matter where Turks find themselves, they take a moment to go out and make the tremendous noise my friend later described. "Truck horns blare, car horns bleat, all the ships on the Bosporus blow their stacks." Maybe this is not religion in the usual sense, but there is certainly something very religious about it.

Once inside the immaculate, Muzak-filled confines of the Point Hotel, I don't hear a thing. The Point is one of a new generation of high-end Istanbul lodgings—most within a few blocks of trendy Taksim Square—that seem to cater to travelers who do not want to know they are in Turkey. To enter the lobby from the predawn din is suddenly to inhabit another universe, one equipped with a Japanese restaurant, a "wellness spa," and molded plastic furniture apparently borrowed from the lounge deck of the Starship *Enterprise*.

In the suites above, a group of Christian tourists is hoping to glimpse another vision of the future. Traveling with a Seattle-based touring company called Ultimate Journeys, they have come to Turkey for the "Seven Churches Experience," which allows scripture-toting adventurers to visit the seven cities addressed in the closing pages of the New Testament, the Revelation of Saint John the Divine, also known as the Apocalypse.

Featured prominently in a text that many believe foretells the end of the world, the ancient Turkish cities of Ephesus, Smyrna, Pergamos, Thyatira, Sardis, Philadelphia, and Laodicea were home to first-century churches that now lay in ruins. Naturally, they now all welcome postcard-buying visitors in hopes of reaping a few lira from their place in the earliest history of Christendom.

In the world of spiritual tourism—travel to places known for either their religious significance or ethereal emanations—Turkey is sometimes called the Second Holy Land. With more biblical sites than any place outside Israel, the western region of Anatolia has for centuries attracted pilgrims in search of contact with the origins of their faith. Of the many faith-based tours of the region available—ranging from reenactments of the travels of Saint Paul to pilgrimages in Antioch, where followers of Jesus first called themselves Christians—I'm most interested in tracing the Revelation route because, wherever I go in the world, small "r" revelation is part of my reason for traveling. Too cynical to expect life-changing experiences every time I hop on a plane, I hope instead for feelings of connection, inklings of what it might have meant to live in another place or time, flashes of significance that let a world teetering on meaninglessness make sense, if only for an instant. As soon as I heard that groups of tourists were looking for big "R" Revelation explicitly—in the land of Revelation no less—I knew I had to have a look.

When Ultimate Journeys agreed a few days before to let me tour with them, I supposed their sense of revelation and my own would be very different. After all, to travel across ten time zones just to see the places mentioned in a biblical book that also speaks of Armageddon, the Antichrist, and the Great Tribulation, I guessed they must be Christians of the *Left Behind* school: jet-setting holy rollers out to get a leg up on everyone else awaiting the End of Days. Did these faithful come to Turkey—a vibrant, modern nation at once fiercely secular and 95 percent Muslim—to experience the country as it is, as it was? Or rather only as it exists in relationship to their faith? And what, I wondered, would they make of the call to prayer? I expected to find pilgrims so focused on the spiritual dimension of their trip they would be blind to the practical reality around them. What's more, part of me hoped this would be the case. Though I didn't share their faith, I thought proximity to their search for Revelation might provide me with some revelations of my own.

I am scanning the lobby for wild-eyed zealots when Russ Good-man appears at my side. Together with his wife, he's the force behind Ultimate Journeys. A barrel-chested fellow with a graying crew cut and matching mustache, he wears navy blue shorts and bright white sneakers that seem right for a day of walking in the Aegean heat, but not quite appropriate for the churches and mosques on today's itinerary. He holds out his hand and shakes mine like he means it.

"I am fired up for this tour," he says with a football coach's pep. He is the dictionary illustration of a practical man at leisure: polo shirt tucked in, two cell phones on his belt. He's the past president of Seattle's Space Needle and seems very much a man who can keep the elevators running on time. His plan is to spend a few hours showing the sites of Istanbul before leading the group off for the main event: a weeklong bus trek between the seven cities of Revelation, all about a day's travel to the south.

Russ checks his watch, scrolls his BlackBerry, then looks up in the direction of the balcony above the lobby. "Here come the troops."

Twenty-nine women and men ranging in age from early twenties to mid-sixties descend the Point's floating staircase to the polished floor below. To my surprise, they do not look like people eagerly anticipating the end of the world. Pale legs and fanny packs, cameras and wallet holders and water bottle slings around their necks, they look like people eagerly anticipating a day at the beach.

In the beginning, Revelation was essentially a book of comfort. Most think of the Apocalypse of Saint John as a text that tells how the world will eventually come to a frightening end; yet the intention of its author, John of Patmos, was more immediate than that. He mainly wanted to cheer up early Christian communities as they suffered religious persecution. In letters addressed to the "seven churches of Asia," and then in an often inscrutable prophecy depicting a battle between Jesus Christ and a beast that scholars now say symbolizes the Roman Empire, John offers assurance that hard times will soon come to an end.

On the Ultimate Journeys chartered bus, comfort comes without the wait. We ride through a hot morning in near-cryogenic air conditioning, listening to a local guide the tour organizers hire whenever they are in town.

A smiling Turk in a plaid shirt and khakis, Ali keeps up a steady patter of Turkish history even as those in his audience press their noses against the windows and talk among themselves. He calls the streets through which we roll "Constantinopolis," as if this group of twenty-first-century Christians might still hold a grudge eighty years after Atatürk permanently unseated the Christian emperor Constantine as the city's namesake. I'm sitting next to Rikk Watts, who is probably the only one to notice. A professor of the New Testament who will take over tour guide duties once the group is on its way to the seven churches, he has done this trip before with Ultimate Journeys and so he knows Ali's script well. Just now Ali is holding up the umbrella we are to look for if we get separated from the group.

"We call him Ali Poppins when he's got that umbrella," Rikk says. "He seems to like it, but I'm not sure he gets the reference."

Rikk teaches at Vancouver's Regent College, the kind of religiously affiliated institution that requires a yearly signing of a statement of faith by all faculty members. Regent in fact is the main reason the seats around us are full. Rikk is among the school's most popular professors, a dynamic speaker who, more than one tour member tells me, "makes history come alive."

That Rikk and his students believe in Revelation goes without saying, but he is an academic at heart and so seems far more interested in context than prophecy. Within minutes of introducing himself, he is explaining to me that many of the sites on which the seven churches were built once held pagan temples.

"What you need to understand," he says with the urgency of

an evangelist, "is that these temples were built along lines that were considered almost like a power grid. Rituals were performed to coax power out of the earth, out of the gods. It was inevitable that Christian churches would end up there."

As Rikk speaks of pagan temples giving rise to churches that would later make way for mosques, Ali is at the front of the bus explaining that, indeed, "Constantinopolis" was once a Christian city, before it became an Islamic one. The only inevitable change, it seems, is change, one faith morphing into another.

As if to prove it, our first stop is the Aya Sofia. Built as the world's largest church by the Byzantine emperor Justinian in the sixth century, it was converted into the world's largest mosque by Mehmed the Conquerer in 1453. Not long after Atatürk's secular government took over following the fall of the Ottoman Empire, it was converted again. Since 1935, it has been a museum of its own history, proudly displaying both ornate Arabic calligraphy and painstakingly restored Byzantine mosaics destroyed or obscured through the centuries.

We are deep inside the Aya Sofia when I meet two more members of the Ultimate Journeys group. David and Tamara Duke of Seattle both work in construction. She's a project manager for industrial building; he oversees major public works projects: highways, bridges, tunnels. I ask Dave what he thinks of the tour so far.

"Impressive," he tells me. "I keep looking at this place, and all I can see is the cost!"

He pats a carved stone column the diameter of a California redwood.

"Jeez, just think of the infrastructure this must have taken! Build something on this scale today, we're in the billions, right? And think of the overpass you'd need!"

It seems a rather secular preoccupation for a member of a faith-based tour, and so I begin to wonder if I've stumbled into the wrong group, or if I've just asked the wrong member. Fishing for something that might connect the people I'm with to what I suppose to be the spiritual goals of their trip, I ask another of the Ultimate Journeys travelers—Robert Ralston, a fiftysomething fellow also dressed in shorts, sneakers, and a polo shirt—if he has come to Turkey for religious reasons.

"Well, sure," he says. "But that's like saying you get married for religious reasons. That may be part of it, but you also want to have sex, right?"

"This way," Ali calls out, and we all follow his umbrella out through the gates of the Aya Sofia, back out to the street. "This way, everyone! We go now to the Blue Mosque."

The Sultan Ahmed Mosque—also called the Blue Mosque for the cerulean tiles decorating its interior walls—is just a short stroll away. With six minarets and a vast marble courtyard leading to its main entrance, it is easily the most impressive of Istanbul's thousands of religious buildings. It is also the only Islamic site Ultimate Journeys will visit while in Turkey.

Ali leads us across the courtyard to the non-Muslim entrance, where a team of sextants waits to inspect the tourists and ensure that they are dressed appropriately. Judging from their exasperated reaction, the Ultimate Journeys group is certainly not.

"Please, please," the men at the door call out, frantically handing electric blue headscarves to the women of the tour, asking them to cover their hair, their shoulders, their legs. Then they look down at the bare knees of Russ, Dave, and nearly every other man in the group, and they begin handing out headscarves to them as well, urging the men to wrap the lengths of fabric around their waists like sarongs. "Please be so kind to cover!" they shout. "Please be so kind to cover!"

Once through this gauntlet, we search for Ali's umbrella and join him beneath the hundreds of hanging lamps that light the mosque. He begins his tour again as soon as a dozen or so have found him.

"The front section is for the men doing their prayers," he says. "The rear section is for the ladies. The question is often asked, why they cannot pray together? The answer, very simple: How you can concentrate on God when a lady does like this in front of you?"

Ali bends over prayerfully then makes a show of wiggling his khaki-clad behind in our direction. The men of Ultimate Journeys seem to find this very funny. Inspired, Rikk Watts spots a few male members of the group standing near each other in their blue modesty skirts and can't resist capturing the image. "Get together now, gentlemen," he says with a grin as his camera jumps to his eye, "or dare I say *gentlemen*?" Russ and Dave and Robert pose next to each other, each pulling the hem of his skirt up to show a little ankle.

"You all seem to get along so well, for a tour group," I say to Tamara Duke, who likewise has been watching the show.

"Oh, a bunch of us have been traveling together for years now," she tells me. "We don't just go on religious trips. We also play golf."

Why am I disappointed? Despite myself, I feel snookered. Revelation, after all, implies intensity of experience, heightened awareness, at least the possibility of life-changing discovery. John of Patmos is said to have been in a fever dream when he composed the prophetic parts of his book. His vision tells of a seven-headed, ten-horned beast that was a key to understanding the state of the world in which he and his audience lived. The original meaning of "apocalypse" is *unveiling*: it is the moment at which the seeming reality of things falls away and the hidden truth is made known.

So far my time among those preparing for the Revelation trail has felt less like an unveiling and more like an ice-cream social. There is a lot of talking, a lot of gawking. We travel through Istanbul as if behind glass, insulated not just by the tour bus but by the very fact that we are a tour—a self-contained unit that has no need to meet or interact with anyone who lives among the sites we see.

After a long day with the group, I decide to set off on my own. Maybe solo revelation would be easier to find.

The city of Smyrna, like all the locations named in Revelation, now has a new name: Izmir. Once the most important coastal city in Asia Minor, it remains Turkey's third-largest metropolis, yet is visited by tourists almost exclusively for its airport. I rent a Ford Festiva from the Hertz counter and ask for a map.

"Where do you go?" one of the two clerks on duty asks. "Efes?"

Of the seven cities mentioned by John of Patmos, Ephesus—now called Efes—is the only one non-Revelation-seeking travelers flock to. It is considered a high point of any trip to Turkey and so I plan to go there last.

"Yes," I say, "but first I will go to Pergamos, Thyatira, Sardis, Philadelphia, and Laodicea."

The Hertz clerks look at me as if I have just rattled off the moons of Neptune. The old names mean nothing to them. I dig out a list of the modern names and the clerks help me plot a course from the airport. With the seven churches marked with red dots on my map, I see now that they make a rough circle. Really, it's more of a kidney shape, but still I am pleased to see I will be able to start and end just where I am standing.

The clerks, however, are less happy with my plan.

"There is nothing to see here, here, here, here, or here," one of them says, pointing at five of my seven dots, which is to say every site with the exception of Efes and Izmir. He puts two thin fingers on two of the dots, reconsidering. "Here, there is a little something. Maybe here."

The second clerk disagrees. Now that they have something to talk about it seems they don't need to include me at all.

"No, there is nothing there also," Clerk #2 says. "He should go to Efes. Efes is a good trip. These other places, this is not a good trip."

"Or maybe go Efes, then another place, then back to Efes, then another place, then back to Efes."

"I only have a day," I say.

They look down at the map, then back up at me, then down at the map.

"One day?"

It's true: for a variety of reasons—money, a two-year-old daughter back home, and maybe a peculiarly American wish to supply with speed the intensity I'm afraid history won't provide—I have about twenty-four hours to see all seven cities of the Book of Revelation. I have the next day's plane ticket out of Izmir in my pocket.

The clerks talk briefly between themselves and then reach a consensus. "One day? Efes."

It is already late in the evening when I pull out of the parking lot. I make my way into the first city of Revelation in darkness.

Because of its airport, Izmir is the beginning and end—the alpha and omega, to use John's language—for most seven churches tours. Yet there is really not much to see. The modern city has been so thoroughly grafted onto the ancient one that signs of the community addressed in scripture barely exist. I discover this by the headlights of the Festiva as I cruise through downtown. I head north in hopes of crossing two of the seven churches sites off my list before I can drive no more.

The road between Smyrna and Pergamos is both antediluvian and postapocalyptic. Izmir may be a thoroughly modern urban center, but it is bordered by a shantytown filled with homes that seem made of mud, concrete, and salvaged materials. Satellite dishes spring up even here, and as I drive by I can see a warm glow emanating from windows cut in walls of corrugated metal. It seems desolate until I am beyond them, when the permanent haze of television radiance mixed with cooking fires gives way to empty night.

When I reach Pergamum, "where Satan's throne is," according to John—it's now called Bergama—four hours and several wrong turns later, I find a closet of a hotel room with a dirty orange carpet, a leaky sink, and no windows, and I don't mind at all.

The next morning I get an early start for the long day ahead. Bergama's main archaeological attractions are high up on the hill that overlooks the town, but the site of most interest to faith-based tour groups is down a quiet road just off the main drag. As Rikk suggested, the visible remains of the Christian community are located on ground that once held a pagan temple, then a church, and now a collection of half-collapsed walls and broken building stones that seem all but forgotten. The ancient buildings felled by history are nearly indistinguishable from the buildings of more recent construction that have fallen from simple neglect. The Church of Saint John the Theologian, as Bergama's main seven churches site is known, sits catty-cornered to an abandoned storehouse, a crumbling barn, and a dusty field where a skinny horse scrapes for grass in the hot morning sun.

I linger for an hour, then climb back into my car. The skinny horse has moved closer to the Festiva, but otherwise there has been no action in Bergama. Despite the rising temperature, this morning the Revelation trail seems cold, indeed.

With five more stops to make, I push on, setting out to check off first-century ruin sites like items on a shopping list. From Bergama I head east, then south, beginning what will quickly turn into several hours of hard driving through a landscape of arid-looking earth that nonetheless has been coaxed to agricultural life. Along the roadsides, women work in green fields with their heads wrapped in blue, red, and black scarves.

Driving five hundred miles in a single day in Turkey is not unlike driving five hundred miles in a single day anywhere in the world. The radio plays different music, but the drivers are just as impatient with foreigners slowing to read every sign, ignorant of all etiquette of the road. It is not long before I learn my first lesson in Turkish driving. Back home in Washington, the car horn usually means something simple and not very expressive, like *Watch it, buddy.* Here, it means something closer to *You'd better get ready because I'm going pass you on either the left or the right; I haven't decided which yet, so if you're smart you will slow down a bit and drive as straight as possible while my truck full of chickens roars by.*

My only breaks from the road are at remnants of civilizations long gone that dot this region like strip malls. I stop first at Thyatira (Thus spoke Saint John: "I hold this against you, that you tolerate that woman Jezebel"), then Sardis ("If you are not watchful, I will come like a thief"), then Philadelphia ("Because you have kept my message of endurance, I will keep you safe"), and I am surprised to find, at each spot, that I am the only soul there. I had heard—from Ultimate Journeys and others—that business was booming on the seven churches trail. So where were all those walking in the footsteps of the people for whom Revelation was born?

I am somewhere on the highway south of Philadelphia and have two church sites to go: Laodicea (now Laodokia), which is near the modern city of Denzili, and then finally on to Ephesus, which has become a beacon in the mist of this long, hot, and mostly fruitless day. The roads wraps first to the right, then to the left, and I ride it as Wile E. Coyote might ride a mine cart down a mountain pass—faster and faster until the dusty world around me seems to be an endlessly repeating backdrop of yellow and brown. I take a hairpin turn which suddenly slopes into a winding valley road that speeds traffic only to throw a stoplight up at the bottom of the hill. Hitting the brakes, I lurch to a stop so sudden it kicks up a storm of sand and stones around me.

And then I see them. As if they have been formed within the

dust cloud, they stand like a mirage in the near-desert landscape. Three men, two women, all in crisp white shirts and navy blue pants or skirts that make them seem like a lost field trip from a Catholic high school.

When the stoplight changes, I begin to roll forward, but then stop again. One of the men in the group has raised his hand into the air, calling to me. I roll down my window and he leans in, smiling with relief as he says, "*Wa salaam aleichem*" ("And to you, peace"). I know that one should answer "*Wa aleichem salaam,*" but I haven't spoken to anyone all day and I can't help but blurt out "Hello!"

"English?" he says, then he turns to the others. "*Englitze,*" he calls to them.

Another young man steps forward and also puts his head through the window.

"We are schoolteachers," the second one says. "The autobus goes."

"Went," the first schoolteacher says.

"Where are you going?" I ask.

"Denzili."

I lean across the passenger seat, push open the door, and wave inward, offering what I hope is the international sign for "get in."

"We *all* are schoolteachers," the second one says, as if my offer of a ride was limited only to the educators in the group.

So far on this trip the Ford Festiva has seated one comfortably. Now, we would see if it could live up to its festive name. The five schoolteachers pile in without a second thought.

"Denzili?" I ask.

"*Evet, evet,*" they say. Yes, yes. "Denzili."

From the backseat there soon comes a period of spirited discussion I cannot understand, followed by flashes of carefully considered questions and comments intended for me.

"What is your name?" they ask slowly, rolling each word like a letter in a spelling bee.

I tell them, and soon they tell me theirs as well. In the passenger seat next to me is the young man who first put his head through the window: Mehmet. Directly behind me, with his head pushed up against the Festiva's ceiling because he is seated on a lap, is the second man, Esra. Under him is the third male teacher, Ihsan. The women are Gokcen and Ulas. It takes about twenty minutes to convey all this but we are still forty kilometers from Denzili, which is another ten kilometers from Laodokia, so we've got nothing but time.

Once names have been established, there follows another five minutes of intense Turkish debate. Finally Gokcen tries her hand at a translation of what they have been saying. She says haltingly, "We . . . love . . . you . . . Peter."

Ulas laughs and buries her face in Gokcen's ear. In the rearview mirror I see her turn red.

"For the driving we are loving you," she says. "For the driving."

"Thank you," Mehmet suggests. "She means to say 'Thank you.'"

Every English word is followed by what seems to be a fierce disputation on grammar and vocabulary. They have all had plenty of instruction in the language, I gather, but rarely get to speak it.

Gokcen is the most fearless: "Peter, are you drinking something?"

Ulas covers her face to stifle more laughter, but Gokcen forges ahead.

"Do you like to drink something? Liquids? Soft drinks, or tea?"

"Do I like drinking liquids?" I ask. There's nothing like travel to cause you to answer questions you never thought to consider. "Yes, I do like drinking liquids," I say. "When I am thirsty."

"We would drink anything with you."

I check my watch—four o'clock—and tell them that in fact I need to get to Laodokia and then to Ephesus before my flight out of Izmir late that night.

"We drink something to thank you," Mehmet says, and all in the backseat make sincere sounds of assent.

On the outskirts of Denzili we stop at a Burger King, where we pile into a small booth. Only after we have all crammed in together does Esra extract himself to order six Cokes at the counter.

Each of the schoolteachers takes a turn trying to tell me something in English, and then I try out a bit of my guidebook Turkish. When I have said my three words and they have blushed through their quiet but useful English vocabularies, we fall into a pleasant silence.

"We want to speak," Esra says, "but we cannot."

Then it seems to be Gokcen's turn. Everyone watches her, waiting.

Finally she opens her mouth to speak.

"The words," she says.

She seems about to add a verb to her noun but instead she breaks into a wide smile that turns into a laugh. In a moment we're all laughing. At what? The words, and the space between them.

We finish our Cokes, climb back into the Festiva, and continue in the direction of Denzili. As Mehmet directs me, I make one stop, then another, dropping off Gokcen, Ulas, and Ihsan near their homes.

"Where now?" I ask, expecting that I will now drive my last two accidental fares to their destinations.

Mehmet and Esra share a few words conspiratorially in Turkish.

"Laodokia!" they shout.

We drive on, out of the city, beginning on a boulevard that thins as it carves through hills of green and yellow. The land is beautiful, the road a labyrinth. There is no way I could have navigated this part of the trip without them. Turning left off the pavement, we bump down a narrow channel of stone and dirt, finally rolling through a chain-link gate pulled halfway across the road. Out before us the sky opens behind fallen white columns and the remnants of buildings that look like Atlantis pulled up from the sea.

"We're here?" I ask.

"No problem," Esra says, and then they both grin. This site is as neglected as the other seven church sites. In fact there is a far more impressive site just down the road—Pamulkake. Not only is it a favorite of the guidebooks, it is also a place locals are just as likely to visit as tourists. But Laodokia? Mehmet and Esra smile at each other at least in part because they have no reason to be here other than that they happened to cross my path.

I park the car and we set out on foot, walking among the ruins we saw from the road.

My new friends jog from shattered statues to building remnants to broken slabs of ancient roadway, occasionally grabbing my hand to show me something they are afraid I might miss. Beyond the ruins we make our way up a slight grassy slope. Soon we stand on the cusp of what was once a vast open-air theater, a steep hill with stone benches set deep enough in the earth that they have not budged in two thousand years.

We walk back through the ruins, entering a wide thoroughfare with white marble columns on either side that provide the sensation of walking through the husk of a giant whale washed up on shore.

Esra puts a hand on one of these bones of the civilization that once stood here, pats it heartily, grinning. His look says he desperately wants to tell me something about this place. He is a schoolteacher, after all.

"History!" he finally says. "History!"

Then he laughs at the absurdity of it. We all laugh.

"History!" I agree.

"No problem!" Mehmet says.

"Laodokia!" Esra shouts, with a tone that is unmistakable: Why on earth are we here? There are other, better ruins not far away.

"Why come Turkey, Peter?" Mehmet asks.

I try to explain. "Well, there were these seven churches," I say. "And this guy John, he wrote them each a letter, and those letters ended up in a book of the Bible. Some people believe that book tells how the world will end."

I give up there, and we all laugh again. Standing in a place that was once a city center but now is thick with weeds and silence, we all know that the world is too flexible to ever end—at least not in the ways any book could foretell.

Dusk is approaching when I drop Mehmet and Esra back in Denzili. I have about a hundred kilometers to go to reach Ephesus by nightfall and I push the Festiva hard to make it. Miraculously, I do not get lost.

Except in my thoughts: I think about the local people to whom John of Patmos once wrote, and I wonder if they remained, like the arid yet fertile land of Anatolia, virtually unchanged as creeds came and went through the centuries. If that was the case, then my new friends—Turks, Muslims, schoolteachers—though separated by faith and language might be the closest living relatives of those for whom Revelation was written.

I miss my two accidental tour groups—both the one I went looking for and the one that found me—but I am glad now to be on my own. I am not a believer in prophecies. I am not a speaker of creeds. I never met a church, mosque, coven, or temple I wanted to join.

And so it makes a certain amount of sense to me that I would need to leave one country caught in a seemingly endless struggle between the religious and the secular and come to another caught in a struggle very different but much the same, in order to make sense of the desire to enter into the story of other people's faith, only to move on to another story, and another story, and another. I put my foot to the floor of the Festiva and revel in the feeling of racing toward the setting sun in a foreign land, thinking about friends just made who likely will never be seen again.

The ruins at Ephesus are closed by the time I get there. The sun hangs low in the sky, and the only people around are armed guards smoking cigarettes in the parking lot.

With nowhere else to go, I keep driving toward what is left of the sun.

A mile or two beyond Ephesus, the road to Revelation ends at a beach. I park the Festiva, walk to the water, and strip down to my boxer shorts.

I wade into the sea, sinking in over my head just as the last light of the sun and the soft breeze turn the surface a rippling orange and red. The wind whistles faintly on the water. It's not quite a revelation, nor a call to prayer. But it's close.

Searching for Sufis

Jill Hamburg Coplan

Istanbul, Turkey, autumn 1992: I withdrew a thousand dollars from the last ATM for three thousand miles and hid it all over my body. I was a novice American reporter out of Jerusalem, a town full of big-time correspondents—bottomless expense accounts, satellite phones, prime ministers' home numbers. They were always rushing off to meet nuclear arms traffickers or Muammar Qaddafi at his private compound. A lowly stringer, I never got invites.

I was no good at pack journalism, anyway. It was time to begin a mission of my own: crossing four or five civil wars in newly independent Central Asia to find a Sufi master.

I was raised with two religions, neither one Islamic: Judaism and Zionism. In fact, I'm a not-so-distant relative of Israel's founder, David Ben-Gurion. Probably it was rebelliousness, but I'd always felt a gravitational pull toward the Arab and Muslim side of things. Late in 1992, with Communism's fall, I suspected that, as two minorities ("nationalities" was the preferred Soviet term), the Jews and the Muslims were heading for interesting times. Central Asia was also appealing as the birthplace of Sufism—mystical, ecstatic, meditative Islam. I'd read that Sufi mathematics, medicine, and poetry, developed in the medieval courts of Avignon and Andalusia, had spread from there to permeate Europe's Enlightenment. Sufi masters were jesters and folk heroes. Carl Jung equated their mental healing techniques with psychotherapy.

And how about this: through the centuries, wherever Sufism held sway—like Ottoman Turkey—Jews could find safe haven. If I could find a Sufi, I thought, I could approach him with genuine respect, bringing my own real curiosity about mysticism, and produce for American newspaper readers a kind of encounter that might help them understand Islam in a different way than a demonizing story about a radical hostage taker or half-crazed suicide attacker ever could. And if not, well, Judaism reserves its mystical texts and practices for old male scholars who've mastered everything else. Perhaps the more tolerant Sufis would open a door for me.

There was little sanctuary, however, in Istanbul. The Berlin Wall's fall had launched millions of Eastern Bloc youth into almost an outer-space orbit—homeless, penniless, stateless, jobless, confused. Many had ended up here. I gathered courage for my journey from Mari, a skinny Romanian maid in my cheap pensione. We were both twenty-six, empty inside, tethered to nothing. She'd gone weeks without food, determined not to cave in to the pimps and the brothels, yet I was the one feeling depressed. She had the guts to believe in her destiny. Now it was my turn.

Much later, a Sufi would tell me that waking up with an overpowering feeling of being drawn toward your destiny is completely natural and normal. Once awakened, you must jump in, "learn how to swim," according to the symbolism of one teaching story. Pursue adventure, guided by love. Knights' quests are rooted in this: both chivalric customs and wandering troubadours' love laments come to us from the Sufis of Islamic Spain.

In an icy drizzle, I hugged Mari good-bye and booked a third-class sleeper going east. I spent my last hours drifting around Istanbul's antique book bazaar, pondering my crazy quest.

The odds were long. It was unclear, first, whether any Sufis had survived Stalin. They were persecuted for centuries—by Crusaders in the Levant, by the Inquisition in Iberia. They were hunted down on their home turf only in the twentieth century, when the Communists took power. From 1917 to about 1929, the Sufis inspired Islamic rebels (the Russians called them *basmachi*—bandits) to fight the modern era's first jihad. In response, the Red Army bulldozed four thousand Central Asian mosques and shrines.

I wandered into a charming old courtyard, down a short flight of stone stairs rubbed round by centuries of slippers. One small, cozy shop beckoned. Inside, a dark-eyed, bearded young man with a velvety buzz cut sat on a stool. Soggy and getting cold feet in every sense, I pulled up to his stove and spilled my story. The empty feeling. The weird quest. The frightening bloodletting on my intended route.

Karabakh, for example, was the scene of terrible mutual slaughter between Azeris and Armenians, neighbors and former friends —of mob attacks and scorched earth. Tens of thousands had fled. There was also a lot of death and displacement in Georgia, which was a lawless and frightening place, lots of organized crime violence, murder just for the money. Also in Abkhazia, Daghestan. And the civil war in Tajikistan displaced about one-quarter of the population. In perfect English, the shopkeeper said to be careful, but he didn't try to dissuade me. Then he leaned over his dusty books and, without a word, fastened something to the front of my sweater: a bunch of tiny plastic grapes surrounded by little blue, white, silver, and purple beads, threaded onto a tiny gold safety pin.

Travelers' suitcases often jingle with little amulets, and I had my share, but more as kitsch than out of real belief. A quarter-sized medal of St. George (patron saint of travelers) buried somewhere. A gold-plated hand-of-Fatima, a Moroccan-Jewish pendant, in another pouch. The grapes, I assumed, were some kind of Turkish good-luck charm. I had little opportunity to think more about it—hours later, I was sitting between exhausted Armenians hauling crates of cooking oil and chickens on an old Turkish train rumbling toward the long-closed Iron Curtain, into the bowels of a disintegrating empire.

That night, our train smacked into a winter storm over Mount

Ararat, where the Bible says Noah's Ark made landfall. Like the Ark, we stalled in the weather, though the blizzard lasted only two days. I shared my high-tech sleeping bag with an elfin teenage Armenian priest-in-training. At night, he sang lullabies of haunting liturgy.

When the storm lifted, I got moving again. And I searched for my Sufis. In wintry Armenia and Georgia, bombed buildings smoldered. In Azerbaijan, leaking refineries stank of oil. I visited mosques, shrines, and grave sites. In Daghestan, Turkmenistan, there was little heat, medicine, or fuel. In the breadlines, Soviet scarcity had turned into full-blown hunger. Three months passed without a Sufi in sight.

In Uzbekistan, I lunched with the leader of a banned Islamic movement. The future he envisioned had no room for pluralism, no place for the resident Russians, and even less room for Bukharan Jews, whose houses of worship, even skullcaps, could pass for those of the Muslims. The Bukharans wanted what he wanted, peace and quiet, to worship and to prosper. But he didn't see it that way. I began accepting, then, that I wouldn't find Sufis. Only the vacuum, the intolerance, growing in their absence.

Toward the end I reached Ferghana, a valley of failing farms where the Basmachi had once held fast. Now, again, it was embattled. Soldiers had opened fire there on Islamic demonstrators, jailed and disappeared students (and would again later, in 2005, killing thousands in cold blood). I met one young man patiently repairing a ruined mosque. He'd learned the Koran as a child from a wandering teacher who would gather up the village children in a barn. Parents paid the old man with bags of rice and lodging.

A Sufi! I thought, feeling the trail finally get warm. Perhaps I'd find him after all.

But the old man, he said, was long gone. The youth had new mentors: the Saudis, and perhaps Pakistan and Iran, according to other farmers' reports. It seemed to be a replay of what had happened during the 1980s, when the United States used those countries to flood the region with holy books—packed in the same cases as weapons, destined for the Soviet–Afghan war. The legacy of such gifts, we now know, was Osama bin Laden.

Were the Sufis complicit? Had they simply died out?

My last stop was the Pamir Mountains, Kipling's "Rooftop of the World," home to shaggy black Bactrian camels and sacred yak tails fluttering on stakes, towering amidst prayer flags. Russian pilots were strafing the villages. The goal was to flush out Islamists, but it was mothers and children I met, fleeing down trails waist deep in snow. But it turned out the rebels were up there, too. I hitched a ride on a farm cart bringing them fresh supplies of shoulder-fired missiles. They were holed up in an abandoned village's police station, wearing frankly theatrical gold lamé turbans and bandoliers strapped across flowing black blouses. These men were Soviet-schooled soldiers, experts in war, not piety. What they wanted was funds, political power, resources.

I'd been five months on the road and had found no Sufis. Just confusion and strife.

It was just before spring. I'd already had several run-ins with the Uzbek KGB and now they'd begun deporting reporters. My time was up, which meant facing the facts. I'd documented intolerance. Filing stories that brought attention to little-known cases of human suffering had restored my sense of purpose. In a sense, I'd succeeded. But what the hell was I thinking? That some weathered old Sufi, a master for decades at evading the secret police, would suddenly emerge after seventy years underground just for me?

But guess what? I'd been hoodwinked.

I met an American diplomat, perhaps a spook. Certainly a senior Asia hand, fluent in Turkish, Farsi, and Urdu, a former academic with a PhD in Persian literature. He noticed my little grapes amulet, still faithfully pinned to my only sweater. He asked where I'd gotten it and I explained.

"In the book bazaar? You mean the little shop on the left? Down the stairs?"

Yes. But how did he know?

The diplomat was an expert on classical Persian poetry, most of it religious, so he knew the Sufis well. The place where I'd met the handsome bookseller, he said, was the understated headquarters of a Sufi order that had inspired the Basmachi. The one I'd set out to find. I thought I'd found no Sufis, yet they had found me, before the train I'd taken to reach them had even left the station. Hidden so well, I didn't notice even when he pinned his logo right above my heart.

Jesters, indeed. He had made me the fool in a mystical fable. I could find what I was after only by looking at myself.

Later, of course, more questions arise. For example: Why grapes? One answer came in Sheikh Idries Shah's book *The Sufis,* which has a whole chapter called "The Travelers and the Grapes." It includes this famous Sufi tale:

Four traveling companions, one Persian, one Arab, one Greek, and one Turk, become hungry. With just a coin between them, they begin to argue.

"I want *angur*," says the Persian.

"I want *uzum*," says the Turk.

"I want *inab*," says the Arab.

"But I want *stafil*," says the Greek.

A Sufi takes their coin and shortly, returns with grapes—*angur* in Persian, *uzum* in Turkish, *inab* in Arabic, *stafil* in Greek.

It spoke to me of my quest, of the splintering nations that are the legacy of the post–Cold War world. And of this country's pervasive, post-9/11 concern with the "enemy religion."

We're all seeking something greater, the Sufi says. It is only our surface differences—and a world that can resemble a pileup of horrors—that blind us to the essential sameness of our need.

A Sufi might call this common need a drive toward union with the divine. The secular might call it the drive for wisdom, or peace. Reporters call it a great story. If your turn of mind is therapeutic, it's healing. They all begin in self-knowledge. Look down at the pin, you rookie.

Barbershop Dharma

Jeff Wilson

For a lot of folks, knowing the Bible is about inspiration and faith. But for some of us, it's about survival.

It's getting on in the afternoon as I step into the Friendly Barber Shop here in Carrboro, a small town a little ways down the road from the University of North Carolina. As I sit down to wait, I glance over the magazine rack filled with issues of *Gun & Ammo* and *Hunting Magazine*. *Gun & Ammo* is extolling the virtues of the thirty-ought-six; all the covers feature gigantic firearms aimed at the reader. *Hunting* promises tips on how to stalk a giant mule. I'm a former subscriber to *Field and Stream,* but even I can't imagine why anyone would want to stalk a humongous jackass. I picture Robert Shaw from *Jaws* rolling up his pants leg, pointing to a semi-circle of badly healed welts: "Aye matey, forget about sharks. This is the real deal. See that there? Giant mule. Nastiest critter on God's green earth."

There are three men sitting next to me, and two others are getting their hair cut in the barbers' chairs. Another man comes in with two young boys. There's no sign outside, but it's understood that this is a gendered space. Men get their hair trimmed here at the barbershop—women go down the street to the *salon*. Maybe it's racialized too. Looking around, I notice that everyone in here is white, and as I think about it, I can't recall ever seeing a black or Latino person in here, even though people of various races amble slowly by in the heat outside. All of this makes me aware that I'm violating a third, unspoken law of admittance to a place like this. I slip the beads off from around my wrist and into my pocket, out of sight. No sense making waves.

One of the customers pays and leaves, and a barber calls out for me. I leave my bag and stroll over to the big chair. The barber is about forty, with a bright pink complexion and short-cropped sandy hair. "I hope you're doing fine today," he says as I sit down. I suppose I am. We discuss how I want my hair cut—real short, off the ears, off the neck. "Hey, you got a sticker on your back," he says. Visions of a "kick me" sign flash through my mind, but turns out it's only a tag left over from the store. This is the first time I've worn this shirt since I got it at Wal-Mart, I explain, and we get a good chuckle out of it.

"Where're you from?" he asks as he starts working a razor over the side of my head. I was raised in New England by Texan parents, so my accent is hard for most people to place—but it's easy for a North Carolinian to tag as "not from around here." "Chapel Hill," I say, eyes closed to keep falling hair out. That's as true as other answers I might've picked. "I've lived around here for years. Used to work down the street at the Inter-Faith Council. We run the soup kitchen."

We're quiet for a minute, but I can sense he'd like to chat. A haircut is a moment of intimacy between strangers, where bodies meet and are reshaped, one of the only times a man is able to touch another man without the threat of danger.

"It's been two months since my last cut," I say. "I was down in Texas visiting my family for Christmas. Do you know I was getting my hair cut, and the lady asked me where I live, and when I said 'North Carolina,' she said, 'Oh, you live in the North'!"

This gets the anticipated laugh. "I guess everything really is relative," I add. "When you live in Houston there's an awful lot of North."

After another minute, the barber asks me what I do, as brown hair falls in clumps into my lap. I know from years of living in the

South that this is where the dance begins. I've got choices to make. Decline his offer, or follow him out onto the floor. I already know where each choice will lead. "Right now I'm an instructor at NC State," I say after considering my reply. "I teach religion."

There's a pause as he reflects on this. Finally, very seriously, he asks, "Would you say that teaching religion has strengthened your faith?"

Has it? I think for a moment. His Christian vocabulary needs a little internal translation before I can decide—faith isn't quite how I think of my religion. But at least now I'm clear about the terms under which our conversation will be conducted. "Yes," I say at last. And it's true, in its way. "Learning about the different religions is interesting, it helps you understand other people better." This seems to satisfy him.

The dance continues with a quicker tempo. "Religion is important," he says. It's not a question. I tell him I agree.

"What do you teach?"

Here it is. Don't slip up. "Right now, I'm teaching Buddhism. And in the summer I'll be teaching American religion at UNC." I don't tell him that I'll be teaching on liberal traditions in American religious history, and therefore my students will learn about how many of the Founding Fathers held beliefs that most folks around here wouldn't even consider Christian.

"Do you teach theology?"

"No, history. We're a state university, we can't teach theology." Not precisely accurate, but it deflects the issue. "We learn about the history of religions. So now we're learning about Buddhism. It's a very old religion, interesting stuff. Lots of compassion."

"I hear that China has more Christians than America," he offers.

"I don't know. They've got 1.5 billion people, so even if one or two percent are Christian, that's a lot of folks. We've only got 300 million people." I decide to put out a feeler, just to check and see if I've understood the actual boundaries of our relationship. "And these days, many of them aren't Christian. Plus, we've got all sorts of Christianity. There's a lot of different ways to be religious these days."

"It worries me," he says, and by his voice I know it's true. "I worry about it a lot. What if God takes away his blessing from America, and gives it to India or China? I don't think we're headed in the right direction." I agree, but for very different reasons. Almost imperceptibly, the scissors have slowed. "What about all those efforts to take God's name off our money?"

"I know what you mean," I tell him, and start rooting into my outsider's knowledge of the Bible to see if I can say what I mean in a way that will be heard. "But I've never understood why it says 'In God we trust' on our currency. That doesn't really jive with the Sermon on the Mount. There's God and there's Mammon. Which one's being served by combining them together like that? I don't think it belongs on there."

Out of the corner of my eye I see him thinking, and then he nods slightly. "Well, what about the courts and the Ten Commandments and all that? All that stuff down there in, where is it, Louisiana?"

"Alabama. I've got family there. They all think the Ten Commandments should be in the courthouse." His scissors are working furiously now; I close my eyes again. The dance continues. "But not me. I don't think we should mix up religion and the courts like that. It's not fair to non-Christians. We're a secular nation with a lot of Christian citizens. The courts need to be free, they need to be fair to everyone. But if anyone tells you that the Bible isn't an important historical source for American justice, they're just plain wrong."

I pause for a breath. The vocabulary is his, but the sentiments can still be mine. "You know, all of this is why I teach American religion. I just find it all so fascinating. Religion's such an important part of American life. Every week I can bring in the newspaper and there's guaranteed to be a story that my students can discuss. There's so much controversy. And as America becomes more diverse, it's important that we understand each other, that we respect our neighbors. Here in North Carolina, most of my students are Christians. But I also get a few Muslims or a few other kinds of folks. Even Buddhists. Things are changing around here too, and we've got to learn about each other." Left unsaid: I'm part of that change.

"I'm a Southern Baptist," he says, "but I guess you figured that out." No kidding, buddy. My bait is left untouched.

"Some of my father's people are Southern Baptists," I say. "My mother's folks are Methodists." I don't mention that my parents became Unitarian Universalists many years ago.

"I think one of the biggest controversies that's brewing is between traditional and modern worship styles," the barber says. "I go to Providence Church over in Raleigh, and they've got three services. Two of them are modern, and one of them is traditional. And some people don't like one kind or the other. I don't know what to think." From his tone, I can tell that he's actually asking me to provide a little direction. I'm a professor of religion, after all, and for some that's at least halfway to being a pastor.

I've never set foot in a megachurch like Providence, but I also don't have the luxury of not knowing about what's going on with the local Christians. Turn on the TV or radio, or just go out shopping long enough, and you'll pick it all up by osmosis. "I've heard about this," I reply. "Churches like Providence are the hottest trend in American religion, and they've mainly grown by offering contemporary worship. But some of them are starting to offer traditional styles too." Time to lead. "I like that. The way I see it, more approaches to religion means you're more likely to find something that fits. And I'd hate to think that someone didn't get religion because they were only allowed one way to worship. It would just be arrogant for me to say everybody's got to do it *my* way."

"Amen," he says, and starts loosening the towel. "You're done.

You sure had a lot of hair." I do feel lighter, as a matter of fact. I pay him and hand over a tip, and he shakes my hand with a smile. "Nice talking with you," he says. "You have a real nice day, you hear?"

Outside, the evening is growing darker, and orange and purple clouds hang in the western sky. As I start the long walk back toward home, I think about how nearly every interaction as a Buddhist in America is an interfaith encounter. When you practice Buddhism, especially in the South, you know each morning when you get up that you'll be living with other people's religion all day long. And they outnumber you a hundred to one. Like it or not, it's here on the ground that dialogue really occurs. I'm sure there's some benefit to groups of liberal Christians and Jews getting together with groups of liberal Buddhists to find out what we can all agree on. But real dialogue happens in the barbershop, on the bus, in the cafeteria, on line at the DMV, and these aren't safe, intentionally ecumenical spaces. It happens out of necessity, and sometimes your partners don't even know they've had an interfaith experience.

Because of my profession, I've talked to a lot of barbers about religion. Christians around here get to assume everyone is just like them, and to get through the day, sometimes you have to play along. Being a religious minority means learning to speak in the parlance of the majority. And in America that means becoming biblically fluent, because the Bible isn't just a book—it's a whole world, a universe that other people live in even as they share the same streets and neighborhoods with me. Or perhaps they're not even the same streets, since we map them differently, by the Bible or the sutras. In order to get along, you have to learn to speak biblical English, a particular dialect just as surely as Ebonics or Creole.

According to tradition, whenever the Buddha preached, the audience heard his sermons as if he spoke to each of them alone, saying exactly what they needed to hear in their own language. There's a similar idea in the Bible, when Jesus's disciples were gathered together after his death, and they were suddenly filled by the holy spirit and began to speak spontaneously. A crowd formed, and though the people were from many countries, amidst the babble they all understood as if the disciples were speaking in their own languages, and many converted.

These were words that didn't merely communicate, but actually transformed the listeners. Words inspired by the wonder beyond ourselves, what in the Bible is called God and in Buddhism is called Other Power, Buddha-nature, and many other names. The word "inspiration"—literally "breathing"—is important here. Not simply the breathing of beings, but of God. As 2 Timothy 3:16 puts it: "All scripture is God-breathed and useful."

This is a deep statement that moves even a Buddhist like me, particularly when you realize that God only breathes a single time in Bible. As the story of Genesis opens, God creates all things, and names them good. Then, from the humble dirt of the ground, God molds Adam, and pressing over his face, breathes into him the kiss of life. Breath and life are the same, it seems to say. To say that all scriptures are God-breathed is to say that they are living documents, not dead letters. Like living things they grow, change, adapt, struggle, and cry out with joy at the gift of life. If we let them, all scriptures—biblical and Buddhist—can reveal themselves to us as inspired, breathing, living words, with the power to speak to us in our particular situations and with the teachings that we each need to hear.

But inspiration is also a luxury. As a non-Christian in a Christian world, learning the Bible is more about just getting by. Stand out too much as a religious "other" in some places, and there can be consequences. It's a lesson that can come as a shock to a white guy, to follow your wandering soul out beyond the bounds of unacknowledged privilege, until an ugly encounter brings your newly marginal status home at last. You used to get a pass; now you have to learn *how* to pass, how to dance with partners who don't know a thing about your religion, and don't have to.

As I pass the bus stop, some kids are playing around. One keeps climbing up on top of the trash can, until his mama hollers at him. Night is almost here and through my headphones Johnny Cash is singing about heaven. A breeze touches my scalp where this morning there was hair.

It's a hard life for Christians too. I have to live in their world, but we've all got to live in *the* world, and it's tough going. Sometimes you have to use the Bible to nudge a Christian ever so slightly in the direction you wish he'd go. Other times, a Christian sings out of the depths of his heart and makes an impression on you. With conviction, Cash declares to me, "I'm just an old lump of coal, but I'm gonna be a diamond some day."

You and me both, Johnny, I think as night comes on, with the dogwood blossoms luminescent in the twilight. Buddhists, Baptists, Muslims, atheists. We're all struggling here with each other, struggling together. And still, all beings, we're gonna be diamonds some day.

The Doctrine of Sugar

Catherine Allgor

On Ash Wednesday this year, I decided to move from Boston to California to take a new job. Over a glass of wine, I told a friend that I was planning, in the good old American tradition, to re-create myself in the West. "Don't do it," he said.

I told him how nineteenth-century pioneers would sell and give away belongings before they set out on the Overland Trail to California, packing only what they needed for their new life. Of course, that included luxury items that conveyed civilization, objects that no doubt seemed even more significant as the pioneers faced an uncultivated world. But as they traveled, they needed to lighten their loads. They dumped silverware, china, even pianos all along the trail. Purged, the westerners arrived at their new world baptized by hardship, divested of the possessions that bound them to their old one.

My friend nodded. "That's the mistake people make," he said. "They don't realize that they're going to need everything. Even their sins." I rolled the wine in my mouth and thought about what I'd like to leave behind.

When I was a child, Saturday night was fried onions and hamburgers—a glory of flesh after a meatless Friday. After dinner, Daddy would pile us all into the Country Squire wagon and drive us to confession. My memories of the time in the Black Box are like those of most Catholics—vivid, specific, and trite. I was never terrified—after all, this was a weekly event and besides, I had a crush on Father O'Brien—but just nervous enough to want to pee my pants a little. I worried that by not remembering all my sins in accurate quantities, I was inadvertently lying to Father O'Brien and God. But Jesuit training came to my rescue, and I hit on the technique of ending each confession with a request for God to forgive me for "all lies of omission and commission."

Friends who have experienced Protestant adult baptism—the kind with white robes and total immersion—tell me about the unbelievable feeling of renewal and regeneration they felt after that single dramatic event. But I reckon you can't beat that post-Confession feeling I had, every week, as we pulled out of the church parking lot, heading downtown on a Saturday night. Tumbling back and forth between the station wagon seats, we were as lighthearted as Luther, clean-souled and off the hook. And the first act of our new life was going to Hyatt Drugstore, where Daddy bought us candy, three or four bars each to last the week.

Daddy loved candy the way he loved doctrine, with a rigorous joy born of suffering. His stories of the Depression did not focus on the lack of necessaries, though often he had no shoes, and malnutrition, rather than candy, had deformed his lower jaw and teeth. For him, the story of his poverty was his longing for refined sugar. The relatives who took him in after his parents deserted him baked with molasses and tried to pass off raisins as candy, but he wasn't fooled. He had tasted just enough of the real stuff to hate raisins forever, and when he grew up he ate real candy and ice cream. Other dads smoked and drank on a Saturday night, but he lined up with us at the candy racks, blinking in Hyatt's fluorescent light, and made his selection.

I had a sophisticated palate, actually enjoying Good & Plenty and developing a taste for licorice Allsorts. But on Saturday—chocolate. Hershey's with almonds, Calvinist in its harsh pairing of raw nuts and stark chocolate, without the mediating grace of even a layer of caramel. The effete Three Musketeers—sleek, fluid, supple. Sky Bar promised four candy bars in one. Each bar divided into four pouches, one plain fudge, the others filled with caramel, peanut butter, marshmallow fluff. Like most committee efforts this one failed to satisfy—the pockets were too small and the chocolate definitely inferior. But its promise of total fulfillment lured me, and I bit, every time.

We got to eat one of our bars right away in the car, though I often waited until I got home for the first bite. Partly, it was the exquisite agony of pleasure deferred; partly, I wanted to extend the moment of grace and purity. For chocolate was not an unambiguous good. Not forbidden, not a sin, nonetheless when Lent came, it was the first thing to go. Not only for us children, but for Daddy. And we all suffered.

The wine stung the back of my mouth like cheap chocolate. I made a face. What spoils my western saga, I told my friend, was that the newly purged pioneers did not appreciate their baptized state, but set about importing luxury from the East as soon as they could. My friend nodded, as though it was just as he expected. "Have you ever heard the expression 'Old sins cast long shadows?'" he said.

I learned early that Lenten sacrifice was not just about subtracting a pleasure. A candy-less forty days loosened the tie that bound your spirit to your body. You could also gain Lent points by addition —going to early Mass or saying extra rosaries. Taking on pain or discomfort—like standing up to do your homework—and offering it up to the souls in Purgatory also counted. Novitiates began their marriage to Christ by taking on the hardest, most menial jobs, trusting that mortifying the physical self would ready them for ultimate transcendence.

I had absorbed this complexity with the Host I swallowed without chewing, and one Ash Wednesday I announced that I would devote my Lent to learning to make piecrust. My mother looked at me hard and then looked away. Since I could walk, she had been training me for my future life as a good Catholic wife and mother. This training centered on the acquisition of housewifely skills. In the world we lived in, these master skills involved the manipulation of white flour, sugar, and fat. Thus far, I had been a recalcitrant pupil.

But now I went straight home from school every day and sifted flour and experimented with varying combinations of lard, butter, and Crisco. I learned about the crucial action of iced water on flour and fat and the goal of a "short" crust. Sometimes piecrust crumbled through my hands; at other times, it stuck to my fingers. Once it just lumped up, a white blob on crumpled wax paper, stuck to the red Formica counter. "Jesus, Mary, and Joseph!" Getting it into the pan was a whole other skill, but about halfway through Lent, I got it.

The first pie that worked was a cherry pie (Daddy's favorite). The filling was too-sweet, too-red stuff from a jar, but the crust held together as my mother sliced into the pie and lifted the first piece. On the plate, it crumbled at a touch. My mother put down her fork and said, "Good. This is good. I couldn't make this." I baked pie all that Lent. Apple, lemon meringue, coconut custard. For Easter day, I made a big chocolate pie for Daddy and my brothers and sister, and a small raisin pie for Mom and me. She loved raisin pie, but wouldn't make it for herself. "Good. This is good."

When I became a teenager, I stopped baking pie and made my last confession at sixteen, with Father Flanagan. My mother took my piecrust recipe and became a superb pastry maker. Her crusts were so good you forgot the filling. One of my boyfriends actually wept a few tears after tasting her strawberry pie.

In their fifties, my parents became fundamentalist Christians, and, later, became perpetually disappointed when I married a Jew. I made hamantashen for my husband's Hebrew class all through Lent, and on Thanksgiving and Christmas we visited my parents' silent house. My stepdaughter loved the pumpkin pie and unstintingly praised my mother, who glowed, and always sent a pie back home with us—"for later."

I'm a historian, and my job involves the relationship between now and then and later. As a historian and an atheist, I'm a true believer, firmly focused on the human, convinced that the past provides lessons that we can choose and change to fit our lives. And I still don't know what to do with my own history. My parents are thrifty, parsimonious people, pack rats. Their solution was to keep everything and transform it—my father tried to turn suffering into candy, my mother tried to turn me into her dream of a happy woman.

How do I choose what to leave behind and what to transform? Can I choose? Will I lose parts of my past without realizing it? What old pianos await me—out of tune and warped by the sun—when I get to the end of my Overland Trail? Faith. That was left behind long ago. But, I realize, so was sin, or rather, the sense of sin. Though it seems I spent most of my childhood feeling guilty, there was no sin there—not on my part nor on the part of my parents. No sin, no sinners, just shadows I can't shake.

Jesus Is Just Alright

Mark Dery

California is America's cultural hothouse. Maybe it's the state's anything-goes permissiveness, a legacy of its frontier days. Or its historical role as a launch pad for utopian experiments—the last, best hope for a fresh start in a nation consecrated to new beginnings. The state has long been synonymous with America's kookiest cults, wackiest fads, freakiest subcultures, and sickest crimes, not to mention a bumper crop of nano-celebrities and Incredibly Strange Creatures Who Stopped Living and Became Mixed-up Media Zombies, from our national plastic-surgery disaster, Michael Jackson, to Hollywood's unofficial mascot, Angelyne, a mega-bosomed sexpot who resembles a reanimated Jayne Mansfield, brought back to life (or, at least, undeath) through the heroic efforts of a beautician and a taxidermist. As the novelist Paul Bowles once told me, "California brings up strange flowers. It nourishes mutations—human mutations."

Bowles's remark was inspired by his friend Christopher Isherwood's interest in what Bowles called "Eastern philosophies"—an interest Bowles apparently found somewhat curious in an otherwise respectable, upper-class Englishman. After moving to Southern California in 1939, the author of *Goodbye to Berlin* (the inspiration for the musical *Cabaret*) worked as a screenwriter, hobnobbed with a glittering expatriate circle, underwent the usual Californian paradigm shift, and emerged a devout follower of the Hindu sage Swami Prabhavananda.

A few of California's holy men (and, occasionally, women)

have been pure of heart, but most have been grabby of wallet: Werner Erhard of EST, Scientology founder L. Ron Hubbard, Hollywood "spiritual teacher" John-Roger, "Crystal Cathedral" televangelist Robert Schuller. Some have been hairy-eyed nutters, such as Jim Jones of the People's Temple or Marshall Applewhite of the Heaven's Gate cult; others have been lovably loopy, such as the late Ruth Norman, founder of the El Cajon–based Unarius Academy of Science.

Dearly beloved of TV reporters the world over, Norman spoke in a fruity warble and wore jaw-dropping costumes that suggested the Good Witch Glinda on Moonbase Alpha. Norman's "Cosmic Generator" getup was typical: a voluminous skirt festooned with comets and brightly colored planets, a blouse dominated by a massive "sun collar" with glittering extensions (solar flares?), a peaked cap bedecked with tiny lights. Somewhere, Liberace is *shrieking* with envy. In her devotees' eyes, however, Norman was the Archangel Uriel. To her, and her alone, was vouchsafed the mind-shattering revelation that Space Brothers from the Interplanetary Confederation will touch down in El Cajon in 2001, heralding a Renaissance of Spirit that—*hey, wait a minute!*

Obviously, it's easy to mock the failed prophesies of a batty old lady in a mylar gown and tiara, gushing space-cadet flapdoodle to goggle-eyed acolytes. But what about the cosmic log in your own eye, brother? For instance, one of my San Diegan relatives got his ontology steam-cleaned when a higher power communicated to him through an eerily repeated number sequence on his digital clock. Now, he believes in a channeled entity who goes by the suspiciously *Star Trek*-ian name of Kryon, perceives extrasensory "energy frequencies" invisible to most mortals, and keeps his cancer in remission through sheer psychic willpower.

Easy for me to roll my cynical, godless eyes *now*, of course. But long, long ago, in a universe far, far away, when the zeitgeist came in harvest gold, burnt orange, and avocado green, I was a teenage fundie. A fundamentalist. One of the Jesus People. A Jesus Freak. A cross-wearing, Bible-believing, born-again Christian.

It was 1973, and I wasn't the only American teenager with heaven on my mind, as Judas sang, in *Jesus Christ Superstar.* As the religious scholar Stephen Prothero recounts in *American Jesus: How the Son of God Became a National Icon,* the late sixties witnessed the emergence of a countercultural Christianity. "The Beatles sparked a guru vogue when they went as pilgrims to India in 1968," Prothero notes, but for every seeker who embraced Zen or the Buddha, scores more "tuned in to the Bible and took Jesus as their guru. . . . These Jesus fans were the praying wing of the Woodstock nation."

California, where I grew up, was ground zero for the Jesus movement. For most chroniclers of the phenomenon, its genesis begins in 1967, in San Francisco's Haight-Ashbury neighborhood. Joined at the hip to hippiedom, the movement was midwifed by Elizabeth and Ted Wise, twentysomething ex-druggies who opened an evangelical coffeehouse called the Living Room and a Marin-based Christian commune, the House of Acts, modeled on the supposedly communal living style of the early Christians. Rejecting the bring-downs of old-time religion (with its Scared Straight threats of hellfire and its Calvinist doctrine of original sin) and the hypocrisy and hollowness of the only-on-Sunday "Churchianity" they had grown up with, the Wises and their brethren took back the messiah, saving the Savior (as they saw it) from the church.

The countercultural Christ of the Jesus movement was "a drop-out, an outlaw, and a revolutionary who scoffed at the religious establishment of his day," in Prothero's words. A "Wanted" poster popular among Jesus People depicted Christ, looking like a cross between Che Guevara and Mister Zig-Zag, accompanied by the warning that this "typical hippie type—long hair, beard, robe, sandals" was the "notorious leader of an underground liberation movement," wanted by the authorities for "practicing medicine,

winemaking, and food distribution without a license" and "associ-
ating with known criminals, radicals, subversives, prostitutes and
street people." The poster warned, "He is still at large!"

This radical-chic Jesus spoke to the disaffected youth of the day,
to whom the church of their parents seemed as phony and out of
touch as the square suburbanite in *The Graduate* (1967) pompously
offering recent college grad Benjamin Braddock (Dustin Hoffman)
the "friendly advice" that he pursue a career in plastics, the Next Big
Thing. The countercultural Jesus was *one of us*—misunderstood,
hassled by The Man for his radical lifestyle and his rage against
the machine, whether it was the law-and-order Mayor Daleys and
Governor Reagans of the Roman Empire or the spiritually empty
religious sects of his day, the Pharisees and the Sadducees. As well,
the hippie Jesus was every teenager's dream of a cooler-than-God
big brother, someone who understands the changes you're going
through, dude, but never judges, just folds you and the other Jesus
Freaks into one big group hug. Awesome!

In 1973, I was one of those disaffected teens, with the requisite
slouch, witchy Charlie Manson stare, and David Cassidy shag gone
feral. When I told my parents that I didn't want to be dragged to our
Lutheran church anymore, I was duly informed that churchgoing
was mandatory, but that I could attend any *Christian* church of my
choice. Naturally, I picked the fringiest church in our San Diego
County suburb, just to set their hair on fire. Since there weren't any
snake handlers in the Chula Vista Yellow Pages, I chose a Baptist
church that had a Friday night "coffeehouse" youth service.

Despite its name, nothing but bread and Welch's grape juice
(communion wine for minors) was on the menu. Nonetheless,
the service rocked: a long-haired electric band cranked out full-
throated versions of hymns such as Sydney Carter's "Lord of the
Dance," people prayed with palms uplifted like the disciples in
medieval tapestries, and somebody spoke in tongues, a cascade of
spooky-sounding glossolalia that lifted the hair on the back of my

neck. In an instant, my irony turned to ecstasy. Faster than you could say *Maranatha!* (Aramaic for "Our Lord cometh," a New Testament catchphrase appropriated by those of us who *knew* the Second Coming was right around the corner), I had Accepted Jesus as My Personal Lord and Savior.

For the rest of that year and much of the next, I was in a state of grace. I read the get-down version of the Living Bible, *The Way.* Illustrated with black-and-white *Life* magazine–type photos—U.S. grunts in Vietnam, a pimply hippie holding a cookie jar marked "opium"—and explicated with rap-session commentary from the editors ("We watch friends trip off into despair, finding no wholeness, no health, no meaning. Is there a way to *life?*"), it was the kind of Bible Linc on *The Mod Squad* might have read, if he'd found God (and if his series hadn't been canceled that year). When I wasn't rejoicing in God's Word, I read inspirational books such as David Wilkerson's *The Cross and the Switchblade* (1963), about a preacher who beards inner-city gang members in their den, with only his faith as his armor; saw Christian movies such as *The Hiding Place* (1975), about the Dutch Holocaust survivor Corrie ten Boom, whose belief in God sustained her through the horrors of the concentration camps; and wondered what I'd wear to the Rapture, so thrillingly described in *The Late Great Planet Earth* (1970), pop eschatologist Hal Lindsey's runaway bestseller.

By '74, however, I, like many of the Jesus People, was losing my religion. In retrospect, the movement's glorious ascension into the national media consciousness marked the beginning of the end, as is almost inevitably the case with subcultural phenomena. In 1973, the Living Bible was the bestselling nonfiction book of the year (as it had been the year before), moviegoers were thronging to *Jesus Christ Superstar* and *Godspell,* "Jesus Is Just Alright" by the Doobie Brothers was climbing up the charts, and Chuck Smith, the youth-friendly pastor of Calvary Chapel in Costa Mesa, California, was baptizing kids by the hundreds in the nearby Pacific Ocean. But by decade's end, the late, great awakening of the early seventies was a fading memory, consigned to the dustbin of pop theology along with cultural relics such as the hippie Bible *The Message,* whose Mister Natural messiah taught his disciples to pray, "Our Father in Heaven, reveal who you are. Set the world right; do what's best—as above, so below. Keep us alive with three square meals. Keep us forgiven with you and forgiving others. Keep us safe from ourselves and the Devil. You're in charge! You can do anything you want! You're ablaze in beauty! Yes. Yes. Yes" (Matthew 6:9–13).

Bit by bit, the fire in my mind died out. The trouble was Christianity, not Christ. "More than any other group in American history," Prothero argues, the Jesus People "boiled Christianity down to Jesus alone," a radical doctrine known as *solus Jesus.* Delving into the scriptures expanded my focus, beyond the movement's tight close-up on Christ. With that wide-angle perspective came the disconcerting realization that social conservatism was hardwired into Christianity, from the Bronze Age homophobia of the Old Testament lawgivers to the toxic misogyny of the appalling Paul. In a divine irony, the Bible was the poisoned apple on my Tree of Knowledge.

Then, too, as my mental universe expanded, the born-again worldview felt more and more like the intellectual pinhole it was, too constricted to admit the dangerous ideas and perverse pleasures of secular culture, from *National Lampoon* to *A Clockwork Orange, Ziggy Stardust* to *The Omega Man* (that movie's way-heavy use of Charlton Heston as a Christ figure notwithstanding).

One Friday night in 1974, I broke bread at one of my church's communal households. Touted as a model of Christian living, it impressed me, up close, as a theocratic horror. The commune was headed by church elders whose edicts were treated as holy writ (though not without the occasional grumble from the insufficiently humble of spirit). They micromanaged people's lives, appropriated and allocated the monies earned by those who worked, even (rumor had it) instructed husbands to spank insubordinate wives.

Everyone ate in phlegmatic silence, unresponsive to my conversational probes about current events. Suddenly, a cadaverous Richard Nixon materialized on a nearby TV, looking nigh unto death as he announced that he would resign the presidency, "effective at noon tomorrow." The son of staunch McGovernites, I was in ecstasy; the prime-time mocking and scourging of the loathsome Nixon was divine intervention, if ever anything was. Incredibly, my sullen tablemates ate on, unmoved; worldly affairs were of no consequence to those whose minds were fixed on the Kingdom of Heaven. Looking into their gazeless eyes, unclouded by doubt, I realized I was no longer one of *them*. Better to reign in hell than serve in heaven, I thought, pedaling home on my bike.

Since then, I've relived Paul's conversion on the road to Damascus in reverse. When the scales fell from my eyes, I was transformed from true believer to tireless scourge of everything that hates free will or fears the skeptical question, especially those viruses of the mind known as religious beliefs that (with apologies to Tom Paine) shock our reason or injure our humanity. As a writer, I've fancied myself a cross between the devil's hitman, Ambrose Bierce, and the Darwinian evolutionist T. H. Huxley riding into battle against Bishop Wilberforce, champion of biblical literalism.

Still, tireless scourging is thirsty work; after a few decades, the whip hand tires. Of course, I can't undo my unbelief, rewind the movie of my intellectual life so I fall from grace in reverse, back into faith. Sometimes, though, I remember what the mysterium tremendum (or at least the seventies Southern Californian version thereof) felt like. Meditating on the portrait of Christ I'd taped to my bedroom wall, a detail from a Renaissance painting, I'd pray until tears ran down my face, pained by a toothache sweetness that can only be called love, something between eros and agape. Even now, my Kevlar cynicism isn't proof against the nostalgia that tugs at me when I hear Yvonne Elliman singing "Everything's Alright" from *Jesus Christ Superstar*—nostalgia for a lost time when people walked into the ocean and came out reborn, convinced they could build a revolution not on ideology, but on love. "California," said Christopher Isherwood, "is a tragic land—like Palestine, like every promised land."

The Lost Temple
of the Pennytitties

Peter Manseau and Jeff Sharlet

According to James Crocker, Tucumcari, New Mexico, is a town named for the Indian word for a woman's breast, but you won't find many people willing to talk about it. Crocker, however, knows a thing or two about the power of telling stories. He's the town photographer and camera shop owner, and when we stopped in to buy a disposable camera last week, he happily boasted that with his pictures he wrote and rewrote the history of the town. Two years ago, for example, when the town's sad-sack high school football team missed the state title by an inch, he printed photos of the team and labeled them champions. "Who in a hundred years will be able to say otherwise?" he asked. He bounced with excitement over his deception.

We told him we were traveling and looking for stories about believers. He pointed us to Route 104, which consists of 104 miles of high plains and mesas between Tucumcari and Las Vegas, New Mexico, and nothing else. Well, some other things.

"Got some folks out there who still do human sacrifice," he said.

If we were taking 104, he told us, we should be sure to stop at the "Temple of the Pennytitties," where "Mexicans" sacrifice their prettiest virgins on a concrete slab in the back. Then we should drive past the turnoff road for the nuclear hideout of the Scientologists; they come and go by helicopter and don't maintain the road to keep everybody out. The few that do brave the bumpy ride or the ten-mile hike, the Scientologists menace with guns. He knew dozens of local men who'd helped build the compound and they swore that several times a day the Scientologists would make all the workers close their eyes and plug their ears while they performed secret ceremonies.

Tucumcari itself had just as much intrigue. A group called LU-LAC, he swore, was trying to "brown" the town as part of one unified Brown nation from Patagonia all the way up to—well, his town of Tucumcari, as a matter of fact. He knew that sounded unlikely, but he had much photographic evidence. To wit: he produced a photograph of the town in 1947, population 12,700. Today?—5,200. Why, 3,000 had disappeared in just the last six years alone, ever since the soldiers of LULAC arrived with their "book on how to take over towns" and "Mexicanized" the city council with their "third-class style of government."

Crocker showed us a photograph of his father's house and said that across the street had stood a dancehall owned by a little roly-poly Mexican man known as the "Mayor of Northside," for his ability to send votes in any direction like he was a strong wind. When the photographer's father died, the Mayor of Northside himself paid a visit.

Crocker puffed out his belly and hunched his shoulders and affected a remarkably nuanced and subtle Mexican accent: "'Your daddy was the only Anglo I ever liked. I don't want nobody to know it, but I loved him as a good man. So I want to give you something in his memory. I'm going to tell you the secret of how I became Mayor of Northside. You want to know that?'"

Crocker bugged out his eyes. "Hell, everybody wants to know that."

"'It was the coming of the voting machines,'" he said, "'the finest invention of my life. Election day, my men, they go into the voting booths, mark the levers for my choices with a bit of axle grease. Never goes away, but stains whatever touches it. Then we go outside and announce that we were paying five dollars to everybody for being such good citizens by voting. Hold out your hand, we say, and when they did we'd check for the axle grease. If it was there, they got the five dollars; if not, they got a beating.'"

Crocker broke character to grin at this. Whether the story was his invention or the Mayor of Northside's, we couldn't tell. He slumped and went back to his accent.

"'And that's how I convinced the people of Northside that I could see everything,'" Crocker said. "'And that, my friend, is why they made me mayor.'"

"Now I'm counting on you boys not to write about what I'm telling you," Mister James Crocker of Ledeane Photography in Tucumcari, New Mexico, told us. "Those Mexicans will burn my store down. They'll kill me. They'll pour out my developing chemicals. They'll take me out on 104 and leave me without any water." He smiled nervously. "I have no choice but to play along, you see. I let them cheat me. I make their pictures for cheap, cheaper even than Wal-Mart. These people, they're so irresponsible, they don't even care."

Crocker pointed to a bin of white photo envelopes. "Those are all unclaimed." Half of them contained photos of white people, people who'd fled; the other half were of Latinos, and who knows what'd become of them.

Just then a pretty Latina woman came into the store. The photographer brightened like the sun popping up over the horizon and proceeded to call her all kinds of nice names, and we slipped out the door and onto 104. It was more or less as he'd described: a few very modest ranch settlements, a handful of stone houses, and a "resort" around a lake that from the highway looked like pale green stone slowly creeping across the grassy desert; its shores were rimmed with salt.

Before long we found a tin-roofed church we thought might be the Temple of the Pennytitties, but when an old Latino couple appeared, they said it was just an ordinary Catholic Church: ten or twelve people served by a priest who sometimes came from Las Vegas. They never knew when he'd arrive, so when he did, they'd call the congregation and sit silently while old worshippers drove an hour or more to church.

We got back in the car and drove on. For forty miles or so we drifted behind an eighteen-wheeler hauling coffins for a funeral supply company ("Drive Safely; Heaven can wait," the back of the trailer read), and finally found it: the Temple of the Pennytitties. A few hundred yards off the road a tiny building perched on a boulder. Inside, Santeria candles burned, freshly lit though there was no one around. From the ceiling, over a statue of the Virgin Mary, bundles of feathers and bones hung by strings of twine. Beside the little building, like the fence around a horse corral, was a thirty-foot string of giant wooden beads tied off in a triangle by a big wooden cross—a giant's rosary, apparently prayed by marching around it.

Behind the temple stood a concrete platform, high up the steep mountainside, that really did look as if it was designed for human sacrifice, for Abraham to give Isaac the knife. But then, that's what every altar is, and an altar is all this was, one belonging not to murderous Pennytitties, but to a Catholic brotherhood called the Penitentes, who continue the medieval practice of self-flagellation during lent. Bloodthirsty perhaps, but only for their own.

Seeing the altar we knew for certain what we'd supposed before: that the photographer's stories of human sacrifice were, like all his tall tales, racist libels—lies made "true" in the telling, like his legend of the winning football team. We knew now that this "temple" was just an ordinary shrine to the Virgin Mary, placed here to mark the entrance to the Sangre de Cristo Mountains. What we didn't know, and what we only later asked ourselves, was why we looked for blood.

The Only Jew for Miles

Gordon Haber

On a bright but astonishingly cold morning, at the ungodly hour of 10 a.m., I was shivering on the train from Krakow to the nearby city of Czestochowa. I had taken a kind of commuter train for students, on which the railway authorities had cut back on luxuries like heat and comfortable seats and toilets. And I, a man well into his thirties, felt out of place among all the kids frowning over their textbooks and text messages. Even the nun across the aisle, bent over her rosary, had more reason to be here. For Czestochowa is known for two things: students, and the Black Madonna, the miraculous painting of the Mother of God.

Some say that the painting—a graceful portrait of Mary with the infant Jesus—was painted by Saint Luke. Art historians describe it as a Byzantine icon that was completely repainted in the fifteenth century. Either way, the Black Madonna is purported to have cured the blind and the deaf, healed the sick and the lame. Her intercession is said to have helped the Poles against every country on their long list of invaders, most notably when Jasna Gora, the monastery where she resides, repelled a massive Swedish siege in 1655. The power of the Black Madonna even worked against the Communists. In 1920, the Soviets were close to Warsaw, but they threw down their weapons and fled when her face appeared in the sky.

Did I believe any of this? Not a word. I'm a Reform Jew, which can be described as someone who loves God, tradition, and shellfish. But even in reproductions—which I had seen in homes all over Poland—Mary projects an undeniable serenity. And apparently lots of Poles believe in the power of the Miraculous Painting. Over five million people visit the monastery each year, thousands making the pilgrimage on foot. Even if I was a skeptical Jew, I was here to see Poland on its own terms, to try and get beyond the usual Jewish or American stereotypes. There would be no understanding Poland without understanding Polish Catholicism, so I realized that I had to make my own mini-pilgrimage to see the Madonna for myself.

The train pulled into Czestochowa, and I filed out with the nun and the students. I had originally planned to walk up to Jasna Gora, for at least a small taste of an actual pilgrimage, but it was just too cold. After only a few seconds outside, my ears burned with it, and even my eyelashes felt frozen. As my own religious temperament precludes suffering of any kind, I found a cab in front of the station.

In most Polish cities, the older buildings look better than the newer ones. An eighteenth-century church appears as if it was put up last year and repainted last month, but the Communist-era structures—the boxy concrete office blocks and the boxy concrete apartment blocks—look patched and peeled, with an invariable patina of soot. This can get depressing. The architecture constantly reminds you of an imposed ideology, of drabness and despair. Most Polish cities, however, also have some architectural marvel, some astonishingly well-maintained edifice that delights the eyes. In Czestochowa, it was Jasna Gora.

In Polish, *jasna gora* means "bright mountain." The monastery is atop a large, sloping hill; and its stolid tower, with its oxidized green dome, is visible from miles away. Below the tower, the cluster of domes and spires brought to mind a compact city of God. But with its massive walls and sharply angled bulwarks, Jasna Gora is really more of a fortress—which probably helped along that miracle against the Swedes.

I paid the driver and he pointed out the entrance for me, through a series of ornate sixteenth-century gates. With sudden excitement—I was going to see the Black Madonna!—I walked quickly upwards. It seemed as if I had picked a good day for my mini-pilgrimage, as there were only a few dozen people going in or out. That is, until I reached the top and saw, among the dense jumble of baroque architecture, hundreds of teenagers. They were all standing around to no purpose, save for trying to look cool and getting in my way. Over their heads I saw a sign for the information center, and I pressed my way through.

It was like any other busy office, with workers on the phone or hustling in and out, papers in hand, except they were all nuns. One came forward.

"Good day," I said, which was, I would later learn, a faux pas. One in supposed to greet a member of the Polish clergy by saying *Niech bedzie pochwalony Jezus Christus,* "Let Jesus Christ be blessed," to which the priest or nun replies, *Na wieki wiekow amen,* "Forever and ever, amen." It's just as well I didn't know this at the time, because I wouldn't have been comfortable saying it. But it does explain why the nun had a touch of frost in her voice when she said, "I'm listening, sir."

"I'd like to see the painting," I said, thinking: I'm speaking to a nun. Never did that before.

"Of course," said the nun. "But today there is a youth group from all over Poland, so the Chapel of Our Lady will be very crowded. It's almost noon—if the gentleman can wait until two, there will be fewer people at Mass."

Mass? Why would I want to go to Mass? Then I realized that from her perspective, no one would want to be at Jasna Gora and *not* go to Mass. Not for the first time in Poland, I was the only Jew for miles.

I thanked the nun and looked over the map she had given me. There was a museum and a treasury; or, if I liked, I could schlep up to the top of the tower. I was here to see the Black Madonna, so it was the noon Mass for me.

Jasna Gora is a bit of a maze, and it was slow going through the crowds. I threaded my way through the throngs, glimpsing the occasional priest or gray-robed monks. The walls were high and gray. Their blankness looked strange to me—outside of the monastery, any wall would be covered with graffiti.

I came to a large chamber with a vaulted ceiling. The chapel was straight ahead, but I stopped when I saw that a nearby wall was decorated with crutches, perhaps fifty of them. Set among the crutches were pendants shaped like hearts, hands, and legs. Another wall had triangular pendants with eyes on them: strange, disembodied eyes, alone or in pairs. These were all offerings, of course, evidence of individual miracles or the least the desire for one. Part of me found this bizarre, but I had to admit that it also gave me a chill. Each silver heart, each cane, represented some intense emotion: supplication or belief or perhaps a desperate and final form of hope.

The students were flowing in, and a song began from up in the gallery, an acoustic guitar and a chorus of young voices. And I felt another chill when a man on crutches went by, with the stuttery gait of someone with muscular dystrophy. His friend went before him, gently tapping the shoulders of those who blocked their way. I trailed them past ornately carved altars of wood and marble that brimmed with gold leaf. The pews were packed, the students coming in droves, hundreds already kneeling in fervent prayer. This was the place: the spiritual heart of a nation. Everyone gathered here was Polish and Catholic; in the Black Madonna they had a symbol to draw them together and closer to God, a way of combining religion and patriotism. For them, Mary was *alive,* bearing an infinite capacity for love and tenderness. And yes, she loved the Poles most of all, for their centuries of sacrifice echoed her own. I was a secularized American Jew; I believed in a remote and unknowable God. Still, I closed my eyes and I asked Him to heal the sick man, to let his crutches go up on the wall, and to let me be here to see it. At the very least, it would make a really good story.

But where was the Black Madonna? There was an ornate black gate at the far end of the chamber; through the bars I saw the Chapel of Our Lady. I pushed my way through the crowds. The chapel had an imposing ebony altar with elaborate silver accents; fresh flowers were everywhere. Men in spotless blue uniforms, with gold braids that ran from an epaulet to a buttonhole, busied themselves with dustpans and whisk brooms. One of them even had a dustbuster.

Again, where was the Black Madonna? On one side of the gate, a line—or what passed for one in this country—was forming. The pilgrims were kneeling before a door in the gate, crossing themselves, then shuffling toward a low opening to the left of the altar, then, still on their knees, emerging from the other side. Maybe she was back there, *behind* the altar, and you were supposed to see her on your knees? When in Rome, I thought, and slipped between two young women. When it was my turn, I knelt and trundled forward.

I noticed very quickly that marble is hard on the knees. Presumably, that was the point—a Christian pilgrimage is supposed to have some echo of Jesus's agony. But I was a Jew, for God's sake; what the hell was I doing? I rounded the corner behind the altar. A narrow hallway, a profusion of glittering plaques—one, I saw, from the firemen of Gdansk. But no painting. No *painting*. The pain was awful and I wanted to get up. No, I told myself. Show some respect. After all, Mary is a Jewish mother. But I was weak. Hoping that I wasn't committing blasphemy, I got to my feet and proceeded in a half-crouch, trying not to fall onto the girl in front of me. And I thought of the girl behind me, who had come all this way, and all she could see was my big, American ass.

Oh shit, the next corner. Back to my knees, hands clasped to keep them from flailing. Finally, after thirty seconds that seemed like an hour, I was past the altar gate. I hobbled off to a corner to collect myself.

The blood slowly returned to my legs. Somehow I had gone half the distance to the exit. I didn't have the energy to force myself forward again. I looked around for the man on crutches, but there was no finding him in this crowd. When I looked back at the altar four priests had appeared and a bell rang, reverberating majestically, and that song—which had been going for so long that I had ceased to notice it—was replaced by a flourish of trumpets and a drum roll. I felt the collective excitement (yes, the hairs stood up on the back of my neck), and something moved at the center of the altar. A silver screen that raised to reveal—the Black Madonna.

I thought: you schmuck! How could you have missed the screen? Squinting, I tried to discern some detail of the painting, maybe the famous scars from a Hussite's sword. But at that distance I could only see the vivid blue of her cowl and her face as a dark smudge.

I felt a sudden emptiness around me: everyone, perhaps a thousand people, had knelt. Everyone, that is, except me. And just as I made it to my knees, everyone stood again. I did the same, feeling like an idiot. I was attracting attention, just a few curious stares, but I didn't want to distract anyone during the service. Better to leave. Now that I knew the drill, I could return early for the next Mass and position myself right by the gate.

I made my way out of the monastery and headed down the hill. The ferocious cold had eased somewhat, and it felt good to walk, as my knees were still smarting from that trip around the altar. Below the monastery there was a lovely park. Old women in heavy coats—the hallmark of all Slavic countries—walked their dogs or chatted on the benches.

At the bottom of the hill, a wide, tree-lined boulevard began —the Avenue of the Sainted Virgin Mary. While waiting for the light to change, I noticed that the windowless side of the building across the street was covered with graffiti. Reappearing among the usual scribblings—"Tomek was here," "Krakow Wisla Football Hooligans"—there was a pictogram. It was a stick-figure drawing of a scaffold, like in the hangman game; but dangling in place of a head, there was a six-pointed star.

Now, I had grown almost used to anti-Semitic graffiti, to the point where I could be amused by how often some cretin misspelled a simple Polish phrase like "Jews to the gas." And, although I saw this sort of thing fairly often, it wasn't every day; and I didn't feel that it reflected the beliefs of 35 million Poles.

But none of these mitigating factors occurred to me when I saw the hanged *Mogen Dovid*, because the past few weeks had been a strange and infuriating time. For example, a Krakovian architect told me that Daniel Libeskind had won the World Trade Center design competition because of the "Jewish lobby." And I had seen a book called "the Polish Holocaust," which contained chapters on the "Judaization of Christianity" and "Jews in the Catholic Church." And I had also seen a seventeenth-century painting that depicted Jews slitting the throats of Christian babies and collecting the blood for matzo. And in Belzec, where my grandfather's family had been gassed, I saw a fat little man let his dog piss in the woods, among the mass graves of a hundred thousand Jews.

So when I saw the repeated images of the hanged Jewish star in Czestochowa, all I thought was this: "These *fucking* Poles. They'll *never* learn." And I knew that I wouldn't be going back to Jasna Gora for the two o'clock Mass. Instead, I wanted to—I *had* to—do something Jewish.

On the avenue the sidewalks were busy and the shops were full. Poles, going about their business, while my stomach burned with anger. I found a taxi line and got in the first car. The driver was about my age, with ginger hair and a mustache; he listened politely as I asked, in my execrable Polish, if there was a Jewish cemetery in Czestochowa.

"Yes," he said.

"Good," I said. I asked him to drive me there, to keep the meter running while I prayed, and then to take me to the train station. He looked taken aback, but to his credit he recovered quickly.

"No problem," he said. "I think it's near the steelworks, but I'll have to ask."

I fished out my notebook, where I had stashed a copy of the Kaddish, the Jewish prayer for the dead. Traveling through southern Poland, I had seen so many sites of Jewish death that I had taken to carrying the prayer around with me.

Meanwhile, the driver had turned the car onto the avenue and gotten on the radio. The dispatcher didn't know the way, and neither did another driver. Then an older voice came on and said, "Take the Avenue of the Sainted Virgin to the bridge. Make the second right after the heating plant, then go exactly two and one half kilometers straight ahead. The road gets bad there so take it slow. You'll see some houses at a crossroads and a little store. Stop there and ask directions."

My driver got off the radio.

"Where is the sir from?" he asked, using the circuitously polite third person.

"New York."

"And the sir's family is from Czestochowa?"

"No, from Jaslo, in the Carpathians."

"So . . . the sir has a relative buried in the Jewish cemetery?"

"No. I want to go because I think . . . no people for long time."

"A-ha," he said, with a nod. "A long time without visitors, right? Okay, we'll get you there."

We came to the crossroads, and he waved over a dumpling-shaped woman with an alarming mustache. I was suddenly tense, expecting—what? That she would send us in the wrong direction? Or point and shriek like Donald Sutherland in *Invasion of the Body Snatchers*?

"Straight ahead to the fence," she said. "Then the sir will have to walk. Make a left and follow the river, oh, for about a kilometer. If you see the bridge you've gone too far."

"Thank you," I said.

"You're welcome," she said. "Good luck."

A minute later we pulled up to the fence. It was heavily wooded to the left; to the right were a couple of houses that looked like they had never seen better days. Not five miles from Czestochowa, and it felt like I was deep in rural Poland.

"Take your time," the driver said. "I'll be here."

I ducked through a break in the fence. Ahead, across a dry riverbed, was an outbuilding of the steelworks; I turned left and followed the path. Walking quickly, I scanned the woods. There was a high shoulder between the path and the trees—I couldn't see much through the undergrowth. When I saw the bridge, a simple concrete structure, I turned around again.

Twice I scrambled up into the woods, looking for some indication of the cemetery. I was hoping for a glimpse of a rusted fence or the hint of a disused path, but there was nothing. I was filled with a sense of futility. I had failed to commune with the Black Madonna; I had failed to find the Jewish cemetery; and I had failed to grow the thicker skin that I would need to get through the months I still had left in Poland. I faced the woods and said Kaddish into the air.

Banana Slug Psalm

Meera Subramanian

Maple. Ant. Robin red breast. These were the names that came first. I would sit in the grass and watch the fat black ants that had made a castle in the crook of the maple tree that lorded it over the front lawn of my New Jersey home. I could stare for hours at the colony's endless marching cavalcade pouring in and out of a crack no larger than the nub of a well-used pencil at the tree's rippled gray base. Overhead, robins appeared each year right around my birthday to decorate the tree's bud-filled branches. They would hop across the well-tended lawn, then stand still, listening through their feet, my mother told me, for the sound of earthworms moving underground. It was a timeless time.

By twenty-one, I'd fled the East Coast and landed in the Pacific Northwest, a cross-country move with a man who was all wrong to a place that was all right. Forest, mountain, and sea fused together in this hidden corner of my country, where there were new names to discover. Old Man's Beard. Douglas fir. Maidenhair fern. I learned the names the way my (once a) Baptist mother had dutifully learned the gospels of Matthew, Mark, Luke, and John. Western red cedar. Trillium. Pacific giant salamander. I learned the names the way my (once a) Hindu father had reluctantly recited the thousand names of God as a small boy in India—Krishna, Kali, Rama, Vishnu . . .

My parents split the difference of their disbelief and joined the Unitarian Church to give my brother and me some semblance of religion. But I was a stubborn child, resisting any notion of God, fighting even the Unitarians' mild form of anti-church, with its lectures instead of liturgy. I saved my reverence for ants and robins, for the wriggling unseen worms.

In Seattle, a friend who called himself Woodsy gave me a copy of Henry David Thoreau's *Walden.* Peering through the door of Thoreau's cabin revealed a transcendentalist world filled with wayward Unitarians like myself whom I had somehow missed in church. Armed with their words, I ventured out of the city with a heavy backpack into those western woods, into the tonic of wilderness, where I found a labyrinth hidden in the forest floor, along a path of broken sticks and banana slugs. As long as my hand, as thick as two fingers held tightly together, the yellow slugs, spotted brown— they really do look like bananas, just this side of rotten—slid across an untended layer of leaf litter a millennium deep, leaving their gelatinous mark upon the world. The silence of the big trees—or was it the reverberations of slug song?—lured me into the forest, where I lost my way with no intention of being found. "Within the woods," wrote Ralph Waldo Emerson, "a man casts off his years and becomes a child, returns to reason and faith and feels that no calamity can befall him which nature cannot repair." I was under the maple tree again.

Three years after I arrived in Seattle imagining I was some kind of pioneer looking for adventure, my friend Evan came to the Emerald City because it had a top-notch cancer research center. I had never not known Evan. Our parents had befriended each other before I was born. When our ages were still in the single digits, Evan and I caught lightning bugs together in my front yard under the ant-filled maple tree and let them loose in the living room as our parents drank wine on the back porch. I thought maybe one day we'd be married. Instead, we grew up. I went west and he went east, to busk in the streets of Paris and fall in love with a Russian. When he arrived in Seattle, the doctors sealed Evan in a sterile room and gave him less than fifty–fifty odds that every last leukemia cell would be vanquished. His wife scowled at them as she held the hand of their young son.

I didn't know how to pray, so I gardened. I lived in a spacious and creaky old house perched on the top of Queen Anne Hill, one of Seattle's many small mountains. Between hospital visits I ripped up a chunk of my lawn when the landlord wasn't looking and knelt in the dirt.

Look here, I can see it still. I have in my hand a mottled piece of the universe, pitted with deep holes and peaked points. It is so small I can barely hold on to it between my two fingers as I press it into the dirt. A beet seed. A tiny world. A sphere of possibilities. It needs soil, light, water, air. It is not so different from Evan or his son. It is not so different from me.

When the bone marrow transplant didn't take, Evan returned to New Jersey, with his family, to his family, to the hometown we'd shared. The robins must have been arriving when Evan died, three weeks before his twenty-seventh birthday, which was two years and sixteen days before mine. His time stopped, while mine continued. I returned to the soil and the dirt to ground me.

My beet seed grew. It sent up leaves that were deep green with blood-red veins. It formed a rough round bulb underground that I dug up with my fingers when the fall rains came. I cooked it and ate it and it turned my pee pink. It wasn't enough. After Evan's death, I was greedy. I wanted more than a backyard garden and weekend backpacking trips; I wanted the big trees, the banana slugs—my forest, my refuge. I drove south, to the end of a dirt road in Oregon where I walked through a grape arbor at the heart of a two-acre garden cradled by towering Douglas fir trees. I emerged from the arbor with the sweet and sour taste of grapes on my tongue and a certainty that I did not want to leave, that I could never return to the pace and lifestyle of a city dweller.

But I did. Eight years later, I wrangled new meaning out of the old texts, Thoreau and Emerson and Muir, as I gave them away, along with the garden tools I had accumulated and a flock of chickens that included a golden hen named Honey I had raised from a chick. "I have learned that the swiftest traveler is he that goes afoot," wrote Thoreau. I twisted the words to justify my decision to leave my forest and move to New York City. I hoped that the god of dirt and trees would remain in my marrow. That the transplant had taken, and I, too, could be a sojourner in civilized life for just a while, just long enough to learn yet another language, which I found myself hungry for again. An insatiable appetite for new words. Q train. Chinatown. Journalism school.

Days before I left, as the moon reached its fullness in a sky littered with stars that I would no longer see, my friends and I disappeared into the woods one last time. We hiked in at dusk, setting up camp on the edge of a dark lake. I slipped off my sweaty clothes and sank into the cold black water. I felt the salamanders slipping away like mercury as lake mud squished between my toes.

The next day, we descended down the steep ravine where Opal Lake spilled into Opal Creek. We were in search of a tree that stood apart for its size even amidst the surrounding grove of giants. Below us, tree roots intertwined, feeding off fungi and rhizomes and an endless supply of water from cloud and creek. Soil, light, water, air. We wrestled through four-foot ferns and then scrambled to the top of downed trees that created superhighways through the thicket. I have heard them when they topple, with a deep thunderous sundering sound, the sky separating from the earth—their fallen bodies settling to serve as nursery logs for the next generation. All together, the young and the old, the healthy and the fallen, form the only church I've ever felt at home in.

We found the tree—a fir wolfy with age, cloaked in lichen—and collapsed into the soft earth, looking up into infinity from its base. From there on the ground, from the vantage of an unbeliever, I imagined that this is what finding God must be like. Or rather, not finding but feeling found. Falling into something as timeless as a slug path, with hidden meanings revealed in the pattern of broken sticks. A coming home, even as I prepared to leave. My friends and I rose, to see if we could circle the tree, all four of us with arms stretched taut, faces pressed against the rough bark, linking our hands to form a current. That's what God is, right? Something so big that you, alone, can't wrap your arms around it. Something that stays with you, no matter where you go. Right?

Seeing Things

Bia Lowe

. . . and then your arms miraculously found me.
Suddenly the sky turned pale.
I could see the midnight sun.

JOHNNY MERCER

Some years ago I went with my brother to see an IMAX film about
life in the sea. It was a spectacle in 3-D, the screen one hundred feet
high. My brother and I sat in the huge theater, with 3-D visored
helmets over our heads. We must have looked like space travelers,
vintage Buck Rogers, ready to scale the night sky.

In the depths above us, clouds of metallic mackerel, drawers
and drawers of silverware, sliced through the cobalt water. Thousands of squid spawned, then died, their tissuelike corpses tossing
on the ocean floor. Throngs of creatures careered and dove, feasted
and rose. The action was larger than life, a vision of enormities,
galactic entities soaring across the deep.

Here is the part I can never forget: a legion of spiny sea stars,
seemingly fashioned out of pastel pipe cleaners, scrambled to escape
a giant sea star. Like animated tumbleweeds, each personalized by
its own ache to survive, they scurried to outrun the colossus bearing
down. In the frantic scramble I began to feel a serious dread, as if
I too were one of the spidery creatures. They were hands dragging
themselves along the ocean floor, their appendages gripped and
crawled—so many fingerlike limbs trying to amble faster, so much
unsuccessful effort. Ironically the whole escapade was impossibly
beautiful, the spindly froth of kicks and curls was like a puppeteer's

chorus line. The red star was an indiscriminate killer. It mowed and devoured, and kept on mowing.

Why did this vision undo me? Where in my soul had I known such ultimate resignation . . . or such tyranny? Were these entities lodged in my limbic system, the atavistic Titans of eat-or-be-eaten? I constellated some terrible meaning out of that footage. I saw something in those stars.

A constellation is an event in the mind, a configuration, a grouping of random occurrences, lassoed by the viewer into an image. Light travels from a few bright suns to our eyes, photons settle like dust motes onto our retinas, and we construct an assemblage, bigger and more congruent than the sum of its parts. And if there is no one in the woods to perceive it, it never happened. "To constellate" is what we do. It is the reason I write, to aggregate disparate elements, to configure a similarity, to essay meaning. It is also the reason you are now reading. It is the course and purpose of our flinting synapses.

The seven brightest stars in the constellation Ursa Major compose the Big Dipper, otherwise known as the Plough, the Chariot, the Drinking Gourd. This first constellation I ever identified as a child is still always the first that I see. Last August, Sinnead, the young girl who lives across the road from me in Ireland, peered up into the night sky and, pointing to that configuration, exclaimed, "Look! The Sauce Pan!"

Because the ancient Arab astronomers were the most thorough in the task of naming the heavens, the stars in my connect-the-dots pot have Arab names. Alkaid is the first star in the panhandle. Where a cook's thumb might go, at the curve in the grip, is actually a binary star, celestial Siamese twins, Mizar and Alcor. Alioth continues the line of the handle to the rim. Megrez at the rim of the pot down to Phecda at the base. . . . Phecda to Merak at the bottom of the pan . . . then Merak up to Dubhe at the lip. Voilà! A line from Merak to Dubhe extends to the North Star. Which is how, by following the Drinking Gourd, American slaves were able to plot their way to freedom in the North.

What human could amble out from her home, be it cave or condo, gape up at the star-strewn night, and not configure the constellations? Who could peer into that fathomless glitter and not hallucinate a form, a face? The sky demands our projections.

Love, too, incites our imaginations. Its promise and mystery hover out of reach like a prize hidden behind a curtain. Beyond that veil we envision a world of enchantment and terror. Celestial seraphs and submarine phantoms enact our primal psychic dramas. The beloved, the object of our desiring, is continually transmuted by our imaginations, one minute a goddess, the next a gorgon. Who is that woman? Indeed who am I? How can one take the trance—transference, transmogrification—out of loving? Can we see the beloved free and clear of all our gobbledygook? Free from the habit of finding her both ruthlessly, and rapturously, divine? How, if sight is ever restored to us, do we know the other?

Imagine for a moment a tale of such a paradox. You are an adventurer, a sailor, drawn to a shore by a woman's beautiful soprano. You are desperate to find the angel whose melody pulses like a beacon from the harbor. You moor your ship as night falls, and follow her song. At last you come to a tower surrounded by brambles, her candlelit chamber like the moon against the starry night. You search the undergrowth in vain for a doorway at the base of the tower. And then you hear the other voice: "Let me up, you insufferable cunt!" The beautiful singing stops, and in its place is a rasp like rough stones ground into gravel. "It is time for your dinner, bitch. Let your hair down!" What monster could make such a fearsome racket? "Now! Or I swear I'll let you starve!"

From your hiding place in the shadows you can see the ladder of tresses cascade, shimmering like sea foam. You see the crone scramble up like a crab.

What an envious witch, to keep such beauty hidden from view! Poor maiden, you whisper, to be held as a hostage, to be so alone.

For a fortnight you spy on this captive and her keeper. By day the maiden sings, then at night the crone comes to silence her. Oh to touch that delicate skin, her full soft lips, her long fingers. You know you cannot live without holding this angel in your arms, without seeing her dear face in the moonlight. How could you doubt her beauty?

Projections anticipate the external world. Snouts, hairs, tendrils, and thorns all extend through space in order to make contact. They jut and jab, grope and wriggle, for the simple goals of Being: to feed or to fight, to know or be known. Projections also exist in the invisible, though no less real, world, predicting droughts, bear markets, an early frost. They cast themselves into the future or the past, scheming for ends, both good and bad, and rehearse or review the means. Projections are the limbs of the imagination, the antennas, the horns, the strong legs and opposable thumbs.

One night you stand at the foot of the tower and call up to her. The witch has not yet come and there is still time. You know how to cause your beloved's hair to spill from the sky: you recite the crone's words. "Rapunzel, Rapunzel, let down your hair!"

It falls like bolts of fabric around you and you begin to hoist yourself up. Your fists make ropes of it. It is like a great net and you, you are its catch. You pull yourself higher, closer to the stars. Oh, it will be heaven when you reach the top, when, at last, you behold each other!

Look up at the sky, doesn't that cloud look just like a snail? A galloping steed? A smoking gun? Jesus's face was recently captured inside the froth of behemoth cosmic clouds—"star nurseries" they were called by the astronomers who were His unwitting paparazzi.

To my mind those clouds looked like coral reefs in some intertidal zone, and the face, well, to me it looked more like Lincoln's. *De gustibus.* Hallucination is part of our natures; the universe is our Rorschach.

Who can blame us for casting the stars in our personal dramas? It cannot be entirely misguided to believe the elements of the cosmos are interconnected, wound in an enormous contraption: each cog—ourselves included—made up of the same stuff. It stands to reason, given this common denominator, that the arrangements of heavenly bodies reflect something of our own minuscule fates. "I wish I may, I wish I might . . ."

We try, as Shakespeare said, to find fault—and lost possibility—in a skyful of twinkling stars, a.k.a. those behemoth nuclear furnaces. Yet, as Shakespeare went on, the accusation is best turned toward ourselves for the cause of our limitations. The stars are stars; constellations are mere figments of perspective, constructs of a vivid imagination.

From *Antony and Cleopatra*:

Sometime we see a cloud that's dragonish;
A vapour sometime like a bear or lion,
A tower'd citadel, a pendent rock.

Projections are our forte, but also our downfall. Our imaginations play tricks on us. How many entities, separate and distinct from ourselves, have been mistaken in nearsighted folly? If we, like Narcissus, cannot see the pond for our reflection, how can we know the depths beyond our skin? How can we hope to distinguish marshland from mirage? Mermaid from manatee? Lingcod from Loch Ness Monster? Friend from foe? Projections are meant to inform us about the Eden outside the sheath of our flesh, but more often they describe the interior into which we've been exiled.

History has a way of showing us how misled we have been—

how confident we are that this year's fashions will endure, only to find ourselves by next year an emperor in imaginary finery. Zeitgeist is merely the breath of the time, yet, my God, how it feels like *Truth*!

We see, often, too often, what we want to see. Even the bellowing specter of self-made hell must be fussed over like a fetish, as precious and potent as any great work of art. We choose to commit ourselves to it, if only because, like the Big Dipper, it is what we revisit each night, the habit by which we familiarize the dark. The Promethean gift of our imagination is found at the heart of most tragedy, the real weapon discovered at the crime scene. Why would we fashion such horrors?

How did this happen, that the very organ of our humanness—as nostril is to dog, as sonar is to bat, as pupil is to owl—would dead-end us with confusion, false information, self-obsession? Would an elephant hang itself with its trunk?

We project—at the very least—to anticipate and taste what we cannot touch, molecule to molecule, and—at the very best—to live out the Golden Rule, heart to heart. We each spend a lifetime struggling to bridge our detachment, to belong at last—to know the Other.

So what gives? Why do we do such a dismal job of it?

How do we become so dazzled, so blinded?

It was, by Helen Keller's own description, a life on ice, a bleak wintry world. There was no experience of past, present, or future. She was imprisoned by silence and a never-ebbing dark. Even those who most loved her had lost hope. Then, as she put it, her "brain felt the impact of another mind."

Most of us know the story, how the teacher, the miracle worker, spilled water into one hand, while into the other she spelled "water." The moment rang with its synergy between the two parallel realms of experience, one corporeal, the other cerebral. The marriage of left and right hemispheres resounded. It shone, it glowed, it thawed Helen's landscape and set her free. It brought her into the life of being, in her words, "human."

This was a miracle to be sure. But that's only half the story.

A woman is impregnated without insemination. A man walks on water. A loving touch restores mobility to the lame, vigor to the plague-ridden, eyesight to the blind. Bushes, trees, stones, even people spontaneously rupture into flame. The sky lets fall fire, toads, bread soaked with honey. Worldwide, on the same day, statues of a Hindu god drink milk their supplicants leave in bowls. In Spain seventy thousand witness the sun dancing before them. A comet announces the birth of the messiah.

Statues turn to flesh. They weep, they rock, they whisper. Flesh turns to salt, to stone, to ash. Armies are summoned by the Virgin in the clouds. Seas part.

People are abducted by alien creatures and taken onboard spacecraft for medical experimentation. Elvis is spotted in a midwestern mall. Patients in psychotherapy recover memories of Satanic ritual abuse in childhood, and uncover a demonic conspiracy to take over the world. Children accuse their teachers of sexual abuse and the school staff is put on trial. Sympathizers are blacklisted. Witches are broiled at the stake.

Hysteria is Faith's stepsister.

Wheat from chaff. Forest for the trees. Baby from the bath water. How do we know the difference, extract blessing from curse? How can we correct our perspective?

You climb over the window ledge, and peer into her chamber. You can see her silhouetted there, against the far wall. Her hair is like a carpet rolled out before you, a channel of silks stretching to the dark portal of her face. Your arms open to bring her near, to hold her close, to taste her perfection. "It is I . . . your love," you say by way

of introduction. The room has an echo. It is colder than you'd expected and there is an unpleasant smell. The scratchy drone of rock
begins, "I don't know you," it says. It is deafening, this grinding
sound, why is it here among all this softness? "I know my room, my
tower, my song, and my keeper . . . but you . . . you are an intruder!"
She moves toward you and into the shaft of starlight falling from the
window. "I should kill you," the hag grumbles. Her face is grotesque,
her flesh scaled like a fish, her hair an enormous tangle of kelp. What
choice do you have but to throw yourself out of this tower, away
from this horrid sight, and into the brambles?

Once, all creation was oracular. The skies told stories and issued
commandments. Stones, plants, and animals divulged their secrets.
In that awesome cosmos, miracles happened every day and we were
wholly engaged, not yet detached from nature. We belonged to that
wise and animate world, and those conversant, if somewhat psychotic, voices had not yet exiled us into the secular quiet.

   Now we know too much. Fascination recedes. The sky is mute.
We are able to know our "selves" as perceivers. Nothing speaks to us
because we have come to an understanding that the external world
is soulless, that "myth" now means unfounded, fictional, untrue. As
Annie Dillard says, "It is difficult to undo our own damage, and to
recall to our presence that which we have asked to leave. It is hard to
desecrate a grove and change your mind. The very holy mountains
are keeping mum."

   We can no longer enter into enchantment with life, we enter
into a metarelationship with it—we "interpret" our dreams, reconstruct the narratives of our pasts, hold ourselves at arm's length. In
the doldrums between the psyche and world it inhabits, imagination exists like a creature in a zoo exhibit, subject to the scrutiny
of the intellect, deemed to be both quaint and a curiosity. With no
access to its natural habitat, the psyche paces without purpose or
dignity. Like Rilke's panther in the Paris Zoo, its circumambula-

tions are "a dance of strength about a center / in which a mighty will stands stupefied." Imagination is trapped, obsessive, unable to fulfill its nature.

Metaphor, of course, survives as a shard from our former preternatural genius, but few experiences still invite that specialism in us. Only love demands the full lexicon of enchantment. We may pathologize this mania from one end of Bedlam to the next, recoil at the way it seduces us, sucks us into its illusory muck. It *is* madness to be sure . . . in love we step into the vital heroism of our dreams. Love is feral and frothy and full of grace, and, by god, it is our muse. We see things in it.

Look: we are suddenly no longer living in, say, Los Angeles, circa 2000; we are instead living inside a fairy tale! We are given to another sight. Yes, we have become blind to our solid and steadfast habits, blind to the familiar precincts of our limitations, blind to the outward appearances of our selves! We no longer recognize our faces, nor are we recognized by those who knew us. We step into living and become transparent; we . . . disappear!

It is very dark, but she finds you. The brambles have cut your arms, legs, and chest, but especially your face, and your eyes. My God, after seeing such a fright, all else might as well be gouged away. Your faith in everything—by which you mean your faith in love—has been torn. You are as blind as Oedipus at Colonus, Milton in Paradise, Monet at Giverny.

You cry for lost beauty, and that's when you feel her hand on your brow—and something other than your own tears. It is her tears, and they plop, one by one, into each of your eyes, washing it clean, restoring your sight.

At first there are just the simple shapes, the movement of light against dark. Her face radiates above you. You strain to see her. It seems her expression is both candid and alien, as familiar and fathomless as the moon.

* * *

Helen's second awakening occurs years later. She is sitting in a library, absorbed in her own imagination. "I have been far away all this time, and I haven't left the room!" she exclaims to her teacher. She has just been, for all practical purposes—as physicists say of quantum phenomena—in Athens! How is it she is able to travel beyond the confines of her body, to penetrate—like the mercurial neutrino—the walls of the library and soar across the seas? The spirit, she answers herself, must have its own life.

Only months before she had asked her teacher, "Why can we not see God?"

The physical world, her teacher explained, the world of appearances, the world known through the limits of the senses, is a kind of veil. To demonstrate this, the teacher made Helen stand on one side of a screen, while she stood on the other. "She could not see me and I could not touch her," Helen said. "Yet by little signs I knew she was there, only separated from me by the 'veil' of Japanese paper."

People will always see things: the ghoul in the pinewood paneling, the genitalia in the river rock. Jesus's face appears one week on a refrigerator door, the next in a photograph of newly hatched galaxies. Mary demurs from a tortilla.

We not only see the things we believe in, we also believe in things we do not see. Black holes are, as far as most of us can comprehend, as fantastic as any sci-fi schtick; so too are subatomic particles, the unconscious, the superego. Nevertheless these "entities" shape our world as surely as any vengeful Deity who sent forth a scourge of plague upon the flat earth ever did. The more closely we examine the physical world, the more we surrender to our observations that things are actually "tendencies," "probabilities." We find ourselves at the mercy of our atavistic metaphors, all the while sensing the existence of things beyond our limitations to perceive them.

Technology boasts the authority and ability to cause the unseen to appear before us. Yet tomorrow, say, we might watch the film *2001* or the explosion of the *Challenger,* and wonder which is the more virtual. Which happened, really? Men walked on the moon? Buddha dispelled an army of demons by touching the earth?

We are in the dark, grasping at holographic straws. Can we explain how the parts of the atom are pulled together? What exactly is that cosmic muscularity that forces mass into attraction with mass? What exactly causes the northern lights? Indeed, what is light? How do we know another human being? Indeed, why are we curious, fascinated, determined to know Her despite our formidable handicaps?

One November night last year I was in a jet from Ireland to New York. I peered out the teeny window to find the northern lights undulating in Day-Glo green below me. The drapery was hung from the bowl of the Big Dipper, and both seemed to be suspended below the horizon, an apparition in what I assumed was the sea. I had lost the horizon, was entirely disoriented in the night sky, like those pilots who aim their planes into a fatal nosedive. It was a spectacular vision, but one that filled me with dread. The curtains of the aurora unfurled and furled like sheets of cream poured from the lip of a saucepan, but did this portend disaster? Where did the sky begin and the sea end?

I thought about my beloved and the undersea things of our relationship. Such dread I've anticipated at the bottom of our love: a shark's fury, an eel's grin, the defeat of a legion of sea stars. I could sink and drown at such depths.

It is one thing, one quite horrible thing, to be lost amid the hall of mirrors of one's own feeble sight, to suspect that your feeling of disorientation is not merely a trick of the mind. You know you have the Mortal Dread within you, and you know how it can cause you to envision the worst: ghastly chimera over the sea and in the skies. It can contaminate the very thing you hold dear, make love itself seem monstrous, unworthy of your best efforts to see beyond and through its most despairing mirage. It can, in effect, make you believe in witches, and in lovers forever held hostage by their own limitations.

It is quite another thing to accept your sight for what it is, to know the ways in which you will hallucinate, either out of love or out of fear. Was it necessary to always "understand," was it necessary to always find a "meaning"?

I beheld the Drinking Gourd, the beacon that guided refugees from human bondage. And there, at its rim, was the enigmatic veil, the aurora borealis, rippling in its own mysterious breezes. What did I make of that iridescence? Love or fear? Fear or love? What I saw from the porthole of that plane was an invitation to enter into a world I cannot control or "understand," to follow love's perplexing song and let it undo me, if need be.

"No pessimist ever discovered the secret of the stars," Helen Keller reminded me. " . . . Or opened the doorway for the human spirit." Either sunk in our privacies, or soaring in our efforts to touch, the blind lead the blind.

Acknowledgments

Let us begin by listing a few of our shortcomings. First, this book is much too brief; we didn't have room to include all the writers we've been delighted to publish during the first eight years of *Killing the Buddha*. Moreover, the vagaries of rights and publishing prevented us from including many of our favorites; we're particularly ashamed of this collection's lack of Muslim voices. And some of the contributors we're proudest of are absent because the emphasis of this collection, first-person essays, excluded genres such as traditional reportage, criticism, fiction, and poetry, as well as scholarly writing, pranks, and the unclassifiable work of Holly Berman and Francine Travis, correspondents for *Killing the Buddha*'s recipes department, "Eat God Now." The selection reflects only our judgment of which pieces would work best together, but there have been enough splendid stories written for *Killing the Buddha* to fill another book, and we hope they will in the future.

Secondly, "eight years" is a bit of an exaggeration; there was at least a year in there when the magazine lay in limbo, as first Peter Manseau, Jeff Sharlet, and Jeremy Brothers, and then Paul Morris, Laurel Snyder, Jeff Wilson, Patton Dodd, Irina Reyn, and other contributing editors moved on to books, babies, and honest work. Several months ago, a new crop of editors—Meera Subramanian, Ashley Makar, and Marissa Dennis—took it upon themselves to resurrect the Buddha so they could kill him again. It's to their initiative that this book owes its existence—and to our editors at Beacon Press, Amy Caldwell and Alexis Rizzuto, to whom it owes its publication with one of the last great independent houses in publishing. But these names are only part of the story; it would take a Book of Numbers to list all those whose efforts were required to produce even this slim volume. "The fiction that artistic labor happens in isolation," notes playwright Tony Kushner, "and that artistic accomplishment is exclusively the provenance of individual talents, is politically charged." All art, especially that of anthologies, is a form of collectivism. So, to the *Killing the Buddha* Borg, whose names are legion: thanks!

Contributors' Notes

After a career in the theater, **Catherine Allgor** attended Mount Holyoke College in South Hadley, Massachusetts. She received her PhD with distinction from Yale University. Professor Allgor's first book, *Parlor Politics: In Which the Ladies of Washington Help Build a City and a Government,* won the James H. Broussard First Book Prize from the Society for Historians of the Early American Republic. She is currently a professor of history at the University of California. Her latest book, *A Perfect Union: Dolley Madison and the Creation of the American Nation,* was a finalist for the George Washington Prize.

Daniel S. Brenner is a Reconstructionist rabbi and occasional playwright who lives in Montclair, New Jersey. Much of his writing can be found on his blog, Reb Blog.

Seth Castleman is cofounder and guiding teacher of Nishmat Hayyim: Breath of Life Jewish Meditation Collaborative of New England. Seth founded and directed programs for incarcerated youth in New York City and women in California prisons. Castleman is published in a dozen anthologies, magazines, and newspapers, and for many years performed for audiences as a critically acclaimed storyteller. He is currently working on a literary memoir on the spiritual path of brokenness.

Jill Hamburg Coplan is a writer and editor living in Montclair, New Jersey. She teaches a religion reporting course for New York University's Department of Journalism.

Mark Dery is a cultural critic and the author of *Escape Velocity: Cyberculture at the End of the Century* and *The Pyrotechnic Insanitarium: American Culture on the Brink.* Raised in San Diego, near the Mexican-American border, he is writing *Don Henley Must Die,* a meditation on the cultural psyche of Southern California. He teaches media criticism and creative nonfiction in the Department of Journalism at New York University.

Patton Dodd is the author of *My Faith So Far: A Story of Conversion and Confusion.* He is writing a book on New Journalism and religion. (Really, it's a dissertation, but "book" sounds more readable and fun.) Patton is a senior editor for Beliefnet.

Rebecca Donner was born in Canada but spent her formative years in Los Angeles, an experience that inspired her first novel, *Sunset Terrace.* While enrolled in the MFA program at Columbia University, she was literary director of the renowned KGB Fiction Series and editor of *On the Rocks: The KGB Bar Fiction Anthology.* In June 2008 DC Comics published her graphic novel, *Burnout.* Rebecca has taught writing at Wesleyan, Columbia, Barnard, and the New School, and writes songs for Symphony Space. She lives in the East Village in New York City.

Elizabeth Frankenberger's essays and reviews have appeared in the *Jewish Daily Forward, Publishers Weekly,* and *Quest* magazine, among other publications. She and her husband live in New York.

Martha G. is anonymous.

Gordon Haber's fiction and criticism have appeared in a variety of newspapers and journals, including the *New York Sun,* the *Jewish Daily Forward, Zeek,* the *Nebraska Review,* and *Heeb.* Currently he is at work on a novel about the Jewish messiah.

Erik Hanson volunteers as "Friendly Adult Presence" for the high school program of the Religious Society of Friends (Quakers). He works as the undergraduate advisor in the Department of Anthropology at the University of Maryland.

Bia Lowe is the author of two collections of essays, *Splendored Thing* and *Wild Ride,* which won the QPB New Visions Award for creative nonfiction.

Ashley Makar, an editor of *Killing the Buddha,* is a poet and literary nonfiction writer. Her work has appeared in *American Book Review,* the *Birmingham News, Search: The Magazine of Science, Religion, and Culture*, and the *Revealer.* She has taught writing and Middle Eastern literature at Hofstra University. She's currently studying religion and literature at Yale Divinity School's Institute of Sacred Music.

Peter Manseau cofounded *Killing the Buddha* with Jeff Sharlet and Jeremy Brothers in 1999. He is the author of a novel, *Songs for the Butcher's Daughter,* and a memoir, *Vows: The Story of a Priest, a Nun, and Their Son,* and is coauthor with Jeff Sharlet of *Killing the Buddha: A Heretic's Bible.* He lives with his wife and two daughters in Washington, D.C., where he studies theology and teaches writing at Georgetown University. He is also the editor of *Search: The Magazine of Science, Religion, and Culture.*

Paul W. Morris, a former editor of *Killing the Buddha,* was an editor at Viking Penguin and *Tricycle: The Buddhist Review* before becoming a freelance gun for hire. He killed time at *Entertainment Weekly* and Martha Stewart Living Omnimedia staring into the abyss, but nothing stared back. He has written for the *Village Voice, Yoga Journal,* and other periodicals, and his essays have appeared in the anthologies *Blue Jean Buddha* and *Before & After: Stories* *from New York.* His introduction to a new translation of Hermann Hesse's *Siddhartha* was published in 2002 by Shambala Sun. He is currently the director of special projects at *Bomb* magazine, an arts and culture quarterly founded in 1981. He lives in Manhattan.

Quince Mountain splits the year between Adirondack Park and the Wisconsin Northwoods. He doesn't recommend joining the military, but would consider sending his kids to church camp.

E.J. Park lives in Chicago.

Michael Allen Potter is an MFA candidate in the Nonfiction Writing Program at the University of Iowa, where he is at work on a memoir about the search for his family.

Stephen Prothero is a writer and a professor in the Department of Religion at Boston University. His books include *American Jesus: How the Son of God Became a National Icon* and the *New York Times* best seller *Religious Literacy—What Every American Needs to Know, and Doesn't.* He has also written for the *New York Times, Wall Street Journal, Newsweek, Slate,* and *Salon.* But his real claim to fame is a brief yet shining appearance on *The Daily Show* with Jon Stewart.

Irina Reyn's first novel, *What Happened to Anna K.,* was published last year. She is also the editor of *Living on the Edge of the World: New Jersey Writers Take on the Garden State.* Her work has appeared in *Tin House, Post Road, One Story, Nextbook,* the *Los Angeles Times,* the *San Francisco Chronicle,* and *Town & Country Travel* as well as other publications and anthologies. Born in Moscow and raised in New York City, she is currently an assistant professor of English at the University of Pittsburgh.

Ben Rutter teaches English at Saint Ann's School in Brooklyn.

Naomi Seidman is Koret Professor of Jewish Culture and director of the Richard S. Dinner Center for Jewish Studies at the Graduate Theological Union in Berkeley, California. Her first book, *A Marriage Made in Heaven: The Sexual Politics of Hebrew and Yiddish*, appeared in 1997. Her second, *Faithful Renderings: Jewish-Christian Difference and the Politics of Translation*, was published in 2006.

Jeff Sharlet cofounded *Killing the Buddha* with Peter Manseau and Jeremy Brothers in 1999. He's the author of the *New York Times* best seller *The Family: The Secret Fundamentalism at the Heart of American Power* and, with Manseau, coauthor of *Killing the Buddha: A Heretic's Bible*. A visiting research scholar at the Center for Religion and Media at New York University, he's the editor of *The Revealer* and a contributing editor for *Harper's* and *Rolling Stone*. He lives with his wife in Honeoye Falls, New York.

Laurel Snyder, a former editor of *Killing the Buddha,* is the editor of *Half/Life: Jew-ish Tales from Interfaith Homes* and the author of a collection of poems, *The Myth of the Simple Machines,* as well as a number of books for children. She lives in Atlanta.

Meera Subramanian writes about culture and the environment for the *New York Times, Audubon, Salon, Grist, Search,* and other publications. Based in Brooklyn, she seeks out the wild world hidden within the urban landscape and can be seen sneaking around the city with binoculars as she works on a book about the peregrine falcons of New York City, a not-so-subtle means of adapting to the city after living in the woods of Oregon for nearly a decade. She became an editor of *Killing the Buddha* in 2008.

Danielle Trussoni has written for the *New York Times Book Review, Tin House,* and the *New York Times Magazine,* among other publications. Her first book, *Falling Through the Earth: A Memoir,* was awarded the 2006 Michener-Copernicus Society of America Award and was chosen as one of the *New York Times* ten best books of 2006.

Timothy B. Tyson is a senior scholar at the Center for Documentary Studies at Duke University and adjunct professor of American studies at the University of North Carolina at Chapel Hill. He is the author of *Blood Done Sign My Name: A True Story* and *Radio Free Dixie: F. Williams and the Roots of Black Power,* winner of the James Rawley Prize and cowinner of the Frederick Jackson Turner Prize. Tyson is also a coeditor of *Democracy Betrayed: The Wilmington Race Riot of 1898 and Its Legacy.*

Mary Valle lives in Baltimore, Maryland. She is working on another novel.

For **Jesse Maceo Vega-Frey**, a life of liberation is crafted in the negotiation between strength and suppleness, struggle and laziness, wisdom and love. To this end, he has spent the last few years committed to deepening his training in practicing and teaching meditation and facilitating group process for social justice activists. Jesse is part of the guiding leadership for The Stone House, a center for spiritual life and strategic action in Mebane, North Carolina. He is a board member of the Buddhist Peace Fellowship, an artist, and a war-tax resister.

Hasdai Westbrook's work has appeared in the *Washington Post,* the *Nation,* and *Nextbook.* He is currently writing a novel about gangsters and Gilgamesh.

Jeff Wilson is an assistant professor of religious studies and East Asian studies at Renison College, University of Waterloo. A former contributing editor for *Killing the Buddha,* he has published over fifty articles and three books: *Buddhism of the Heart: Reflections on Shin Buddhism and Inner Togetherness, Mourning the Unborn Dead: A Buddhist Ritual Comes to America,* and *The Buddhist Guide to New York.* A lifelong Unitarian Universalist and longtime Buddhist practitioner, he currently lives in Canada with his wife and son.